Visions of Council Democracy

Series Editors: Alex Thomson, Benjamin Arditi, Andrew Schaap
International Advisory Editors: Michael Dillon, Michael J. Shapiro, Jeremy Valentine

Offering new perspectives on contemporary political theory, books in this series 'take on' the political in accordance with the ambivalent colloquial sense of the phrase – as both an acceptance and a challenge. They interrogate received accounts of the relationship between political thought and political practice, criticise and engage with the contemporary political imagination, and reflect on the ongoing transformations of politics. Concise and polemical, the texts are oriented towards critique, developments in Continental thought, and the crossing of disciplinary borders.

Titles in the *Taking on the Political* series include:

Polemicization: The Contingency of the Commonplace
Benjamin Arditi and Jeremy Valentine

Cinematic Political Thought
Michael Shapiro

Untimely Politics
Samuel A. Chambers

Speaking Against Number: Heidegger, Language and the Politics of Calculation
Stuart Elden

Post-Marxism versus Cultural Studies
Paul Bowman

Post-Foundational Political Thought: Political Difference in Nancy, Lefort, Badiou and Laclau
Oliver Marchart

Democratic Piety: Complexity, Conflict and Violence
Adrian Little

Gillian Rose: A Good Enough Justice
Kate Schick

Ethics and Politics after Poststructuralism: Levinas, Derrida and Nancy
Madeleine Fagan

Space, Politics and Aesthetics
Mustafa Dikeç

History and Event: From Marxism to Contemporary French Theory
Nathan Coombs

Immanence and Micropolitics: Sartre, Merleau-Ponty, Foucault and Deleuze
Christian Gilliam

Shame: A Genealogy of Queer Practices in the 19th Century
Bogdan Popa

Visions of Council Democracy: Castoriadis, Lefort, Arendt
Benjamin Ask Popp-Madsen

https://edinburghuniversitypress.com/series-taking-on-the-political.html

Visions of Council Democracy

Castoriadis, Lefort, Arendt

Benjamin Ask Popp-Madsen

EDINBURGH
University Press

To Otto and Pelle

Edinburgh University Press is one of the leading university presses in the UK. We publish academic books and journals in our selected subject areas across the humanities and social sciences, combining cutting-edge scholarship with high editorial and production values to produce academic works of lasting importance. For more information visit our website: edinburghuniversitypress.com

© Benjamin Ask Popp-Madsen, 2021, 2022

Edinburgh University Press Ltd
The Tun – Holyrood Road
12(2f) Jackson's Entry
Edinburgh EH8 8PJ

First published in hardback by Edinburgh University Press 2021

Typeset in 11/13 Sabon by
IDSUK (DataConnection) Ltd

A CIP record for this book is available from the British Library

ISBN 978 1 4744 5631 9 (hardback)
ISBN 978 1 4744 5632 6 (paperback)
ISBN 978 1 4744 5633 3 (webready PDF)
ISBN 978 1 4744 5634 0 (epub)

The right of Benjamin Ask Popp-Madsen to be identified as the author of this work has been asserted in accordance with the Copyright, Designs and Patents Act 1988, and the Copyright and Related Rights Regulations 2003 (SI No. 2498).

Contents

Acknowledgements

While writing this book and thinking about democracy in the past and present, I have been extraordinarily fortunate to receive the support, engagement and critique of numerous colleagues, interlocutors and friends, who shaped this project in uncountable ways, and who have been exemplars of truly inspiring and caring scholars, without whom this book would never have been written. I first began to contemplate on what would become the main themes of the book as a Master's student at The New School of Social Research in 2012–13. At The New School, I learned that political radicalism, engaged citizenship and erudite scholarship are not opposites, but mutual preconditions for understanding, and perhaps changing, the world. The true institutional home of the book, though, has been the Department of Political Science, University of Copenhagen, at which I was a PhD student from 2014 to 2018. I am sincerely grateful to Christian F. Rostbøll, whose motivating clarity and precision continually urged me to provide sharpness to my own arguments. If this book comes across as a piece of balanced scholarly work, Christian is most certainly to be credited for that. Moreover, I would like to express a very special thanks to Lars Tønder, on whom I have unashamedly drawn on at numerous occasions. Lars read an early draft of the book, and his supportive and critical comments helped immensely going forward. At the University of Copenhagen, I would also like to thank Anders Berg-Sørensen, Noel Parker, Ditte Maria Brasso Sørensen, Christiane Mossin, Esben Høgh, Rune Møller Stahl and Mads Ejsing for many interesting discussions and good friendship.

I am greatly indebted to series editor Andrew Schaap, who is the primary reason that this book is being published in its current form. Andrew suggested that the book would fit well in the *Taking on the Political* series, and his engagement throughout the writing has been absolutely critical. I also wish to thank series editor Alex Thomson, whose stimulating comments on the manuscript proved vital for its final shape. Moreover, I am grateful to my editors at Edinburgh University Press, Jen Daly and Sarah Foyle, for competent and efficient cooperation, and to Eliza Wright for careful copyediting of the manuscript.

Writing this book was also made possible by generous funding from the Carlsberg Foundation, which provided me with an International Postdoc Fellowship at Uppsala University in 2019. In Uppsala, I was incredibly lucky to engage with and learn from Sofia Nässtrom, who helped sharpen the argument of several chapters. At Uppsala University, I also wish to thank Jonas Hultin Rosenberg, Gina Gustavsson, Sofia Helander, Siri Sylvan and Oskar Hultin Bäckersten for encouraging discussions. While at Uppsala, I was also a visiting researcher at Danish Institute for International Studies at which the companionship, intellectual discussions and fun times with Manni Crone and Vibeke Schou Tjalve was a welcome distraction from the sometimes very hard job of writing a book. The final editing of this book was done while employed at Department of Management, Politics and Philosophy, Copenhagen Business School. I would like thank Anker Brink Lund for bringing my attention to the living and strong tradition of democracy in my own backyard – the Nordic countries – and for providing a thought-provoking research environment that focuses on the great questions of politics, but with the informal and humoristic approach of good comrades. I also wish to thank Haldor Byrkjeflot, Andreas Møller Mulvad, Mathias Hein Jessen and Anders Sevelsted for their role in this environment. Outside these institutions, where I have been fortunate to work and write, I am also indebted to James Muldoon, Jason Frank, Gaard Kets, Amnon Lev, Mikkel Flohr, Mikkel Thorup and Nis Primdahl for collaboration and critique over the years.

Finally, I wish to thank my family, especially my mother Mette Lissia Popp-Madsen and my father Lars Ask Røgilds, for the curiosity for stories with which they have raised me, and for the support and invaluable help in managing scholarship and life with small children. My deepest thanks and gratitude go to my partner Rikke Popp-Jensen, who for the last ten years has been my supportive, loving and incredibly funny life companion. While I have aspired to put the experiences of one democratic experiment into words in this book, Rikke practises the ideals of equality, tolerance and the search for justice continually and on a daily basis. That is truly inspiring.

I dedicate this book to our two lovely children, Otto and Pelle, with much admiration and even more hope. Throughout the writing of the book, they have been perfect and always welcome disturbers of the peace, and they will most certainly grow up in a world where democracy will not be the only game in town, and where the self-government of the people might only survive by being radicalised.

Chapter 3 has been published in a much-abridged form as 'From Workers' Councils to Democratic Autonomy: Rediscovering Cornelius Castoriadis' Theory of Council Democracy', *Critical Horizons: A Journal of Philosophy and Social Theory*, 21 (4), pp. 318–34, 2020.

   Chapter 4 has been published in an early version as 'The Self-Limiting Revolution and the Mixed Constitution of Socialist Democracy: Claude Lefort's Vision of Council Democracy', in J. Muldoon (ed.), *Council Democracy: Towards a Democratic Socialist Politics*, London: Routledge, 2018, pp. 168–88.

   Chapter 6 has appeared in a different version as 'Between Constituent Power and Political Form: Toward a Theory of Council Democracy', *Political Theory*, [Online First], 2020.

   I thank the publishers for being able to use material in new form in this book.

Benjamin Ask Popp-Madsen
Copenhagen, June 2020

Introduction
Why Council Democracy, Why Now?

This book is about the twentieth-century workers' councils and the theories of council democracy that political thinkers developed from the historical experiences with the council system. It focuses especially on the theories of council democracy developed by Cornelius Castoriadis, Claude Lefort and Hannah Arendt, as they are the most important interpreters of council democracy in the second half of the twentieth century. For about two-thirds of the twentieth century, workers' councils continually emerged throughout Europe, and although in no way united in their specific political demands, the general programme of the European council movements was a deepening of democracy, including the democratisation of the capitalist economy, a dismantling of the bourgeois state apparatus, and the introduction of self-governing practices in most aspects of social, economic and political life. The councils repeatedly challenged hierarchical relations of power in the workplace, in the economy and in political life.

The self-governing neighbourhoods (*sociétés populaires*) of the 1871 Paris Commune, the strike movement and self-managing factories (*soviets*) of revolutionary St Petersburg in the failed Russian Revolution of 1905, the delegates from army regiments and factories (soldiers' and workers' soviets) of Petrograd and other industrialised cities during the Russian Revolution(s) of 1917, the German workers' and sailors' councils (*die Räte*) responsible for the German Revolution of 1918–19, the factory councils of Turin, Milan and Genoa (*commissioni interne*), instrumental in bringing about the Italian *bienno rosso* from 1919 to 1920, and the Hungarian council movement of 1956, which was actively involved in the first Eastern European uprising against Russian oppression, are all examples of nascent council systems in the making (Anweiler 1974; Gluckstein

1985, 2011). By the end of World War I, council movements in Russia, Germany and Austria were responsible for overthrowing three gigantic empires, and during the last hundred years, the council system has been a focal point for a heterodox group of critics of liberal democracy, parliamentarianism, representation, state communism and bureaucratic rule, and has repeatedly been interpreted as the democratic kernel of socialism. The council movements and the subsequent theories of council democracy are definitely interesting in their own right, but why revitalise this specific tradition of political radicalism and democratic experimentation? *Why* council democracy, and why *now*?

Western democracies are facing their worst political crisis since the 1930s. An increasing number of citizens are losing faith in their representatives, political parties and representative democracy as a whole. The dominant post-World War II political regime of liberal democracy, which ascended to total hegemony after the fall of the Berlin Wall, is beginning to disintegrate into its constituent parts, insofar as illiberal democracies as well as undemocratic liberalism attract the minds of voters and politicians (Mounk 2018). In short, citizens in Europe and the US are withdrawing support from their political systems as well as doubting their fundamental legitimacy.

The political background for the present crisis of liberal democracy is indeed multifaceted and complex. One privileged entry point is the growing mismatch between national democratic institutions and globalised capitalism. The financial crisis of 2008–9 and the decision by democratically elected parliaments to, via tax money, bail out the responsible banks, which were considered 'too big to fail', cemented for many the suspicion of a too tight connection between the political decision-makers and the global economic elite. This bailing out of the banks after the financial crisis, though, is only indicative of a larger transfer of political power over the last forty years from political units with a degree of democratic control to political units with much less developed democratic institutions, or with no democratic structures at all. Due to the emergence of a genuinely globalised capitalism, nation-states and national parliaments have gradually lost power, initiative and control to supranational organisations, and also to gigantic corporations, banks and investment funds. In a sentence, the nation-state – that is, the primary carrier of popular sovereignty in modern politics – has lost the relative control over the economy that it enjoyed during the post-war Keynesian compromise between the state and the market. The signs of the political crisis we observe today are responses to this flagrant mismatch between a representative democracy nested in the nation-state and a truly globalised capitalism. Due to this mismatch, national parliaments cannot deliver on the issues that affect their citizens, as they lack the necessary political instruments.

It is within this historical development and conceptual frame that we should understand claims such as 'the end of politics', 'post-politics', 'the end of ideology', 'the extremism of the centre' and 'the politics of necessity'. Since national, democratic politics has largely been deprived of the issue over which different political parties earlier debated fiercely, politics has been reduced to a strategic game without substance or actual choice between distinct political alternatives. As a result, many citizens of Western democracies have either become apathetic and disinterested, or they have grown weary with their political systems and withdrawn their support by voting for populists, who offer to 'drain the swamp' (Donald Trump), 'change politics for good' (Nigel Farage), 'make America great again' (Trump again) and to do politics 'au nom du peuple' (Marine Le Pen). What unites such right-wing populists is the promise of an unrealistic restoration of a homogenous, national people with political and economic sovereignty within the boundaries of the nation-state.

Many new books have surveyed the present political crisis, and the rise of right-wing populism (Levitsky and Ziblatt 2018; Müller 2016; Mounk 2018; Runciman 2018; Finchelstein 2017). They convey the same basic message, namely that the present political situation in the US and across Europe is characterised by a record-high dissatisfaction with elected politicians (Mounk 2018: 99–103); increased enmity between political parties and demonisation of political opponents (Levitsky and Ziblatt 2018: 145–75); and decreasing support for democratic institutions in general (Mounk 2018: 105). With the widespread electoral support of populists like Donald Trump, Boris Johnson, Viktor Orbán, Jarosław Kaczyński, Recep Erdoğan and Marine Le Pen, liberal democracy is either at risk of being replaced by twenty-first-century forms of fascism (Connolly 2017: 1–30; Finchelstein 2017: 175) or mutating into new variants of democracy far from resembling the liberal variant (Mounk 2018: 29–52).

Apart from the resurgence of right-wing populism, another response to the present crisis of democracy is simply to leave behind the ideal of democracy itself and turn to different modalities of technocracy (Brennan 2016). If technocracy could be broadly defined as political rule devoid of democratic legitimacy, then 'technocracy' is only another term for the loss of economic and political sovereignty experienced in contemporary Western democracies. The regulation and structuring of globalised capitalism performed by the EU, WTO, the World Bank, G7 and others is indeed a form of technocratic government or what some have called 'undemocratic liberalism' (Mounk 2018: 53–98), as the political room to manoeuvre for national parliaments has considerably shrunk. The relation between populism and technocracy as responses to the crisis of democracy resembles something like a vicious circle: the more populist parties demand the restoration of economic and political sovereignty, as they harvest votes on a rhetorically constructed conflict between the incorruptible people and the corrupt political *cum* technocratic elite, the more political and economic elites across Western democracies are reassured that popular sovereignty is indeed an inherently unstable force, which can only be alluded to rhetorically but never realised or approximated institutionally. This attitude among political elites, consequently, only fuels further dissatisfaction with liberal democracy and support for the populists, who seek to fundamentally transcend it.

The conflict between 'more democracy' (populism) and 'less democracy' (technocracy) as responses to the present political crisis is indeed a false dichotomy, as neither populism nor technocracy promises ordinary citizens more political participation or experiments with new popular mobilising institutional designs. This argument is obvious in relation to the present technocratic push to move political decisions beyond the arenas under direct popular influence, but neither is populism – contrary to its promise of 'giving back power to the people' – really concerned with the political participation and direct involvement of ordinary citizens (Müller 2014). Instead, as argued by, for example, Federico Finchelstein (2017: xvi) and Jan-Werner Müller (2014), populism entails a distinct understanding of political representation, where the political leader *knows* the demands and desires of the citizenry without the need for their actual participation or for institutional mediation.

In contrast to populism and technocracy, the clearest, most genuinely *popular* response to the uncontrollable nature of twenty-first-century global capitalism, and its gradual eroding of practices of democratic decision-making, has been anti-austerity Square movements like *Occupy* in America, *Indignados* in Spain and *Aganaktismenoi* in Greece, which emerged after the global financial crisis of

2007–8. Such movements criticised the self-interestedness and elitism of political representatives as well as the economic exploitation of neo-liberal capitalism. Together with similar movements during the Arab Spring, in Rojava, Kurdistan and across Latin America, the Square movements have not only criticised the lack of popular participation in representative democracies, and the fundamental divide between politics and economics inherent in liberal democracy; they have also experimented with novel forms of democratic organisation in order to prefigure the free, equal and just society these movements strive to create in the future.

In order to interpret the Square movements and the democratic ideals they practise, increased attention has been paid to council democracy, communal democracy and the workers' councils of the twentieth century (Bonnet 2014; Kioupkiolis and Katsambekis 2016; Sitrin and Azzellini 2014; Dirik 2016; Popp-Madsen and Kets 2020). Moreover, due to the recent centenaries of the Russian Revolution of 1917 and the German Revolution of 1918–19, in which council systems emerged most forcefully and acquired real political power, an increased attentiveness to the Russian soviets, the German *Räte* and their potentialities for democratic politics is clearly visible (Bosteels 2017; Negri 2017; Tomba 2017; Pelz 2018; Kets and Muldoon 2019). In addition, recent books have taken issue with alternative labour history, workers' control and council democracy (Azzellini 2015; Ness and Azzellini 2012; Muldoon 2018; Dubigeon 2017). Hence, the contemporary dissatisfaction with representative politics, liberal democracy and global capitalism provides an initial answer to the question of *why council democracy*, and *why now*. Although the twentieth-century workers' councils cannot provide an institutional blueprint for contemporary democratic experimentation beyond representative politics and capitalism, their history and the theories of council democracy they ignited might guide and inspire contemporary democratic protest and experimentation.

The historical councils emerged at the beginning of the twentieth century in a historical situation not entirely unlike the present legitimacy crisis of liberal democracy. At the beginning of the twentieth century, Europe was, by and large, ruled by sovereign monarchs and emperors, thus making dynasticism the primary legitimating principle of political life. World War I changed that completely, as the Russian, German and Austro-Hungarian empires – helped by various council movements across the continent – came to a halt and were replaced by one-party communism and parliamentary democracy. As a result, the historical period in which the councils emerged was marked by a severe breakdown of public authority, a withdrawal of political support for the existing political regimes, and an intense debate on the various meanings of democracy and its institutional form. It is the argument of this book that contemporary political projects that seek to deepen and widen democratic practices beyond, beneath and besides the institutions of liberal democracy can draw sustenance and inspiration from the tradition of council democracy.

Politics and Vision, Visions of Council Democracy

This practice of drawing inspiration from historical events and half-forgotten political institutions of the past is central to the political thinkers and their theories of council democracy discussed in this book. The title of the book, *Visions of Council Democracy*, refers to a discussion by Sheldon Wolin on the vital importance of *vision* for the political thinker. According to Wolin (2004: 17–19), political thinking is situated in the encounter between two different forms of vision. Firstly, vision is associated with perception, that is, with the observation of facts. But secondly, and more importantly for political thought, vision is associated with something normative – 'I have a vision' – and something imaginative – 'I had a vision'. On the one hand, the political thinkers discussed in this book are interested in the council movements of their time, as well as in the past, as they are recounting the history of prior council systems; on the other hand, they are seeking to *forge* a new reality into being, as they are envisioning a novel political reality through reviewing the possibilities of council democracy in their own present political moment.

In 2016 the journal *Political Theory* published a guide to its archive under the title 'Political Theory and the Untimely'. In the introduction to the volume, the editor Nicholas Tampio writes: 'To be a political theorist is to negotiate the timely and the untimely' (2016: 1). The political theorist must every morning decide whether to enter an untimely space and immerse him- or herself in a classic work of political thought or whether to occupy the space of timeliness and speak to the political issues of the day. The political theorist, therefore, 'must explain how dwelling in the untimely can shed light on contemporary political affairs' (Tampio 2016: 1–2). Although a brief description, it expresses something important about how the political thinkers in this book differ from historians and political scientists. Whereas the two latter primarily occupy *either* the untimely *or* the timely and insist that these domains can be held apart, the political theorist mediates between them, as his or her reflections occupy both. He or she can primarily reflect on timely questions by drawing on untimely resources, and the primary reason for studying the tradition of political thought is to somehow speak to present affairs, if not to intervene directly in contemporary politics. The timely and untimely, the present and past, in other words, are intertwined and entangled. On the one hand, council thinkers are interested in the historical councils of the past – they are dwelling in the untimely, registering facts about prior political institutions, constitutional arrangements and historical events; on the other hand, they are seeking to forge a new reality into being, as they are en*visioning* new political modes of existence through reviewing the councils' relevance for democracy, freedom, equality and justice in their present moment.

With Wolin's dual understanding of *vision*, the analyses of the twentieth-century workers' councils included in this book, as well as this book as a whole, are not just undertaken for the sake of the past itself. Instead, the detailed analyses of the historical councils function as exemplars of more abstract theories of council democracy, which are meant to challenge liberal democracy, political representation, capitalism, bureaucracy and totalitarianism. Maurizio Passerin d'Entrèves argues that in going back and forth between historical events and political theory, the analyses of the council system are able to combine history, theory and politics into a unified reflection on the potentialities of the past and its relevance for the future:

> The Paris Commune, the Russian Soviets, the German Revolutionary Councils of 1918–19, the Hungarian uprising of 1956, all these events possess the kind of exemplary validity that make them of universal significance, while still retaining their own specificity and uniqueness. Thus, by attending to these events in their particularity the historian or judging spectator is able to illuminate their universal import and thereby preserve them as 'examples' for posterity. (d'Entrèves 1994: 114–15)

The following analyses of the council tradition, especially in the work of Castoriadis, Lefort and Arendt, thus investigate the ways in which the detailed historical analyses of the councils become exemplary for broader political projects, which in different ways fundamentally challenge the dominant political systems of modernity.

Council Democracy in the Political Thought of Castoriadis, Lefort and Arendt

Despite the critical importance of council movements for twentieth-century politics, especially in the first part of the century, and even though many influential Marxist thinkers have celebrated the councils, council democracy is, regardless of the newfound interest in the subject, still a marginal topic within contemporary democratic theory. While historical scholarship on the twentieth-century council movements is certainly not lacking (Grunberger 1973; Michell 1965; Hoffrogge 2011; Anweiler 1974; Smirnov 1997; Haumer 2015; Di Paola 2011; Williams 1975; Gluckstein 1985, 2011; Lindemann 1974; van der Linden 2004; Schecter 1994; Rachleff 1976), few scholars have connected the council movements to democratic theory. Moreover, no existing studies provide an overview of the political theory of council democracy from late nineteenth-century anarchist conceptions of communal democracy to the post-World War II rediscovery of the council tradition and its importance for a reformulation of a post-totalitarian vision of democracy different from the constrained, disciplined, minimal ideal of liberal democracy (Müller 2011). This book remedies these shortcomings by, firstly, providing such an overview of the political theory of council democracy, and, secondly, by developing a theory of council democracy as a political form, which combines constituent power and constituted form, thereby insisting on democratic politics' dual commitment to the freedom to act anew and the concern for self-limitation.[1]

I develop this theory of council democracy by engaging with the work of Castoriadis, Lefort and Arendt because they are not only significant political thinkers of democracy, freedom and autonomy as well as critics of totalitarianism, bureaucratisation and depoliticisation; they are also the most important interpreters of the council tradition in the second half of the twentieth century. Castoriadis, Lefort and Arendt followed similar intellectual paths, as all three thinkers began as critics of totalitarianism (Castoriadis 1988c; Lefort 1986a, 1986c; Arendt 1968). Up until the mid-1950s, they displayed no positive evaluations of modern society and little hope of a democratic remedy to totalitarianism. This may come as a surprise, as the three thinkers are generally known for their appraisals of *the political* and for their attempts to restore the importance of popular politics. The fundamental moment of political change for Castoriadis, Lefort and Arendt came with the Hungarian Revolution of 1956 and the emergence of revolutionary councils. It was this experience with the councils that made it possible for these political thinkers to develop new concepts of politics, freedom and democracy.

Castoriadis, Lefort and Arendt are extremely important interpreters of council democracy because the council system in their writings is transposed from a Marxist discourse to the discourse of democracy. The natural breeding ground for the historical councils was the factory shop floor and the production assembly line, as the councils primarily emerged as working-class institutions that sought to enhance the conditions for the working masses. Subsequently, the theoretical interpretations of the council system were primarily carried out by Marxist thinkers, who often saw the council system as partaking in a debate within the European labour movement on organisational forms of the proletariat, the means of revolutionary transformation, the end of capitalist exploitation, and the relations between the communist, vanguard party and the working masses. With Castoriadis's, Lefort's and Arendt's visions of council democracy, the council system gradually loses its firm, exclusive location within Marxism and working-class politics; instead, it becomes paradigmatic for general questions of the political, society's self-transformation and democracy. It is not the case that such questions are entirely foreign to the different Marxist interpretations. Instead, Castoriadis's, Lefort's and Arendt's visions of council democracy come to speak to problems which characterise political modernity as such, not just working-class politics. Questions of totalitarianism, bureaucracy, autonomy, constitutionalism, freedom, conflict, alienation and democracy can be discussed in novel conceptual registers through these thinkers' interpretations of the council system. This book demonstrates the productive relationship between Castoriadis, Lefort and Arendt and the council system insofar as their writings on the councils highlight novel aspects of their work as well as providing new insights into the politics of the councils.

The council system confronts Castoriadis, Lefort and Arendt with the most spectacular of human powers, namely that of the creation of new forms of political regime, as well as the inherent dangers of this power. Their different evaluations of such *constituent power* also make them conceptualise and evaluate the council system differently. Whereas Castoriadis and Arendt advance largely comparable theories of council democracy, namely as a political form that combines constituent power and constituted form in a manner that de-revolutionises the constituent power and makes it accessible to the many through participation in local, decentral and autonomous councils, Lefort's analysis of the council tradition is substantially different. Instead of pitting the council system against other political forms such as the party system, the unions, the state and representative government, as Castoriadis and Arendt do, Lefort argues that the councils – in a spirit of self-limitation – propose a political regime in which parties, unions and workers' councils co-govern in a mixed system. According to Lefort, every political regime in its pure form has the danger of totalitarianism inscribed into it; hence, there is a need for a plurality of political forms to coexist.

Because Castoriadis, Lefort and Arendt evaluate the potentialities and inherent dangers of the constituent power differently, they end up having markedly diverse visions of council democracy. These different interpretations of the relation between the council system and the constituent power also account for the way the chapters on Castoriadis, Lefort and Arendt are organised. I begin with Castoriadis, move on to Lefort and end with Arendt, because this order of investigation allows me to explore closely how the thinkers' changing evaluation of constituent power influences their visions of council democracy. Whereas Castoriadis has a rather uncritical understanding of constituent power, what he calls society's *instituting dimension*, as he locates the dangers to democracy only in bureaucracy or constituted politics, Lefort ends up abandoning the language of constituent power in relation to council democracy, as he sees traces of totalitarianism in this concept. Arendt, finally, is as critical of total politicisation as she is of depoliticisation; that is, she is equally critical of constituent power and constituted power, which is why she interprets council democracy as a combination of both. In order to expand on the different evaluations of council democracy advanced by the three thinkers, it is pertinent to introduce the concept of constituent power and its relevance for council democracy.

The Council System between Constituent Power and Constituted Form

The constituent power is the generative power to constitute the constitutional rules and political form of a polity. It is the power to alter and abolish the existing constitution or create a new one. The constituent power is closely linked to the advent of 'the people' in modern political thought; as 'the people' replaced the 'divine right of monarchs' or the 'natural order' as the legitimising force of politics, constituent power came to denote the self-instituting power of the people to decide on its own modes of collective existence (Loughlin and Walker 2007; Kalyvas 2005). The power to constitute and the sovereignty of 'the people' are therefore conceptually and historically coeval.[2] Moreover, the constituent power is often conceptualised as the superior power of the commonwealth, as the constitution, the legal system and all positive laws are derived from it as well as being subject to it.

As a superior power, though, the constituent power is fundamentally paradoxical. As aptly argued by Filippo Del Lucchese,

> modern theories of constituent power generally agree on its paradoxical essence: a power that comes before the law and founds the law is at the same time a power that, once the juridical sphere is established, has to be obliterated by the law. (Del Lucchese 2012: 182)

Firstly, and most importantly, the paradox lies in the relation between constituent power and constituted powers. Although the constituent power is the origin of the constitution, it emerges only in extraordinary moments of revolution, insurgency and mass upheaval. It is hence an episodic, momentary power, which cannot function in ordinary, normal politics. According to this conception, the constituent power is vested in an extraordinary organ such as a constitutional assembly that grants authority to the new regime; thereafter it is replaced by public officials, political institutions and elected representatives, who take care of the business of politics on behalf of the people. Martin Loughlin and Neil Walker have called this the 'juridical containment thesis', whereby 'constituent power is exhausted and absorbed within the settled constitutional form' (2007: 6). Hence, the difference between constituent politics and constituted politics is often conceptualised as absolute and clear-cut, and the survival of the constituent power in ordinary politics is perceived as a danger to the stability and order of the polity.

The second paradoxical element of the constituent power is its inherent arbitrariness, normlessness and circularity. Even though the constituent power is the origin of all political forms, legal normativity and procedural norms, it is itself often described as formless, normless and arbitrary. As Loughlin has argued, the constituent power is a 'juristic expression' of something that is not itself juridical; a formal expression of something that cannot be formalised, as this form of power is above positive law, and as such 'not easily reconcilable to law' (2003: 100). A simple question asked by Jacques Derrida illustrates the arbitrariness of the constituent power: who signed the American Declaration of Independence? An uncontroversial answer could be 'the American people'. But as Derrida argues, no such thing existed *before* the Declaration, as it was by virtue *of* the Declaration that the British settlers transformed themselves into 'the American people'. 'The signature', Derrida says, 'invents the signer' (1986: 10). This is an affirmation of the normlessness of constituent power, as the legitimate subject of this power ('the people') comes only *after* the very act of constituting. This act must hence by definition be arbitrary, contingent and reliant on force.

If the constituent power is the source of the constitution and its regulation of normal political life, what regulates the constituent power itself? One dominant answer is that *nothing* regulates the constituent power except itself, meaning that it is self-referential and formless. One of the most famous of such formulations was given by the French revolutionary Emmanuel Sieyès in the pamphlet 'What is the Third Estate?' published in 1789 just before the first meeting of the Estates-General of France since 1614, which eventually led to the French Revolution. According to Sieyès, the constituent power is above constituted politics and all forms of instituted legality, as it is itself unbound by law: 'the nation exists prior to everything; it is the origin of everything. Its will is always legal. It is law itself' (2003: 136). Sieyès uses a famous metaphor to describe the formlessness and arbitrariness of the constituent power, namely 'the state of nature'. 'A nation never leaves the state of nature', Sieyès argued, because

> a nation is independent of all forms, and however it may will, it is enough for its will to be made known for all positive laws to fall silent in its presence, because it is the source and supreme master of all positive laws. (Sieyès 2003: 138)

As a twentieth-century update of Sieyès, Carl Schmitt also stressed the formless, arbitrary nature of constituent power, as according to Schmitt, this power can 'change its forms and give itself continually new forms of political existence. It has the complete freedom of political self-determination. It can be the "*formless formative capacity*"' ([1928] 2008: 129, emphasis added).

It is in relation to these two paradoxes of the constituent power –
its antithetical relation to constituted power and its inherent formlessness – that the historical councils, and especially the visions of
council democracy developed by Castoriadis, Lefort and Arendt,
become relevant. The historical councils in Europe oscillated
between being temporary *organs of insurrection* and permanent
organs of public authority. On the one hand, they were spontaneously emerging strike committees, neighbourhood assemblies, rural
communes and factory councils, which due to their organic relation
to ordinary workers, residents, soldiers and peasants could effectively challenge existing relations of power and even overthrow the
existing political systems. The councils were hence revolutionary or
constituent organs. On the other hand, the councils often became
permanent *organs of public authority*, in some places even turning
into state-like organs of public power. As such, the councils were
also *constituted* political forms with certain institutional structures,
hierarchies and schematic modes of operation.

The political and intellectual debate on council democracy
after their widespread emergence in 1917–21 focused directly on
this duality of the councils' practices. Some argued that the councils were effective only as temporary means of insurrection, as pure
expressions of revolutionary constituent power, and that after the
revolution, the councils had to surrender their political power to
more visionary, rational and well-educated political leaders. This
was the argument of Russian Bolsheviks and German Social Democrats alike. Others argued that the council system laid the foundations for a new type of democracy: a proletarian democracy which
distinct institutional structures expressed 'the political form at last
discovered for the emancipation of labour', as Marx (1996a: 187)
had famously proclaimed in relation to the Paris Commune. That
is, the pivotal point of discussion was whether the councils were
expressions of constituent power or whether they were constituted
political forms. This debate on whether the councils were temporary
organs of insurrection or permanent organs of public authority mirrors discussions on the constituent power insofar as it operates with
the same clear-cut and absolute division between constituent power
and constituted form.

In my interpretation, Castoriadis, Lefort and Arendt seek to
develop a notion of constituent power – through their analyses of
the council tradition – that is not inherently formless, not only episodic and momentary and not outright hostile to institutionalisation.

Instead, by revisiting the council tradition, Castoriadis, Lefort and Arendt develop, in very different ways to be sure, a notion of constituent power that bridges the gap between extraordinary and ordinary politics, in order for the constituent power to become a part of everyday politics. Hence, these political thinkers position the council system between constituent formlessness and political form, insofar as the councils acquire the transformatory capabilities of constituent power as well as the stabilising effects of political institutionalisation. They regard the councils as 'formless forms'; as a form of 'constituted constituent power' that combines novelty and stability, order and action, spontaneity and organisation. This position is captured nicely by Herbert Marcuse, according to whom the councils 'express some kind of what I would like to call, and I mean it seriously, *organized spontaneity*' (Marcuse 2005: 126; original emphasis). For Castoriadis, Lefort and Arendt, the councils were certainly both temporary organs of insurrection as well as permanent organs of public authority, as they in different ways understood the councils as both 'organs of order as much as organs of action' (Arendt [1963] 2006: 255). For Castoriadis, Lefort and Arendt, then, it is not the case that the constituent power is completely formless and normless and neither that it is completely hostile to institutionalisation. Instead, according to these thinkers, the councils disclose a version of the constituent power that seeks to combine form and formlessness in order 'to make the *extraordinary* an *ordinary* occurrence of everyday life' (Arendt [1958] 1998: 197; emphasis added). Or as Arendt argued, the function of council-like organs is 'to enable men to do *permanently*, albeit under certain restrictions, what otherwise had been possible only as an *extraordinary* and *infrequent* enterprise' ([1958] 1998: 197; emphasis added).

By situating Castoriadis's, Lefort's and Arendt's writings on the councils, as well as the council tradition as a whole, in the context of the theoretical discussions on constituent power, this book's central theoretical ambition is to contribute to radical democratic theory. Lately, a number of radical democrats have established historical, conceptual and political links between constituent power and democracy. Antonio Negri, for example, claims that 'to speak of constituent power is to speak of democracy' (1999: 1). Sheldon Wolin and Jacques Rancière also contend that democracy is a practice that cannot be contained within an institutional (police) order (Rancière) or a constitution (Wolin), but that instead creates constitutions and their institutional logics (Rancière 2010: 32–3; Wolin 1994).

While radical democratic theories of constituent power do not fall into the Sieyèsian–Schmittian camp, as they are often developed as direct alternatives to the unitary and decisionistic notion of the people and its power in Schmitt, thinkers like Negri, Wolin and Rancière reproduce one of the central tenets of Sieyèsian–Schmittian constituent power, namely the antagonistic relation between constituent power and political form.[3] For Negri (1999: 1), constituent power resists every attempt at constitutionalisation and exists as an external, grounding force to every constitutional order; for Rancière (2010: 32–3, 35, 36–7), politics as transformative and constituent is excluded by every specific institutional order. In Wolin's case, the conceptual opposition is between 'constitutional democracy' and 'democratic constitutionalism'. While the first term designates the constitution's power over the *demos*, the second term implies the power of the *demos* over its constitution and hence its externality to it. From the second term Wolin develops a notion of *formless* democracy: 'I propose accepting the familiar charges that democracy is inherently unstable, inclined toward anarchy, and identified with revolution', Wolin argues, 'and using these traits as the basis for a different, *a*constitutional conception of democracy' (1994: 37).

By advancing a concept of democracy in contrast to any institutionalisable ideal, some radical democrats stress the inevitably inegalitarian form of social organisation that institutions always seem to require. For radical democrats, it is not only the question of exchanging an inegalitarian, oppressive form of government or constituted order for another, more egalitarian and free form of government. Instead, by pointing to the intimate relation between constituent power and democracy, radical democrats are able to differentiate between *any* institutionalised version of democracy and the democratic ideal of popular self-government itself. The problematic consequence of associating (radical) democracy with this specific understanding of constituent power, that is, with the antagonistic relation between constituent power and political form, is, I argue, that democracy itself becomes momentary, unable to ever institutionalise itself. As Wolin himself admits, democracy becomes an exceptional moment, 'revolutionary and excessive, irregular and spasmodic', which essentially makes it a 'bitter experience, doomed to succeed only temporarily' (1996: 48, 43). Consequently, I argue throughout the book that council democratic constituent power provides an important institutional approximation of radical democracy; that is, council democracy discloses a modality of politics both institutional and constituent. While council democracy shares with radical democracy the critique of the impoverished understanding of democracy within liberalism, as well as the critique of the decisionistic, unitary subject in Sieyèsian–Schmittian constituent power, council democracy proposes a historically grounded way to bridge the antagonistic gap between constituent power and political form entailed in many theories of radical democracy. The central theoretical aim of the book, therefore, is to contribute to radical democratic theory by providing a way to understand political institutions apart from domination, representation, discipline and elitism. In short, what does it mean for institutions to be radically democratic? In contrast to other commentators, I do not regard the commitment to constituent power and the lack of institutional focus in theories of radical democracy as essentially disqualifying. It is ultimately not a question of saving democracy from constituent power altogether, but instead of redefining constituent power itself through the experiences of the councils. By intending to let the councils as forms of insurrection *prefigure*, that is, be the *harbingers*, the *germs*, the *embryos*, the *nuclei* of future forms of self-government, council democracy expresses a form of constituent politics that establishes political forms aiming to prevent bureaucratisation, and preserving the constituent power while simultaneously checking its most arbitrary, anarchical and violent potentialities.

As a way of illustrating how the twentieth-century workers' councils could be interpreted as combining constituent power and political form, I would like to call attention to a scene from John Reed's narration of the storming of the Winter Palace, on the eve of the Russian October Revolution of 1917, from his famous book *Ten Days That Shook the World* (1919). Although spontaneous in nature, the storming of the Tsar's palace took place through the workers' and soldiers' councils, which had been created in abundance after the February Revolution of 1917. This scene succinctly expresses the combination of constituent power and political form which is at the centre of the book's exploration of council democracy:

> A number of huge packing cases stood about, and upon these the Red Guards and soldiers fell furiously, battering them open with the butts of their rifles, and pulling out carpets, curtains, linen, porcelain plates, glassware. One man went strutting around with a bronze clock perched on his shoulder; another found a plume of ostrich feathers, which he stuck in his hat.

The looting was just beginning when somebody cried, 'Comrades! Don't touch anything! Don't take anything! This is the property of the People!'. Immediately twenty voices were crying, 'Stop! Put everything back! Don't take anything! Property of the People!'. Many hands dragged the spoilers down. Damask and tapestry were snatched from the arms of those who had them; two men took away the bronze clock. Roughly and hastily the things were crammed back in their cases, and *self-appointed* sentinels stood guard. It was all utterly *spontaneous*. Through corridors and up stair-cases the cry could be heard growing fainter and fainter in the distance, '*Revolutionary discipline! Property of the People*'.

We crossed back over to the left entrance, in the West wing. There *order* was also being established. 'Clear the Palace!' bawled a Red Guard, sticking his head through an inner door. '*Come, comrades, let's show that we're not thieves and bandits.*' (Reed 1966: 108–9; emphasis added)

The scene portrays the symbolic zenith of the revolution, where workers, soldiers and the common people of Petrograd gain access to the grandiose palace, from where the Romanov dynasty had ruled the Russian Empire for over 300 years. Reed depicts what could be called an archetypical image of the act of revolting, of constituent power in the Sieyèsian–Schmittian modality: As political power is incarnated in the monarch's palace, the revolting people must storm this physical space in order to free themselves from the yoke of domination. On the one hand, Reed's description is one of transgression, where the symbols of the old regime are defiled and dishonoured. The images of one soldier with a bronze clock on his shoulder and another soldier with a plume of ostrich feathers in his hat depict a carnivalesque atmosphere of popular liberation. But on the other hand, Reed describes this extraordinary moment of revolt as containing a self-imposed order, self-created councils, even a sense of legality. The joy of spontaneous transgression is immediately combined with a care for structure through the creation of nascent institutions. As the insurrectionists left the Winter Palace, they passed through self-appointed councils and left behind all looted property from the palace.

Actually, Reed's depiction of the insurrection is nothing like the archetypical picture of a founding of a new body politic or of the normless constituent power in the Schmittian register. It is not a description of a popular mob that unleashes its primordial fury on its ancient oppressors, destroying everything in its wake. It is a description neither of a mythical founding moment of patricide, where the sons kill their father, nor of fratricide, where Cain slays Abel or Romulus murders Remus, nor of regicide, in which the multitude kills their king.[4] Instead, it is, I argue, an account of a group of insurrectionists who seem to be well aware of the tremendous power unleashed by their actions, and who realise the immediate need to give form to this constituent power. It is a description of a founding moment in which spontaneity and organisation, constituent power and political form, are combined instead of being experienced as opposites. The rest of the book investigates this combination of constituent power and political form through historical, conceptual and theoretical analyses of the 20th century workers' councils.

Outline of the Book

Chapter 1 discusses the councils in twentieth-century Europe focusing on Russia 1917, Germany 1918–19 and Hungary 1956. The chapter condenses the historical experiences of council politics into several principles, which set the councils apart from parliamentary democracy as well as from Bolshevism.

Chapter 2 reconstructs the political theory of council democracy from the classical anarchists' and Karl Marx's analyses of the Paris Commune over Vladimir Lenin's shifting evaluations of the Russian soviets to the German–Dutch council communists' critique of Bolshevism. The chapter argues that the theoretical discourse on council democracy is structured around concepts such as anti-statism, anti-parliamentarianism, economic self-management and popular self-government. The chapter closes with a preliminary discussion of council politics through the conceptual language of constituent power, which demonstrates how the political discussions on the council system can productively be translated into a theoretical discussion on the relation between constituent power and political form.

Chapter 3 reconstructs Castoriadis's theory of council democracy. The council system in Castoriadis's thought can be understood as an intermediary institution between what he calls the 'instituting power' and 'instituted society', and consequently, Castoriadis understands the councils as a way to institutionalise the constituent power and make it exercisable to all citizens. That is, the councils are spaces where the constituent power can be reactivated continually and regularly. The exposition of the three thinkers begins with Castoriadis, as he most deliberately relocates the council system from a discourse of Marxism to a discourse of democracy, and because he delivers the most optimistic analysis of constituent power and the council system, which both Lefort and Arendt will nuance and critique in later chapters.

Chapter 4 reconstructs Lefort's model of council democracy. I show how Lefort interprets the council system from the outset of his theory of democracy as an 'empty place of power', and how he – in contrast to Castoriadis and the council tradition in general – conceptualises the novel contribution of the councils to democratic theory as residing in their self-limiting proposals of a mixed regime of councils, parties and unions. In contrast to Castoriadis, Lefort is more suspicious of the constituent power due to the spectre of totalitarianism that haunts his political thinking. Therefore, Lefort proposes a set of conflicting political logics to balance each other in order to keep the place of power empty and prevent the emergence of what he calls the 'People-as-One'. Ultimately, Castoriadis evaluates the councils from the perspective of the constituent power, whereas Lefort takes a perspective on the council system as a constituted form. Lefort thereby provides a conceptual movement from the constituent power to the constituted power in analysing the council system.

Chapter 5 re-evaluates Arendt's writings on the council tradition and emphasises how the councils in Arendt's rendition can be understood as an alternative mode of revolution and constitution-making markedly different from liberal constitution-making and permanent revolution in the Jacobin–Bolshevik tradition. Instead, Arendt understood the councils as 'constituted, constituent organs', which were able to stabilise the revolutionary energy of popular foundings without exhausting its creative power. Arendt was as critical of pure constituent power in the modality of the French Revolution as she was critical of pure constituted power such as in the final result of the American Revolution. The discussion of Arendt, constituent power and the council system, thus, combines elements of Castoriadis's and Lefort's analyses by pointing to their internal weaknesses.

On the basis of the preceding chapters, Chapter 6 develops an original theoretical formulation of council democracy, which situates the council system between political form and transformatory politics, thereby incorporating arguments and insights from Castoriadis, Lefort and Arendt. The unique feature of the councils, I argue, is their way of combining institutional structure with an equal access to the constituent power of political transformation. This dual nature is the fundamental principle of council democracy, insofar as it bridges the clear-cut distinction between constituent politics and constituted politics, which I regard as the precondition for the survival of the constituent power after the moment of revolution. Council democracy hence provides an alternative understanding of the exception, extraordinary politics and constituent power compared with the dominant Sieyèsian–Schmittian conception of constituent power. In contrast to this conception, I argue that the experiences with the councils disclose a notion of constituent power that involves *immanent principles*, a *plural political subject*, an *active conception of citizenship* and a *politicised public sphere*. Such conceptualisation of the constituent power is important, because it reassess our evaluation of popular politics outside, below and against established political structures. Moreover, it contributes to radical democratic theory by proposing an institutional approximation of radical democracy. In short, council democratic constituent power expresses how contestation and struggle against established institutions can carry within itself immanent principles of legitimacy and nascent forms of legality.

Chapter 1
The Historical Councils in Twentieth-Century Europe

As all thinkers of the councils use the historical experiences with council organisation from the twentieth century as 'raw material' for their theories of council democracy, it is important to investigate what kind of political bodies the historical councils were, how they emerged, how they were structured and the way they dissolved. As leading historian on the Russian soviets Oskar Anweiler argues, 'the councils as they actually existed must clearly be distinguished from the ideology that subsequently developed. This ideology tries to construct an ideal council system that tends to leave reality far behind' (1974: 5). Consequently, this chapter provides an exploration of three key historical moments of twentieth-century council politics: Russia from 1905 to 1921, Germany from 1918 to 1919 and Hungary in 1956.

Workers' councils appeared simultaneously in many European countries from 1917 to 1921 (for in-depth studies on the council movements of specific European countries, see Carsten 1972; Michell 1965; Anweiler 1974; Williams 1975; Lindemann 1974; Sirianni 1980; Gluckstein 1985, 2011). Countries with vast geographical distance, different traditions of working life and degrees of industrialisation, and diverse reactions to the end of war developed similar institutions of workers' control and representational mechanisms, such as the soviets and their delegates in Russia; the *Arbeiterräte* with representatives, *Obleute*, in Germany; the *commissioni interne* and their *commissario* in Italy; and the *factory committees* in the British mining industries and their shop stewards. The appearance of the councils were sudden, spontaneous and uncoordinated (Gombin 1978: 83; Anweiler 1974: 4–5; Carsten 1972: 323; Michell 1965: 33), and they emerged as local reactions to context-specific problems, often as the institutionalisation of mass strikes concerned with concrete political issues such as starvation, dissatisfaction with the hardship of the war and lack of interest representation in the factories and army regiments.

Although we historically can only speak of a council system in *embryonic* form, as the various council formations never existed long enough for their structures to be fully developed,[1] this massive and sudden emergence of councils throughout Europe ought to be understood against the backdrop of the fundamental changes in the nature of political authority, which followed World War I. The political breakdown of the large-scale, multinational European empires after the war signified the contestation of most of the political ideas and institutional arrangements, which had characterised Europe in the late nineteenth and early twentieth centuries (Hobsbawm 1994: 6). As a matter of fact, council movements were crucial in bringing these empires to an end and initiate revolutionary transformation. The European empires had been authoritarian regimes ruled by royal sovereigns, whose rule had been passed down through generations, and dynasticism had thus been one of the principle factors legitimating political rule in Europe prior to the war (Müller 2011: 16).

The breakdown of monarchy, though, did not mean that new, clearly formulated ideas came to the fore. Questions of how to stabilise the newly constituted polities without a transcendental divine subject such as the monarch occupied the constitutional framers, and an immense degree of political experimentation took place. But the decline of monarchical sovereignty certainly did not mean that democratic ideas instantly became dominant – either intellectually or institutionally. Criticisms of 'mass society' and 'mass man' without the proper intellectual capabilities to deliberate and participate were heard almost everywhere (Jonsson 2013: 16–23), and the election of representatives to govern in the name of the new national people was often deemed inadequate, as real political power was believed to be vested elsewhere, in strong social groups and not least in the highly specialised bureaucracy. Consequently, the restructuring of Europe after World War I happened as a great political, economic and social experiment. Jan-Werner Müller has aptly summarised this period of political confusion on the political right (the now discredited monarchs), the liberal middle position and the communist left:

> Europeans were partly forced to experiment because both tradition and dynastic legitimacy had ceased to provide principles for public order, but new ones had hardly become entrenched. A liberal restoration proved impossible – there were too many new people in politics, too many new claims to be made – but so did the socialist revolution. (Müller 2011: 50)

Whereas liberal ideas of universalist citizenship, parliamentarianism and equal representation proved difficult due to the many new faces in the new national political communities such as women, peasants, workers and ethnic minorities (Carsten 1972: 11), socialists, communists and social democrats were also baffled by the new political order. Two major models of socialist politics became dominant after World War I (Eley 2002: 89): one was the communist position in which a theoretically disciplined vanguard in a centralised party sought to educate the masses and enhance their class-consciousness in order for the laws of history to do their inevitable work and let the working class destroy capitalism and bourgeois society altogether. This was the position of the Bolsheviks in Russia and the numerous communist parties of Western Europe that appeared after the Russian Revolution. In contrast, the other position, held by the social democratic parties, was that parliamentary democracy was an arena well-suited to attaining the goals of the working class. By enhancing power in parliament and by making alliances with non-socialist parties, living conditions, education, equality and freedom could be enhanced for all workers. Representative government and capitalism were thus not something to be destroyed, but something to be enhanced (the widening of suffrage and removal of age and property qualifications) and controlled (the state as an intervening force in the market). The communists were generally shocked by the policies of their social democratic counterparts. Whereas Marxist intellectuals had predicted that World War I would reveal the unity of the working classes across Europe, the social democrats in every European country opted for war and broad national cooperation (Eley 2002: 123). Thus, the two models of socialist politics became more intensively oppositional in the years after the war. The conflict now concerned not only different strategies towards the same political goals, but completely different evaluations of representative government, capitalism and the Great War.

Despite their disagreements, though, the social democrats and the Bolsheviks did agree on central political issues. Both these groups were essentially hierarchical elite organisations, which sought to either mobilise the working masses through the vote or to radicalise them through agitation and propaganda, but neither movement thought the working masses capable of governing themselves. Also, the social democrats and Bolsheviks agreed that the state and its coercive apparatus were of primary importance (Eley 2002: 93–9). For the social democrats, the state was the locus of parliamentary power, thus the aim was to take control of the legal forms of power which dwelt in the state and use them for the enhancement of the conditions of the workers. The Bolsheviks, instead, saw the state as the oppressive objectification of the class rule of the bourgeoisie, thus making it of primary importance to smash the state. The only way to do so was by initially taking over the state itself and asserting the class rule of the proletariat over its former oppressors. As concluded by Nikos Poulantzas, 'both are marked by *statism*, and profound distrust of the mass initiatives, in short by suspicion of democratic demands' (1978: 251; original emphasis).

The landscape of the left, though, was more complicated than the opposition between social democracy and Bolshevism. Other, less political successful strains of leftist thought and practice took part in debates on democracy, the role of the state and capitalism. They especially attacked the centralisation and hierarchy of the social democratic parties, the trade unions and the communist vanguard, the lack of real incorporation of workers and peasants, and the social democratic and Bolshevik preoccupation with the power of the state. Council communists in the early twentieth century rejected the parliamentarianism and elections of the social democrats on the one hand and the elitism, discipline and secrecy of the communist vanguard on the other hand, and instead – as Eley aptly puts it – 'they defended democratic values that socialists . . . tended to forget – local control, direct participation, small-scale community, and federative corporation' (2002: 95). Instead of socialising the economy through the control of the state, council communists valued the rank-and-file workers and shop-floor activity; instead of honouring the parliamentary process, they preferred direct action and strikes; and instead of a vanguard of professional revolutionaries, they stressed mass insurgency.

The widespread appearances of workers', soldiers', peasants' and sailors' councils throughout Europe from 1917 to 1921 took place within this post-World War I crisis. As the old systems of legitimation and modes of political power had died out without giving birth to new modes of stabilising the political communities, revolution and turmoil emerged all over the continent (Lindemann 1974: xiii). The impetus behind the uprisings was in almost every case the social groups that had suffered the most under the harsh wartime conditions such as the factory workers, ordinary soldiers, conscripted peasants, and naval personnel, who completely lost confidence in the established political systems due to the deterioration of their living conditions during the war (Sirianni 1980: 36–9). When the war ended in 1918, many European countries were thus in a revolutionary or pre-revolutionary situation; and already a year before, the revolutionary torch had been lit in Russia with the formation of workers', soldiers' and sailors' councils.

The 1905 Revolution in St Petersburg: The Inauguration of the Council Form

The Russian soviets – *soviet* literally meaning 'council' in Russian – appeared for the first time in the so-called 'failed revolution' of 1905, and consequently, any history of the soviets must begin with their sudden appearance in 1905. The year 1905 was marked by intense unrest in the greater Russian cities, especially St Petersburg and Moscow, where a series of intense strikes took place. In particular, in St Petersburg, the event known as 'Bloody Sunday' on 9 January 1905 – where a group of demonstrating workers led by the priest Father Gapon was fired at by soldiers of the Imperial Guard in front of the Winter Palace – was met by outrage, resulting in mass strikes across the industrialised cities of Russia (Anweiler 1974: 32–3). The strikers' demands were both economic and political: better working conditions for industrial workers, as well as political rights such as freedom of assembly and speech, which did not exist for the working masses in Russia.

Throughout 1905, dissatisfaction among the working masses intensified greatly, due both to external affairs, such as the loss in the Japanese–Russian war in 1904–5, and to the increasing violence of the Tsarist regime. In October 1905, the printers of St Petersburg began to strike in sympathy with their fellow printers in Moscow, who had recently been striking for the betterment of their working conditions. In mid-October, the railway workers joined them, paralysing the entire railway network around the city, and during the strikes on 10 and 12 October, factory workers, small shopkeepers, hospital workers, students and teachers joined the demonstrations against the Tsar (Anweiler 1974: 44). During these mass strikes, demonstrators formed a strike committee with the object of paying a salary to workers on striking days, coordinating the strike activity, and negotiating with the authorities as well as the individual factory owners.

Throughout 1905, many factories in and around St Petersburg had developed the habit of electing delegates to factory committees, which could represent the interests of the rank-and-file workers to the management (Anweiler 1974: 38–9; Smith 1997). On 13 October 1905, during yet another mass strike against the Tsarist regime, the newly established strike committee decided to combine their own efforts with the actions of the factory committees, and issued the following appeal to the St Petersburg workers:

> The assembly of deputies from all factories and workshops will form a general workers committee in St. Petersburg. The committee will strengthen and unify our movement, represent the St. Petersburg workers to the public, and decide actions during the strike, as well as its termination. (Qtd in Anweiler 1974: 46)

With this call, the representatives of the separate factories of the St Petersburg area were to join a city-wide strike committee, which included delegates from trade unions as well as representatives from the three major socialist parties (the Mensheviks, the Bolsheviks and the Socialist Revolutionaries), and hence, the first soviet of workers' deputies – i.e. council – was born. It lasted fifty days from 13 October to 3 December. As Anweiler concludes, 'Whenever such a strike committee – for running a single action, for a limited time – turned into a permanent elected delegation with much broader aims, then we have before us a council (soviet) of workers deputies' (1974: 39). It was precisely such a call for a permanent assembly of factory delegates which was the first action of the St Petersburg Soviet.

The newly established St Petersburg Soviet decided that it was to have one delegate from every 500 workers from every factory in the St Petersburg area, and when it assembled on 15 October, only two days after the initial call for factory deputies, it already hosted 226 delegates from 96 different factories. At its height, the soviet had 400–500 delegates, representing around 200,000 industrial workers. The first council to emerge in history, hence, was born in a revolutionary situation with the immediate aim of coordinating the direction of strikes and uprisings. It appeared spontaneously and without the influence of existing proletarian organisations. In this sense, it was a *revolutionary* organisation – a political organ that emerged in struggle; an organisation well-suited to the hastiness and spontaneous character of an uprising. In 1907, Leon Trotsky, who was elected chairman of the St Petersburg Soviet's Executive Committee, summarised this aspect of a soviet as a revolutionary organisation:

> The Soviet came into being as a response to an objective need – a need born of the course of events. It was an organization which was authoritative and yet had no traditions; which could immediately involve a scattered mass of hundreds of thousands of people while having virtually no organizational machinery; which united the revolutionary currents within the proletariat; which was capable of initiative and spontaneous self-control – and most important of all, which could be brought out from underground within twenty-four hours. (Trotsky 1907)

In addition to being a *revolutionary* organisation, the St Petersburg Soviet also aspired to be an organ of *proletarian self-government*. After the October strikes, the Soviet continued its meetings and assembled broad strains of the labour movement, including delegates from factory committees, borough assemblies, trade unions and parties. Although its immediate activity – the coordination of the strikes – was no longer necessary, as this had waned again, the St Petersburg Soviet stayed in session because its delegates, and the workers they represented, found the Soviet a productive organ for coordination.

From their very inception, then, the soviets contained a dual purpose, which is crucial and will be reformulated by many council thinkers, including Castoriadis, Lefort and Arendt: the councils functioned both for the temporary coordination of the insurrection and as the permanent self-government and representation of workers. The St Petersburg Soviet, though, or any soviet that appeared anywhere in Russia in 1905, did not envision itself as constituting a new form of state power which would eventually replace the autocratic regime. The general politics, which the St Petersburg Soviet pursued, was to convene a Constituent Assembly and advocate for parliamentary democracy. The soviets, the workers thought, were useful for practical organisation and concrete political negotiations (Anweiler 1974: 63). The St Petersburg Soviet existed from October to December 1905 when its leaders were arrested and the factory committees on which the Soviet was built were dissolved by law. Although the 1905 soviets achieved little politically, they stayed in the minds of workers and revolutionaries, so when unrest and dissatisfaction arose in February 1917, the reconstitution of the soviets was the natural response of the Russian proletariat.

The 1917 Revolution: From Organs of Insurrection to Organs of State Power

From the beginning of World War I in 1914, strike activity went on the rise due to the hardship of the war. The popular unrest was felt intensely by industrial workers in the cities and peasants in the countryside, but the group on which the war inflicted the most direct consequences was the common soldiers at the front. As a result, they were to have the most extraordinary influence on the second emergence of the Russian councils in the February Revolution of 1917. Like the St Petersburg Soviet in 1905, the Petrograd Soviet, which was the first soviet to appear in 1917, was essentially sparked into life during the mass strikes of February 1917 that eventually turned out to be the starting point for the February Revolution and the end of the Romanov dynasty. On 24 February, nearly 200,000 workers took to the streets of Petrograd, paralysing the city in a general strike (Anweiler 1974: 101; Smith 1983). Like the 1905 strikes, no leadership directed these mass strikes; the socialist parties did not plan them, nor did the re-establishment of councils appear in the political programme of the major socialist parties (Mandel 2011: 104). Instead, the strikes arose spontaneously through the actions of workers in the industrial parts of Petrograd (Anweiler 1974: 102; Sirianni 1980: 15–16).

On 27 February, as a response to the need to coordinate the mass strikes, workers and revolutionaries formed the Petrograd Soviet at the Tauride Palace. As a first order of business, the newly established soviet called for elected deputies from the factories and army regiments and established a provisional Executive Committee. The factories were to send one delegate for each 1,000 workers, and the soldiers to send one delegate from every regiment, no matter how small the regiment might be. Herein lies the chief difference in composition between the 1905 and 1917 soviets. By incorporating elected soldiers' deputies alongside workers' deputies, the Petrograd Soviet was able to accelerate the revolutionary situation by gradually taking control of the means of violence. The soldiers had already been rebelling at the front, and as most soldiers came from labouring classes, they – as did the industrial workers – had the organisational form of the soviet fresh in their minds and close to their hearts. As Trotsky noted in his history of the revolution, 'the form of organization itself [the soviet] stood clear of all debate' (1932: 174).

As a revolutionary situation often involves the struggle over the means of violence, the High Command of the army, who were loyal to the Tsar, called for discipline in the ranks and obedience from the soldiers. The Petrograd Soviet replied immediately with their Order Number 1. Order Number 1 repeated the call for soldiers' deputies from every regiment but went even further by announcing that these regiments were now under the control of the Soviet. In this way, the Petrograd Workers' and Soldiers' Council acquired control of the Petrograd garrison. Throughout March 1917, after Tsar Nicholas had abdicated and the revolutionary movement was split into two power centres – that is, the Provisional Government centred on middle-class and liberal interests, and the Petrograd Soviet representing the working class and the soldiers – the soviets became a mass phenomenon emerging all over Russia. Peasants' councils were established in the countryside, borough councils appeared in neighbourhoods alongside workers' councils emanating from the factories, and naval councils were established in the fleet. During the months after the February Revolution, a politicisation of society took place, as local grass-roots organisations imitating the structure of the Petrograd Soviet appeared everywhere, giving voice to the subgroups of the population that had hitherto been excluded from political life (Smirnov 1997: 429). Anweiler summarises the political climate in the immediate aftermath of the February Revolution the following way:

> Spontaneously they [councils of every kind] mushroomed everywhere, without theoretical preparation, stimulated only by the immediate needs of the revolution. The council idea – that is, the idea of a revolutionary representative body that could be established simply, quickly, anywhere at any time – seemed to the Russian workers and soldiers automatically the most suitable form of uniting along class lines at a time of political and social upheaval. (Anweiler 1974: 111)

At the centre of this politicisation of society stood the Petrograd Soviet, which by the end of March, only a month after its inception, had 3,000 deputies. The mode of electing deputies involved novel forms of representation – at least in theory. The 3,000 deputies were elected by the local factory committees and soldiers' councils and were answerable to these local bodies at any time. The deputies were under imperative mandate, implying that the elected deputy carried the will of the constituency (the factory or the army regiment) to the central council (the Petrograd Soviet), and if the deputy did not perform according to the expectations of the constituency, they could be recalled immediately (Smirnov 1997: 430). In theory, these mechanisms between the lower and higher councils were intended to ensure that political power stayed at the lowest level possible, so that ordinary workers and soldiers controlled the revolutionary situation. However, as more and more deputies were elected, as the soviet movement spread through the cities and the countryside, and as the Petrograd Soviet acquired further political and administrative tasks due to the breakdown of governmental authority after the February Revolution, leading positions in the Petrograd Soviet were taken up by experienced politicians, primarily Mensheviks and Socialist Revolutionaries, but also some Bolsheviks. The delegates from the factories and barracks often played the role of the legitimising chorus rather than actively participating beyond the plenary sessions of the Soviet (Smirnov 1997: 430; Sirianni 1982: 69–71).

Before June 1917, workers' and soldiers' councils throughout the country sent delegates to the Petrograd Soviet. As an attempt to make the council movement more effective, as well as making it more representative of the entire country, a gradual federalisation between councils took place, and in June 1917, the First All-Russian Congress of Soviets of Workers' and Soldiers' Deputies was held. The All-Russian Congress of Soviets was to become the supreme organ of the revolutionary movement, and this 'in practice [was] the beginning of the creation of a new type of state apparatus' (Smirnov 1997: 431). The soviets, though, did not at first aspire to be permanent organs of state power. This was due to two central elements of the soviets: firstly, the early councils were revolutionary organs, born amidst great upheaval and instituted to direct the revolution forward and take care of practical and economic questions related to everyday life. In all proclamations passed by the early soviets, the central political demands were to end the war and to convene a Constituent Assembly, with the object of deciding on the future constitutional form of Russia. Therefore, the delegates of the early soviets did not aspire to have the soviets take sovereign state power. Secondly, the Mensheviks and other moderate socialists, who did not endorse the Bolshevik slogan of 'All power to the soviets', dominated the Petrograd Soviet (Anweiler 1974: 139). The Mensheviks often adopted a strictly Marxist interpretation of the political situation. According to Marx in his famous 'stage theory' (1996a: 158–63), the passage from feudalism and autocracy to communism could not leap over a period of capitalism and bourgeois parliamentarianism. It would be the internal contradictions of capitalist society which would shape the proletarian consciousness and prepare the proletariat for class war. As Russia was primarily a peasant country in 1917 apart from a few, heavily industrialised areas, the Mensheviks argued that the February Revolution was akin to the French Revolution of 1789, and that a parliamentary democracy with large-scale representation of working-class interests was most suitable for the economic situation as well as for guarding the revolution against counter-revolutionary conspiracies (Anweiler 1974: 141). Thus, while the soviets were certainly revolutionary organs that had brought self-management and interest representation to the working masses, the councils themselves did not seek sovereign power over the country. While local soviets performed bureaucratic tasks that state institutions would normally perform, due to the breakdown of public authority after the fall of the Tsarist regime, this was supposed to be temporary until a constitutional assembly had decided on the political future of the country.

The fate of the Russian councils is linked to the October Revolution, the Bolshevik takeover of power and the subsequent establishment of a one-party dictatorship. The Bolsheviks' relation to the soviets is a much-discussed issue. One dominant view (Anweiler 1974: 144–207) is that the Bolsheviks did *not* play a direct part in the initial creation of the soviets in 1905 or in 1917, that the councils did *not* feature in the political programmes of the Bolsheviks between 1905 and 1917, and that support for the soviets from the Bolsheviks, and especially from Lenin, waxed and waned with their strategic use to the Bolshevik party. Throughout the late summer and early autumn of 1917, as the war progressed and as the dual-power situation was unable to solve pressing political questions, Bolshevik influence in the soviets, as well as in the factory committees and rural communes, was on the rise. Moreover, the Kornilov Affair in August 1917 led many industrial workers to agitate for the full takeover of power by the soviets. The soviets hesitated, but the Bolsheviks did not. Lenin realised that the working masses were tied to the soviets to a much greater degree than they were to the Bolshevik Party. They perceived the soviets as *their own* organisations; hence, a takeover of power, Lenin reasoned, had to be disguised as a takeover of power by the soviets.

On the night before the opening of the Second All-Russian Congress of Councils of Workers' and Soldiers' Deputies, the Bolsheviks alongside armed workers, soldiers and sailors occupied the seat of the Provisional Government, the Winter Palace. Of the 670 delegates of the Second All-Russian Congress, 300 were Bolsheviks and hence they did not have an absolute majority in the Congress of Soviets. But in response to what they believed was an illegitimate takeover of power, the Mensheviks and moderate Socialist Revolutionaries walked out of the Congress. Now, the Bolsheviks had an absolute majority in the Congress, and it declared that the soviets had over-thrown the Provisional Government, and that the soviets were now the sovereign power of Russia (Rabinowitch 1997: 89–90). Lenin opened the Congress triumphantly:

> Backed by the will of the vast majority of the workers, soldiers, and peasants, backed by the victorious uprising of the workers and the gar-rison which has taken place in Petrograd, the Congress takes power into its own hands . . . The Congress decrees: all power in the localities shall pass to the Soviets of Workers', Soldiers' and Peasants' Deputies, which must guarantee genuine revolutionary order. (Lenin 1917g)

Formally, Russia was now a republic of soviets, a *council republic*. But quickly the Bolsheviks took control over the soviets and used their connection to the masses to cloak their *coup d'état* in legal-ity. The Congress declared the All-Russian Central Executive Committee to be the highest organ of state power and established the Council of People's Commissars as the highest executive organ. Lenin was elected chairman of the Council of People's Commissars, which included only Bolsheviks (Smirnov 1997: 432). The bolshevi-sation of the soviets was in full swing, and during the following months, the Bolsheviks came to control most local and regional soviets, thereby establishing a one-party rule through the soviets. The regime they founded, the Union of Soviet Socialist Republics (USSR), retained the soviets in their official name, as well as the formal foundation of power in the constitution of the USSR,[2] but the independent power of the soviets diminished as the Bolsheviks took power.

Ironically, the council movement came to a definitive end in Russia in 1921, when the Kronstadt sailors, who had been loyal to the Octo-ber Revolution, rebelled against the Bolshevik dictatorship by form-ing a new soviet in Kronstadt and demanding new elections in the existing soviets across the country in order for the soviets to get rid of Bolshevik control, and relaunch them as organs of proletarian self-government (Anweiler 1974: 244–53; Avrich 1991). The Bolshevik troops with Trotsky in their lead brutally destroyed the rebellion and the attempt to re-establish and revitalise the soviets. The day after, the Bolshevik leadership celebrated the fiftieth anniversary of the Paris Commune (Figes 1998: 768).

When the period from the failed revolution in 1905 through the two revolutions in 1917 to the repressed Kronstadt rebellion in 1921 is condensed, what can be concluded about the Russian soviets? In the sixteen-year span of their dispersed existence, the Russian soviets took on very different roles and executed diverse functions. They began as spontaneous mass organisations constituted by ordinary workers during mass strikes, as no other organisations represented the interests of the workers (the 1905 soviets). The natural breeding ground for these councils was the strike and the factory shop floor. The councils, thus, were instruments of mobilisation, politicisation and representation; hence, they functioned as a way to give voice to those without political voice. The basic *modus operandi* was to send delegates, elected by ordinary workers in the factories, to a common assembly (i.e. a soviet) to coordinate, deliberate and decide. Hence, the councils began as spontaneous organs emerging in revolutionary situations in order to represent the lower levels of society.

The nature of the 1917 soviets had both similar and different traits compared with the 1905 soviets. The basic idea of a representative organ gathering delegates from workplaces and factories was still central, but it was combined with two additional elements: firstly, these councils incorporated not only workers, but also soldiers and sailors and later peasants, implying that the councils could function as a mechanism for representing the entire lower strata of the population. Hence, they were class-specific modes of representation, which tried to unite the lower classes in one movement, contra bourgeois parliaments, which are – at least in theory – class-neutral organs of representation.[3] Secondly, the 1917 soviets displayed a novel function of the councils that became very influential in subsequent theories of council democracy. The 1917 councils not only functioned as spontaneous strike committees, but became – gradually – organs of state power. Due to the complete breakdown of political authority as a result of the dissolution of the Romanov dynasty, the Petrograd Soviet and later the All-Russian Congress of Soviets performed tasks of state power including control of the army, the upholding of order and the distribution of food. Exercising such state power included the need for an expanding bureaucracy and a more effective leadership through the establishment of the Executive Committee. As the soviets started to resemble organs of state power, their function as organs of proletarian self-government diminished.

The development of the Russian councils shows that every council formation can be placed on a continuum from spontaneous, temporary organs of mass strike to permanent, state-like institutions of public authority.

The 1918–19 German Revolution

Next to the Russian councils, the German councils were the most well-developed councils to appear in Europe, as Germany was officially a council republic from November 1918 to January 2019. Throughout November, December (1918) and January (1919), independent council republics were proclaimed in Brunswick and Bavaria, and workers' and soldiers' councils took charge of various German cities such as Leipzig, Hamburg, Düsseldorf, Kiel, Lübeck and Hanover (Kuhn 2012: xxv–xxvi). All over Germany, soldiers and sailors were mutinying and workers were striking due to the hardships of war. Throughout 1918, the state and Kaiser Wilhelm II lost public authority in the large cities and industrial areas, and the German military high command lost control over large parts of the armed forces. The German workers', soldiers' and sailors' councils were responsible for ending World War I in Germany and for the abdication of Kaiser Wilhelm II, but their story is little known (Pelz 2018). The conditions from which the German councils appeared were somewhat similar to those behind the appearance of the Russian soviets, as was the development of the political situation in Germany in 1918–19, which also passed through phases of spontaneous strikes, the formation of councils, a period resembling dual power between the councils and parliamentary forces and, finally, the dissolution of the councils – not by Bolshevism this time, but by the other historical enemy of the councils: the Social Democratic Party. For the rest of the twentieth century, the political struggle between communist one-party dictatorship and multiparty, capitalist democracy would dominate European politics, but before this political landscape ossified, the councils appeared as an alternative to both.

The spread of councils started with a sailors' mutiny in Kiel and Wilhelmshaven on 5 November 1918, where the sailors, after having refused to take on a last, desperate naval campaign against the superior British fleet, formed a sailors' council, elected representatives amongst themselves and took control over the port, and subsequently the entire city (Eley 2002: 165). Consequently, soldiers and workers organised in councils and seized power over both Kiel and Wilhelmshaven. Popular mass insurgency, primarily due to dis-satisfaction with the war, spread across the country, as workers and soldiers in many places formed local councils, committees and other popular institutions (Schecter 1994: 79; Eley 2002: 165–9; Hof-frogge 2011: 96–8). Mass strikes and dissatisfaction paralysed the economy as well as the state bureaucracy. Although the formation of councils took place across the entire country, events in the impe-rial capital of Berlin were of the greatest significance, and here strike activity reached unprecedented heights.

Facing such massive political unrest, the German emperor Wil-helm II abdicated, leaving Germany in a revolutionary situation without any established political leadership (Hoffrogge 2011: 94). The abdication was followed by the proclamations of two oppos-ing German republics: a liberal and a socialist one. On 9 Novem-ber 1918 in Berlin, member of the Social Democratic Party (SPD) Philipp Scheidemann proclaimed Germany a liberal republic with parliamentarianism as its constitutional form. To the dissatisfaction of many ordinary workers and to the shock of many left-wing radi-cals, the SPD had supported the war, and the party now supported a bourgeois revolution from autocracy to parliamentary democracy.

Hours after Scheidemann's proclamation of a liberal republic, revolutionary leader of the Spartacus League Karl Liebknecht pro-claimed Germany a socialist republic to be governed by a system of sailors', soldiers' and workers' councils (Kuhn 2012: 27). In prin-ciple, the leading organ of the council movement, the Executive Committee of the Workers' and Soldiers' Councils of Great Berlin, just like the Petrograd Soviet, would consist of revocable delegates from local factory committees, soldiers' and sailors' councils. But during the tumultuous days after the Kaiser's abdication and in the absence of established political authority, the real trust of the Berlin workers lay with the so-called 'Revolutionary Shop Stewards', who had been involved in anti-war unionism with the rank-and-file workers, and hence had the confidence of the industrial workers. Throughout the war, the Revolutionary Shop Stewards had frater-nised with the industrial workers of the Berlin area and set up a *de facto* system of factory committees (Hoffrogge 2011: 88–9). In the face of great confusion caused by the dual proclamation of two conflicting German republics, the Revolutionary Shop Stewards called for a great meeting with leaders of the council movement as well as delegates from the social democratic and socialist par-ties. An agreement was reached to form a provisional government consisting of the Executive Committee of the Workers' and Soldiers' Councils and a Council of People's Commissars. Leadership of both organs was divided between the reformist SPD and the more revolutionary USPD (the Independent Social Democratic Party of Germany). The composition of this provisional government demonstrates that historically, there is not always clear-cut opposition between councils and parties, as later theorists of council democracy have often argued. Although the German councils emerged spontaneously through mass strikes and mutinies, they willingly invited political leaders from existing socialist parties to join and often lead the council movement.

The dual-power situation lasted little over a month, not without strikes and unrest, until 16–21 December, when the General Congress of the Workers' and Soldiers' Councils of Germany was held in Berlin. Elections to the congress took place in local factories as well as in army regiments, each of which sent one delegate per 1,000 workers to the congress (Gluckstein 1995: 142). Up till the election to the Congress, the SPD had used its overwhelming party machine to mobilise the working masses in order for the party to secure the majority of the votes. The Social Democrats were successful: of the 490 delegates at the Congress, around 60 per cent were associated with the SPD and thus in favour of a parliamentary system, whereas only around 20 per cent were associated with the more radical USPD, which favoured the establishment of a sovereign council system (Carsten 1972: 133). Consequently, the Social Democrats were firmly in control of the Congress, which quickly decided that a national election to a parliament was to be held as early as 19 January 1919. The Congress furthermore decided that the Executive Committee of Workers' and Soldiers' Councils should be stripped of any independent power and function only as a supervisory organ. The radical elements of the Congress opposed these decisions and proposed a new constitution based on the council system; the proposal was rejected by 344 to 98 votes (Carsten 1972: 134). Faced with this defeat, the delegates associated with USPD and other radical strains of the workers' movement in favour of the councils withdrew from the Congress and handed full power over the German council movement to the Social Democrats. Hence, it was the council movement itself or its delegates at the Congress – heavily influenced by the successful agitation by the reformist SPD – that agreed to its own dissolution and the handing over of power to a parliamentary republic.

During the Congress, Rosa Luxemburg voiced concern about this self-dissolution in the newspaper published by the Spartacus League, *Die Rote Fahne*:

> National assembly or council government? That is the second point on the agenda of the national assembly of the workers' and soldiers' councils. It is also the cardinal question of the revolution right now: we either elect a national assembly or we empower the workers' and soldiers' councils; we either forgo socialism or we engage in uncompromising class struggle between the proletariat and the bourgeoisie. (Luxemburg 2012a: 119)

By 21 December, when the Congress was over, Luxemburg summarised its achievements:

> The first meeting of the Council Congress is over. If you judge the outcome by the discussions that the delegates engaged in and by the decrees that they issued, it was a total victory for the Ebert government[4] and the counterrevolution. (Luxemburg 2012a: 116)

Luxemburg was indeed right, as the SPD controlled the governing organs of the council movement after the Congress. Throughout December 1918 and January 1919, clashes between government troops and armed workers took place due to dissatisfaction with the counter-revolutionary policies of the SPD. The unrest culminated with the assassination of Karl Liebknecht and Rosa Luxemburg on 15 January 1919 after the so-called 'Spartacus Uprising' after which the council movement lost its impetus. The independent council republics in Bavaria, Bremen and Brunswick were destroyed by government troops throughout the first months of 1919. The workers' councils were subdued and became controlled by trade unions which were loyal to the SPD, and with the transformation from the autocratic German Empire to the Weimar Republic, the German council movement dissolved.

The experience of council organisation in Germany, hence, did not go as far as in Russia, and lasted for an even shorter time than the Russian soviets. Like the Russian soviets, though, the German *Räte* functioned as revolutionary organs, which effectively challenged the existing authorities and successfully created new institutions of public power during times of crisis. Like the soviets, the German councils were able to represent and empower the lower strata of the population, giving them a voice on political matters.

The chief difference between these two primary experiences with the council system in the twentieth century was that the German councils somewhat willingly surrendered power to the forces of par-liamentarianism, whereas the forces of Bolshevism infiltrated the Russian councils. In both examples of council politics, the delegates from factories, peasant communities, military units and the navy very seldom spoke of the establishment of a sovereign republic of councils, but instead rallied around concrete political goals such as the betterment of working conditions, the termination of brutalism in the army and more self-management in factories.

The Hungarian Uprising against Soviet Totalitarianism

The experiments with council organisation in Europe after World War I were not restricted to Russia and Germany, as council sys-tems in different forms appeared in Great Britain, Italy, Austria and Hungary, and later during the Spanish Civil War. In view of this, it is remarkable that bottom-up organisations for the representation of workers, soldiers and other marginalised groups did emerge simul-taneously in many European countries around the end of World War I. It is noteworthy that the council form was geographically widespread, politically influential and seemed like a natural organ-isational impulse in the face of the pervasive breakdown of politi-cal authority. I will not provide a detailed analysis of these council formations, as they did not acquire the same political power as their Russian and German counterparts, and as council thinkers in the interwar period primarily developed theories of council democracy based on the Russian and German experiences. Instead, I shall dis-cuss the experiences with workers' councils during the Hungarian Revolution of 1956, as Castoriadis, Lefort and Arendt were tremen-dously inspired by the activities of the Hungarian revolutionaries.

The Hungarian Revolution did not only have a lasting influence on the three main thinkers of this book. The revolutionary days in late October and early November 1956 also had a permanent influ-ence on the lines of conflict within the European communist parties. For many on the left, the end of the Hungarian Revolution, namely the Soviet invasion of Hungary on 4 November and the reinstalment of a Moscow-controlled communist government, meant they were faced with a fundamental decision on whether the Hungarian Revolu-tion, and the establishment of revolutionary councils throughout the country, was the resurfacing of the true ideal of socialist revolution, as the emerging institutions resembled the Russian soviets of 1905 and 1917, or whether the uprising in Hungary constituted a major counter-revolutionary danger (Eley 2002: 334; Müller 2011: 163–5; Fehér and Heller 1983: 42–9). Either one had to remain loyal to the authority of the Party, stressing that, as the Hungarian uprising was directed against the Soviet-loyal government, it could only be a counter-revolutionary moment; or one had to acknowledge that the spontaneous upheaval and the sudden emergence of popular councils was a genuine moment of working-class self-organisation, and as such exemplified the democratic kernel of socialism. In making this choice, many left-wing intellectuals, socialist activists and communist party members were also taking a direct stance on the fundamental issues of the socialist project: who spoke with the *true* voice of socialism – the insurrectionary people or the deputies of the communist party? Which force ought to determine the course of history – the spontaneous actions of people in the streets or the communist leaders with their special insight into the laws of history?

For many members of the communist parties across the European continent, the historical embodiment of the communist ideal – the Soviet Union – lost its innocence and purity as its tanks rolled into the streets of Budapest. What became known as the New Left, with its emphasis on participatory democracy rather than party discipline and loyalty to historical necessity, was very much sparked into being by siding with the Hungarian people *against* the military forces of the Soviet Union (Eley 2002: 336). As aptly phrased by Fehér and Heller, the Hungarian Revolution's 'greatest historical merit was *to question the existing concept of socialism*, and at least to *suggest an alternative one*' (1983: 115; original emphasis). This 'alternative' concept of socialism was not, as we know from this chapter, a completely new one, but rather the re-emergence of *council* socialism. As argued by one historian of the revolution, the Hungarian insurrectionists, 'instead of imitating the Yugoslav model, which was little known, . . . followed the Soviet of model of 1905 and 1917' (Molnár 1971: 175). For Castoriadis, Lefort and Arendt, as we shall see in the coming chapters, the Hungarian Revolution and the re-emergence of workers' councils during totalitarian domination was a pivotal moment in their intellectual developments, which paved the way for their novel visions of politics.

The Hungarian Revolution was the first full-blown uprising against Soviet control in Eastern Europe, although important strikes and protests had taken place in East Germany in 1953 as well as in

Poland in 1956. The Polish Poznan protests in June 1956 began as factory workers spontaneously called a general strike in the city of Poznan, because the Moscow-loyal Polish government had raised the work quota. Students joined the strikers, and the immediate political demands were the betterment of working conditions and the reintroduction of various political rights. The Poznan strike was met with harsh, violent repression by the Soviet-controlled Polish army.

Initially, the Hungarian Revolution began with a demonstration of solidarity with the Polish people organised by students from the Budapest University of Engineering on 22 October 1956 (Fehér and Heller 1983: xiv). The students issued a famous sixteen-point resolution demanding, among other things, general elections to a new national assembly in a multiparty system, a charter of political liberties as well as complete independence from the Soviet Union. The establishment of councils was not a part of the students' demands. The next day, 23 October, around 300,000 demonstrators took to the streets of Budapest demanding the reinstatement of Imre Nagy as prime minister as well as more ambitious demands like parliamentary democracy and political independence (Fehér and Heller 1983: xv). The demonstration ended in a clash between armed protestors and the secret police in front of the State Radio building. The following day, two pivotal events took place. Firstly, the Soviet army – unauthorised by the Hungarian authorities – began to arrest demonstrators and police the streets. Secondly, revolutionary councils in the countryside and factory councils in the larger cities, especially in Budapest, emerged spontaneously without orders from above and without cross-country coordination. Like Trotsky's (1907) evaluation of the failed Russian Revolution of 1905, the most astonishing feature of the council system as a revolutionary organ was once again its ability to be 'brought out from underground within twenty-four hours'. From 24 to 26 October, 'all factories in the country had elected their councils', as argued by one historian of the revolution (Molnár 1971: 174). Moreover, according to the UN report on Hungary, which was published in 1957, revolutionary and territorially based councils controlled many villages and districts in the countryside and assumed administrative responsibilities (UN Report on Hungary 1957: 155). The same federalisation of the many disparate councils that took place especially in Russian in 1917 also happened in germinal form in Hungary, as coordination and collaboration between local councils began during the dying days of October 1956. Some councils even proposed establishing a National Revolutionary Committee, thus drawing inspiration from the federal, pyramidal model of council organisation that the Russian soviets had experimented with (Haynes 2006).

In a speech on 30 October, reinstated Prime Minister Nagy asked for the support of the councils as 'autonomous, democratic, local organs formed during the revolution' (UN Report on Hungary 1957: 155). As highlighted in the UN report, 'no aspect of the Hungarian uprising expressed its *democratic* tendencies or its reaction to previous conditions more clearly than the creation of Revolutionary Councils in the villages, towns and on the county level, and of Workers' Councils in the factories', and so 'the overwhelming support given by the Hungarians to these Workers' Councils confirms the impression that they were among the most important achievements of the Hungarian people during their days of freedom' (UN Report on Hungary 1957: 154, 171; emphasis added). In general, the political programmes of the Hungarian councils until the Soviet invasion on 4 November, although in no way in unison, were a mixture of liberal democratic, socialist and anti-Soviet Union demands. Although the experiences of the Russian soviets of 1905 and 1917 were in the minds of some Hungarian insurrectionists, there were no slogans such as 'All Power to the Soviets' (Molnár 1971: 177–8).

With the Soviet invasion on 4 November and the re-establishment of a Moscow-loyal government, the impetus of the council movement also came to a halt, although a not insignificant number of councils remained in existence in the countryside and sporadically combatted the regime up till the summer of 1957. Although the Hungarian councils had an effective share in political power for an even shorter timespan than their Russian and German predecessors, the development of the councils followed quite similar paths. The Hungarian councils appeared spontaneously without orders from political parties, trade unions or intellectuals. Councils were formed in all parts of society, in the factories, among students, in the army, among mine workers, within government departments, among rural peasants and in different territorial units from small villages to the capital of Budapest. The workers' councils stressed the self-management of economic production, and the territorially based revolutionary councils stressed the people's self-government in political and administrative matters. Moreover, initial attempts were made to federalise and thus turn the council movement into a contender for political power in the national arena. Just as the Russian soviets were dismantled through the Bolsheviks' takeover of power, so did the Soviet army destroy the Hungarian councils. But the Hungarian Revolution of 1956 testified to the almost natural organisational impulse of creating councils during times of revolution and political disintegration. Although the days in Hungary in October and November 1956 were the last time a widespread, broad-based and politically influential council movement appeared in Europe, the Hungarian councils had a lasting influence on a new generation of political thinkers, including Castoriadis, Lefort and Arendt.

Conclusion: Core Principles of the Historical Councils

What are the core principles to be drawn from the historical experiences of the councils? According to Anweiler (1974: 4), the following three general characteristics of the historical councils can be enumerated:

1. The councils are connected to a particular dependent or oppressed social stratum.
2. The councils have radical democracy as their political form.
3. The councils have a revolutionary origin.

Anweiler's first and third characteristics are relatively easy to affirm through historical reconstruction, as the councils emerged in revolutionary situations and were brought into being by social groups without other means of political representation such as workers, peasants and soldiers. But, what does it mean that a political form such as the council system is *radically* democratic? It is very much this question of the relationship between democracy and form – or between constituent power and political form – that I confront throughout the book. It is a question that council thinkers of the interwar period will try to answer, that Castoriadis, Lefort and Arendt will also grapple with, and that I, finally, will contribute to in the last chapter of the book. For now, let me point towards some preliminary features of the historical councils, which can account for their radical democratic form.

Firstly, the historical councils functioned as self-managing organs, taking decisions on their own endeavours on a number of questions (factory councils on economic production, army regiments on political and military support for the revolutionary movements, neighbourhood councils on food supply and infrastructure in local districts). They were thus organs of popular self-government in embryonic form. Secondly, the historical councils elected their own delegates from their organic environments (the factory shop floor, the army regiment, the neighbourhood) and hence decided directly on the personnel who influenced the course of the revolutionary transformations across Europe. Thirdly, the relation between the local (factory, army, neighbourhood) committee and the central council (Petrograd Soviet, Workers' and Soldiers' Councils of Great Berlin) was most often regulated by imperative mandate and instant recall. These institutional mechanisms – which also emerged in the radical politics of popular societies and clubs during the French Revolution, in the Paris Commune and dating to as far back as the government of medieval towns – were a means by which the local councils could instruct their delegates on various matters of concern (i.e. the mandate of the delegates was not free as in parliamentary systems), and could instantly recall them if the trust was breached and elect new delegates (i.e. the temporal term of the delegates was not fixed as in parliamentary systems) (Tomba 2018). The historical councils, hence, sought to develop novel representative mechanisms for retaining power at the bottom of the federal council system, by instructing delegates in advance (imperative mandate) and holding them accountable under threat of re-election (instant recall). When these features of the historical councils are taken together, a preliminary designation of the core principle of historical councils can be suggested. As Anweiler proposes,

> the inherent idea of such councils, which may be called 'the council idea', is the striving toward the most direct, far-reaching, and unrestricted participation of the individual in public life. When applied to the collective, it becomes the idea of *self-government of the masses*. (Anweiler 1974: 4; emphasis added)

Chapter 2
Political Theory of Council Democracy from Bakunin to Luxemburg

After the impetus of the historical council movements ground to a halt at the beginning of the 1920s, the council form was widely discussed across the European labour movement. The councils became a key touchstone for those political thinkers who wanted to develop different conceptions of democracy than the parliamentary variant, but at the same time wanted to criticise the development of communism in Soviet Russia. Moreover, council democracy was conceptualised by different thinkers as being an alternative to most of the fundamental political structures of modern politics such as the state, capitalism, parliamentarianism and the party system. Discussions on council democracy developed into an alternative strain of left-wing thought, which situated the councils well beyond the schism of social democratic parliamentarianism and Leninist one-party rule. Whereas the historical councils are relatively well discussed, the political theory of council democracy has to some extent been neglected. This is primarily because its political and conceptual adversaries – parliamentary democracy and capitalism, and Bolshevik-style communism and state planning – dominated the ideological struggle of the twentieth century. After intense debate on the council system within the European labour movement during the 1920s, as fascism rose in the 1930s, the council system was primarily discussed within marginalised left-wing tendencies (van der Linden 2004). The result is that a historical reconstruction of the political theory of council democracy is still somewhat missing (see Popp-Madsen and Kets 2020).

In this chapter I hope to rectify this by analysing the interpretations of council democracy in relation to three distinct experiences with council politics: firstly, I turn to the theoretical precursors to the interpretations of the actual councils, namely the analyses of the Paris Commune by the anarchists Mikhail Bakunin and Peter

Kropotkin as well as by Karl Marx. I then turn to Vladimir Lenin's two different interpretations of the Russian soviets, and lastly I engage with the so-called 'council communists' – a loosely connected group of thinkers including Anton Pannekoek, Herman Gorter, Karl Korsch, Otto Rühle and Rosa Luxemburg – and their analyses of primarily the German councils, their refutation of Lenin and their development of the council system as an alternative beyond parliamentarianism and party communism. I undertake the analysis by asking two general questions to each political thinker surveyed in the chapter: *firstly*, what is the political function of the council? Is it a class-based, representative institution, an insurrectionary organ of proletarian struggle or a model for a future emancipated society? How and why can the councils perform such functions? *Secondly*, what are the councils alternatives to? Most importantly, what is the relationship between the councils and the state, parliamentarianism, and the communist party?

By discussing these questions, I argue three things: *firstly*, despite the political struggle on the role of the councils, the political theory of council democracy is structured by some regularities. Even though theories of council democracy are developed from markedly different historical experiences, there are certain features and specific institutional arrangements that occur in most theories of council democracy. This regularity shows that despite Hannah Arendt's claim ([1963] 2006: 248–9) that the councils were never incorporated into a tradition of political thought, the main thinkers under scrutiny in this book – Castoriadis, Lefort and Arendt – certainly engage with an intellectual tradition whether they are aware of it or not. *Secondly*, the primary disruption in the tradition of council democracy occurs with Lenin's second interpretation of the councils, which subordinates the councils to the Bolshevik Party, thereby instituting a major split in the council tradition between understanding the councils as a germinal model for future working-class self-government or as temporary instruments of insurrection, preferably in the hands of the communist party. *Thirdly*, the last sustained theorisation of the councils before they fell out of the mainstream left-wing imaginary in 1930s, namely the 'council communists' of the 1920s, conceptualised the council system as an alternative to both social democratic parliamentarianism and Leninism, as a political system *beyond* this dichotomy, which is critical of the statist and hierarchical elements of both these regime forms. Overall, hence, the chapter makes available the intellectual tradition of council democracy which Castoriadis, Lefort and Arendt inherit and reinterpret. Castoriadis, Lefort and Arendt are on the one hand *inheritors* of this intellectual tradition, which has its own components, its own mode of posing problems and providing answers; and on the other hand, they are *reinterpreters* of this tradition, as they provide novel interpretations of council politics.

Anarchist Conceptions of Councils and Communes

The first theoretical discussions on the 'council concept' are reflections on the Paris Commune of 1871. Almost all subsequent interpretations of council organisation mention the Paris Commune as the first moment of council politics. Hence, discussions on Commune's political functions, and the political enemies it was to refute, are a natural starting point for historical reconstruction of the political theory of council democracy. Much has been written on the discussions between Marx and Bakunin and the latter's exclusion from the International Workingmen's Association (the First International) in 1872 (May 1994: 45–6), and the ways in which this split came to influence the history of socialism (Eley 2002). But in regard to the evaluation of the Paris Commune, Bakunin and Marx – as well as Kropotkin – accentuated similar elements in their interpretations. Both the anarchists and Marx saw in the Paris Commune a political form which could enhance political participation and equality, while combatting capitalism and the state. Where they differed the most was in their understanding of what specifically it means that the commune was an anti-statist form, that is, what does it mean to abolish the state? With reference to Nikos Poulantzas's state theory, the anarchists wanted to abolish both the state apparatus and the functions of the state, whereas Marx sought to get rid of the state apparatus, while letting the commune, and hence the working people, perform the state functions.

Mikhail Bakunin and Peter Kropotkin

When evaluating the Paris Commune and its democratised clubs, associations and districts, Bakunin focused on the anti-statist nature of the Commune. In 'The Paris Commune and the Idea of the State', written in 1871 after the demise of the Paris Commune, Bakunin openly asserts, 'I am a supporter of the Paris Commune . . . I am its supporter, above all, because it was a bold, clearly formulated negation of the state' (1871: 87). Where the Parisian Communards differ from what Bakunin calls the 'authoritarian communists' is that they do not wish to conquer the state in order to implement their own policies. 'The state is like a vast slaughterhouse or an enormous cemetery', Bakunin proclaims, 'where all the real aspirations, all the living forces of a country enter generously and happily, in the shadow of that abstraction, to let themselves be slain and buried' (1871: 83). The state, through its monopolisation of power, nullifies the political life of society's local and voluntary associations, and leaves society depoliticised and its members coerced. The Paris Commune is, according to Bakunin, the first attempt to shatter the state and replace it with 'the free association or federation of workers, starting with the associations, then going to the communes' (1871: 84).

Bakunin greatly valorised not only the Paris Commune, but also the communal form as such, as his involvement in the Lyon Commune of 1870 testifies. Bakunin was a co-signatory of the first declaration of the Lyon Communards, which sought to establish an autonomous commune in Lyon. The declaration begins: 'The administrative and governmental machine of the state, having become powerless, is abolished' (Declaration of the Lyon Commune 1870). The articles that follow plea for the termination of the state's court system and its ability to impose taxation and to intervene in private debt – in short, a dismantling of both the state apparatus and the state functions. Instead, 'federated communes . . . will exercise all the powers under direct control of the people' (Declaration of the Lyon Commune 1870). In a letter to the anarchist Albert Richard, Bakunin asserts that the communal strategy of politicising society through a host of bottom-up organs culminating in a federation of communes equals the creation of spontaneous political life: 'There must be anarchy, there must be – if the revolution is to become and remain alive, real and powerful – the greatest possible awakening of all local passions and aspirations; a tremendous awakening of spontaneous life everywhere' (Bakunin 1870).

The spontaneous character of communal organisation is reiterated in Bakunin's evaluation of the Paris Commune and used as a critique of both Marxist propagandists of the dictatorship of the proletariat and bourgeois proposals for a constituent assembly. According to Bakunin, 'our friends, the Paris socialists, believed that revolution could neither be made nor brought to its full development except by the spontaneous and continued action of the masses, the groups and the associations of the people' (1871: 82). Ultimately, the expected political function, which Bakunin attributes to the Paris Commune and to the communal form *per se*, is a political formation that terminates the domination of the state over society and replaces it with spontaneous self-government. Already in the earliest discourse on the communal/council form, therefore, the state appears to be the primary counter-concept to the council.

The understanding of the communal form as anti-statist is equally visible in the evaluation of the Paris Commune by another major anarchist thinker, Peter Kropotkin. Kropotkin also stresses the spontaneous and popular character of the Paris Commune, noting how 'it was born of collective spirit', how 'it sprang from the heart of a whole community'; as 'it was made by the people themselves, it sprang spontaneously from the midst of the mass' (1880: 94). Kropotkin mentions how the Paris Commune serves as a model of future revolutions, as 'it is no longer a dream of the vanquished' (1880: 93) but an inspirational torch for the future of revolutionary struggle. Without underestimating the importance of the themes of spontaneity and inspiration, the most important element in Kropotkin's evaluation of the Commune is, like for Bakunin, its anti-statist character. In language reminiscent of Bakunin's characterisation of the state as a slaughterhouse extracting energy from society, Kropotkin deems the state a parasite that coercively takes possession of all societal wealth. 'By proclaiming the free Commune', Kropotkin declares, 'the people of Paris proclaimed an essentially anarchist principle, which was the breakdown of the state' (1880: 95). This anarchist principle is expressed directly in the Commune, as it entails 'the total abolition of the state, and social organization from the simple to the complex by means of free federation of popular groups of producers and consumers' (1880: 91).

As alluded to, one can distinguish between the state apparatus and the state functions. The state apparatus expresses the idea that the state coincides with certain class interests – what Bakunin and Kropotkin call the 'state parasite' or the state as a 'slaughterhouse'. The state functions cover certain tasks that a society can perform in order to govern itself, such as legislation, executive measures, courts, armies and the police. These two are analytically different, insofar as one could argue – as does Marx – for the abolition of the state apparatus, while acknowledging the necessity of state functions, wanting to democratise the control over these functions. Bakunin and Kropotkin are anti-statists *tout court*, meaning that they disregard both the state apparatus and the state functions. Instead, they argue that in the communal form, the functions of the state will give way to spontaneous, free and non-institutionalised forms of human relationships. It is not merely that the commune democratises political functions, but that it abolishes them altogether. According to Kropotkin, the communards 'will not only break down the state and substitute free federation for parliamentary rule, they will part with parliamentary rule *within* the commune itself' (1880: 100; emphasis added), meaning that institutionalised functions of government will be alien to the commune. Another way to phrase this is that the anarchists are anti-statists, insofar as they reject all forms of institutionalised decision-making, even if these are conceived as democratically as possible. According to Bakunin, 'the sense in which we are really anarchists, [is that] we reject all legislation, all authority, and all privileged, licensed, official, and legal influence, even though arising from universal suffrage' (1970: 35).

This is a very different understanding of the Paris Commune than the one Marx provided, because Marx did not see in the Paris Commune the abolition of legislation, authority and executive powers, but the genuine democratisation of such functions. Despite these differences between the anarchists and Marx, Bakunin and Kropotkin ultimately set the parameters of the discourse on the councils. By proclaiming the state as the primary *counter-concept* to the commune/council due to its separation from society and its dominance over it, the anarchists declared that the *expected political function* of councils was to end the division between society and state, by democratising society in order for self-rule to replace representation and specialised bureaucratic rule.

Karl Marx and the Paris Commune

Karl Marx's analysis of the Paris Commune in 'The Civil War in France' (1871) is the most important document in the history of the political theory of council democracy. Here Marx provides the basic theoretical coordinates through which the councils of early twentieth-century Europe were to be discussed. Almost all subsequent analyses of the councils refer to Marx, often find a basic similarity between the Paris Commune and the councils, and use the same conceptual language as Marx. The core political achievement of the Paris Commune – according to Marx – was to create an *anti-statist* and *truly democratic* polity. The two correlating counter-concepts to these core achievements – the state and parliamentary democracy – would remain the most important conceptual enemies in the tradition of council democracy. Marx proclaimed the Paris Commune a specifically 'proletarian political form', meaning a specific set of functions of government devised for the proletariat to exercise political power, and this idea of the commune as a specifically proletarian form became hugely influential.

Marx acknowledged that the commune would be in the middle of a tense conceptual struggle, as according to him, the Parisian experiment had already been subject to a 'multiplicity of interpretations' and a 'multiplicity of interests which construed it in their favour' (1996a: 187). Marx chose to reject interpretations of the Commune as a reproduction of medieval guilds or as the re-emergence of the ancient struggle against imperial over-centralisation. Instead, he offered an analysis of the Commune as an example of a proletarian, democratic form; a popular polity allowing for mass civic participation in the affairs of public life. Hence, Marx regarded the expected political function of the Commune to be a democratisation of society against the state. This process of democratisation was enabled by a specific constellation of political institutions, which were essentially different from the statist imaginary. Therefore, Marx initially argued that the events in Paris affirmed that the working class cannot take hold of the already established state apparatus, because such an action would not destroy the conflict between society and state. As Marx famously wrote in his 1871 essay on the Commune, 'the working class cannot simply lay hold of the ready-made state apparatus, and wield it for its own purposes' (1996a: 181). The aspiration of the Parisian Communards was an innovation in revolutionary practice, therefore, as it was essentially anti-*Jacobin* in character, meaning that the Parisian populace – in Marx's interpretation – was not concerned with taking over the state apparatus and employing it for their own interests, but instead wanted to transform the state into something different. The entire endeavour of the Commune was, according to Marx, focused on creating a different kind of political structure, which did not alienate itself from society and so dominated it (Marx 1996a: 181; Ross 2015: 78–9). When analysing what he called the *communal constitution*, Marx emphasised the following four, genuinely democratic, anti-statist institutional features: local self-government, the commune as a working body, its generic political form and its status as a working-class government.

Firstly, the Commune was split into local districts, which sent delegates under imperative mandate to central coordinating institutions.

The local neighbourhoods had widespread political and economic self-government, meaning that the political structure of the Commune was pyramidal, with authority, legitimacy and power generated from below and upward (Marx 1996a: 184). In other words, 'the very existence of the Commune involved as a matter of course, local municipal liberty . . . It supplied the republic with the basis of real democratic institutions' (Marx 1996a: 186–7). This implied, according to Marx, the most widespread local self-government in the clubs, committees and associations of each *arrondissement*.

Secondly, the Commune functioned as what Marx calls a *working body*, 'executive and legislative at the same time' (1996a: 184). Marx saw the lack of separation of powers as a rejection of parliamentary democracy: 'Instead of deciding once in three or six years which member of the ruling class was to misrepresent the people in Parliament, universal suffrage serves the people, constituted in Communes' (1996a: 185). In order to let the Commune function as a working body and prevent the alienation between representatives and represented, which Marx saw as inherent in the modern parliamentary state (1996a: 243–58), all public servants were elected under recall, earning only a workman's wage. This included demolishing the professional army and the police, and introducing a people's army, which instead of functioning as the state's instrument in controlling society was 'turned into the responsible and at all times revocable agent of the Commune. So were all officials of all other branches of the administration' (Marx 1996a: 184).

Thirdly, for Marx, these institutional features of local self-government, delegates under instant recall and working bodies without unnecessary professionalisation were to be the model of political organisation in the entire country. Not only in Paris, but from the 'great industrial centers of France' to the 'smallest country hamlet . . . the old centralised government would in the provinces, too, have to give way to the self-government of the producers' (Marx 1996a: 185). Marx imagined that in the entire country, 'rural communes of every district were to administer their common affairs by an assembly of delegates in the central town, and these district assemblies were again to send deputies to the national delegation in Paris' (1996a: 185). Thus, Marx saw in the structures of the Paris Commune a generic form of government to be applied to different political, geographical and historical situations.

Fourthly, and finally, Marx interpreted the Paris Commune as a working-class government. Whereas historical scholarship has doubted whether the Parisian artisans, workers and small shop-keepers can be described as a modern proletariat (Johnson 1996), Marx was convinced of the Commune's working-class character. Famously, he argued that 'its true secret was this. It was essentially a working-class government, the produce of the struggle of the pro-ducing against appropriating class, the political form at last dis-covered under which to work out the economical emancipation of labour' (Marx 1996a: 187). According to Marx, the Commune was the *political form at last discovered* for the emancipation of labour, meaning that it would end the domination that state power and capitalism exerted over society, providing the workers with demo-cratic control over economic and social aspects of their lives. The working-class character of the Commune and its status as a working body with revocable delegates avoided bureaucratisation and would furthermore prevent, according to Marx, the construction of a state that separates itself from society and dominates it.

These institutional features are the core insights of Marx's analy-sis of the Paris Commune. As is obvious, Marx's commune is not a condemnation of the functions of government as such, but a democ-ratisation of these functions. Marx does not imagine that communal society would be without legislative organs, civil servants or the police, but that these would be under the democratic control of the citizens. The most enduring feature of Marx's analysis for the twentieth-century political theory of council democracy is the ways in which the communal form is able to democratise the functions of government; hence the argument that the commune is *anti-statist* and *more democratic* than the façade democracy of parliamentary systems. Everywhere in Marx's analysis is the difference between the modern state and its parasitical domestication of the creative forces of society contrasted with the commune's attempt at constructing a self-governing society, where the functions of public power are con-trolled by the people. According to Marx, 'centralized state power . . . originates from the days of absolute monarchy' (1996a: 181), and so the commune liberates the creative capabilities of the people from the dominance of the state. Hence, the anti-statist nature of the commune is repeated throughout Marx's text, as 'the Communal constitution would have restored to the social body all the forces hitherto absorbed by the state parasite feeding upon, and clogging the free movement of society' (Marx 1996a: 185–6).

Marx's analysis ultimately entails two guiding elements that became almost mandatory for the interpretations of council democ-racy that followed throughout the twentieth century. The *first* is the already mentioned anti-state character of the commune, as almost all subsequent interpretations of council democracy mention how the councils would be the germs of a new political order. As Marx puts it, the commune is 'the glorious harbinger of a new society' (1996a: 207). The *second* important element is the idea that the commune discloses a truly self-governing political *form*, which is far more democratic than parliamentary democracy. According to Marx, parliamentary democracy is based on *separation* – the separation of the represented from the representatives, the separation of the state from society, the separation of politics from the economy and the separation of political power into distinct branches. The result of such a separation is the *pacification* of society in favour of the *domination* of the representatives, of the state and of bourgeois interests. In contrast, the expected political function of the communal form is to overcome such separation and domination and institute forms of self-government on all issues of public importance. Importantly, therefore, the proletarian revolution is not only the movement of negating the existing structures of capitalist domination, but also the process of instituting new ones: 'the lessons of the Commune, at least the one retained by Marx, is that social emancipation of the workers – the emancipation of labour from the domination of capital – can only be realized by the mediation of a political *form*' (Abensour 2011b: 87; emphasis added).

Vladimir Lenin's Dual Concept of the Soviets

To engage with Lenin's interpretations of the councils is to take issue with the course of the Russian Revolution of 1917 itself, as Lenin's assessments of the councils fluctuate with the political situation in Russia. Before the 1917 revolution, Lenin did not devote many thoughts to the councils, Marx's communal analysis or the nascent soviets in 1905, although he wrote some articles on the 1905 soviets; and after 1917–18, when the Bolsheviks had taken control of the state apparatus and its functions, Lenin once again stressed the dominance of the party vis-à-vis the councils. From his position as head of the Soviet Union, Lenin openly criticised the 'left-communism' of Dutch–German 'council communists' such as Anton Pannekoek, Otto Rühle, Rosa Luxemburg and Herman Gorter, deeming their involvement in the council movement of the German Revolution an 'infantile disorder' (Lenin [1920] 1940). In his attack on the council communists, Lenin stresses the superiority of the Party – with its firm leadership and theoretical insights – over the councils as a mode of revolutionary organisation. Ultimately, Lenin's evaluation of the soviets serves the strategical purpose of legitimising Bolshevik leadership; hence, Lenin developed not one but two visions of council democracy. In one conceptualisation from 1917, the soviets are bases of public authority, as they perform the functions of government. Here Lenin is in agreement with Marx's communal analysis, giving the soviets the same expected political functions and counter-concepts. In another conceptualisation, apparent in Lenin's writings both before and after 1917, he undertakes a great political redefinition, as the councils play a more modest role as insurrectionary organs, preferably under the control of the Bolshevik Party.

Lenin's 1917 Conception: All Power to the Soviets!

Lenin was in exile during the February Revolution and watched from afar how a system of dual power emerged between the Petrograd Soviet and the Provisional Government. When he arrived in Petrograd in April 1917, Lenin carried with him his now famous *April Theses*,[1] which was immediately read aloud to the Bolshevik leadership, who were generally shocked by the content. The *April Theses* consists of ten guidelines for Bolshevik politics in the revolutionary situation of dual power. The dominant attitude of the Bolshevik leadership before Lenin returned from exile was to moderately collaborate with the Provisional Government and uphold the situation of dual power. Lenin's theses changed that. Most importantly, he stated – without mentioning a single word about the Bolshevik Party – 'that the Soviets of Workers' Deputies are the *only possible* form of revolutionary government', and all forces should concentrate on 'transferring the entire power to the Soviets of Workers' Deputies' in order to establish a new 'republic of Soviets of Workers', Agricultural Labourers' and Peasants' Deputies throughout the country, from top to bottom' (Lenin 1917f; original emphasis). The attempt to situate the workers' councils as the new foundation of political power certainly reflected their popularity in 1917, so Lenin's commitment to the workers' councils was definitively also a tactical move (Daniels 1953; 1965: 51–2; Anweiler 1974: 161–5; Carr 1952: 233–49). Commentators agree that the Bolsheviks rarely took part in the formation or early development of the soviets (Negri 2004: 109; Anweiler 1974; Smirnov 1997: 429–37); and in addition, before Lenin advocated for the councils in 1917, he regarded them as only temporary organs of insurrection, as purely insurrectional bodies, not as permanent organs for democratic self-government (Negri 2004: 110).

If we momentarily leave Lenin's tactical motives aside, his understanding of the councils – in this positive 1917 evaluation – is in line with Marx's analysis of the Paris Commune. Lenin followed Marx in stressing the anti-statist nature of the Russian councils, emphasising the state as their primary counter-concept, and hence theorised the councils as a way for society to gain control over the state. Moreover, Lenin highlighted the same institutional mechanisms through which the council system would recapture this control: democratisation of the army and police (soldiers' councils), election of officials under imperative mandate and instant recall, self-managing economy (factory councils), and the abolition of parliamentary democracy through institutions of local self-government. Moreover, Lenin emphasises the intimate relationship between the 1905 soviets, the 1917 soviets and the Paris Commune:

> The workers have realised that in revolutionary times they need *not only* ordinary organisation, but an entirely different organisation. They have rightly taken the path indicated by the experience of our 1905 Revolution and of the Paris Commune; they have set up a *Soviet of Workers' Deputies*. (Lenin 1917b; original emphasis)

For Lenin, as the events of 1917 were unfolding, 'the obvious truth [is] that in as much as these Soviets exist, *in as much as* they are a power, we have in Russia a state of the *type* of the Paris Commune' (Lenin 1917c; original emphasis). In Lenin's main theoretical work, *The State and Revolution* (1917e), a basic commonality between the Paris Commune and the soviets is also established. The Russian councils *continue* the communal tradition, they finish the work that the Parisian workers had begun: 'The Russian revolutions of 1905 and 1917, in different circumstances and under different conditions, continue the work of the Commune and confirm the historical analysis given by Marx' (Lenin 1917e: 96). Like Marx, but against the anarchists, Lenin argues that the apparatus of the state needs to be smashed, as it expresses bourgeois interests, but the functions of the state need to be in place and fully democratised. Hence, in the quote below, Lenin does speak of a new form of the state, but he differentiates between the apparatus of the bourgeois state, which is founded upon separation and domination and thus needs to be abolished, and the organs of state power (what Poulantzas calls 'state functions'), which are to be placed in the hands of the people through the soviets:

> We need a state, but *not the kind* of state the bourgeoisie needs, with organs of government in the shape of a police force, an army and a bureaucracy separate from and opposed to the people. . . . Following the path indicated by the experience of the Paris Commune of 1871 and the Russian Revolution of 1905, the proletariat, must organise and arm *all* the poor, exploited sections of the population in order that they *themselves* should take the organs of state power directly into their hands, in order that *they themselves should constitute* these organs of state power. (Lenin 1917b; original emphasis)

This quote from 1917 show how Lenin shares the analysis of Marx, namely that the state and parliamentary democracy, as the primary counter-concepts of the council, rest on mechanisms of *separation* and *domination*. The only way, in Lenin's analysis, to achieve a more democratic regime is to overcome the dominance of specialised bureaucrats and elite politicians and let ordinary workers, soldiers and peasants perform the functions of state power. In doing so, the councils redirect political power to its actual source – the people or the proletariat – and the institutional mechanisms of instant recall, imperative mandate, working bodies, local self-government and the popularisation of army and police ensure that the people retain control over its political institutions.

Lenin's Conception before and after 1917: The Party above the Soviets

If the above conceptualisation were Lenin's final word on the soviets, his understanding would not differ greatly from that of Marx. But Lenin had another understanding of the councils, which he voiced both before and after 1917 and the Bolshevik takeover of power. With this second understanding of the council concept, Lenin redefines both the expected political function of the council as well as its counter-concepts, and from Lenin's second understanding emerges a markedly different interpretation of the council system. For Bakunin, Kropotkin and Marx, the crux of the Paris Commune was that it was an embryo for an emancipated society. Marx, for example, thought of the council form as a *permanent* constitutional form, which through its institutional structures and popular spirit secured self-government in perpetuity – theoretically, at least. The council form, in this version, is both destructive, as it negates the state, but also constituent, as it entails a new political form beyond the state. Lenin's pre- and post-1917 analyses of the councils change this conception profoundly. Instead, once the Bolsheviks had secured power over the state apparatus through infiltrating the soviets and eliminating their *de facto* power, making them merely the *de jure* foundation of the Soviet Union, Lenin argued that the aspiration of the councils was never to become a *permanent* political form, through which the masses could govern themselves. Only the Bolshevik Party with incorruptible, iron discipline could perform such a task. The council form, instead, according to Lenin, is a *temporary* organ for revolutionary upheaval. Councils are flexible institutions that can be created in great haste and effectively organise the masses in moments of crisis. Precisely because of their spontaneity and organic relation to instances of strikes, the councils are not fit to function as permanent governing organisations. They are, in short, *insurrectional* bodies, not constitutional forms. Under this view, it is not the workers themselves – through the soviets – who are to exercise the functions of government, but instead it is the party.

As already mentioned, prior to 1917 Lenin rarely discussed the councils. In the immediate aftermath of the 1905 Revolution, though, Lenin discusses the value of the St Petersburg Soviet. In this discussion, we can see the contours of his post-1917 theory of the councils as instruments in the hands of the Bolsheviks. In a pamphlet from 1905, in which Lenin evaluates the St Petersburg Soviet, he argued against viewing the soviets as organs of proletarian self-government: 'The Soviet of Workers' Deputies is not a labour parliament and not an organ of proletarian self-government, nor an organ of self-government at all, but a fighting organisation for the achievement of *definite* aims' (Lenin 1905b; emphasis added). The definitiveness of the aims of the soviets is a way to argue that the councils are not fit for popular self-government as such, but merely useful in securing specific objectives. As Lenin reflected on the 1905 Revolution, he clearly did not find any occasion to praise the soviets:

> The role played by the Soviet of Workers' Deputies ... in the great October and December [in the 1905 Revolution] days surrounded them with something like a halo, so that sometimes they are treated almost as a fetish ... people imagine that those organs are 'necessary and sufficient' for a mass revolutionary movement at all times and in all circumstances. (Lenin 1905a)

According to Lenin, such an attitude towards the soviets is naive and misses the point that the soviets were merely temporary strike committees, which were only 'necessary for welding the masses together, for creating unity in the struggle, for handing on the party slogans (or slogans advanced by agreement between parties) of political leadership, for awakening the interest of the masses, for rousing and attracting them' (1905a).

The specific purposes Lenin attributes to the soviets in 1905–6 are thus the following: they are *instruments* in order to achieve something else, methods of revolutionary struggle, not germinal models of democratic organs. Because they emerge spontaneously from the insurrectionist actions of the workers and thus enjoy legitimacy among them, councils can be used to create unity, to disseminate vital information from the party leadership and to organise revolts. The councils are training grounds for advancing class-consciousness, not models for proletarian self-government. The overall goal of advancing the revolution, coordinating between the dispersed groups of the population, must be left to the party vanguard and its leaders. After the revolution, the councils must surrender their power to the party; as insurrection is successful, the soviets must renounce their authority. In sum, according to Negri, for Lenin the soviets' 'end was only insurrection' (2004: 111).

Such an understanding of the soviets is obviously miles apart from Lenin's Marx-inspired interpretation in 1917. But after the Bolsheviks had conquered state power through infiltrating the soviets, Lenin reverted to his 1905 position. From February to October 1917, when the Bolsheviks were not in total power and did not have a majority of delegates in the soviets, Lenin tirelessly argued for the total transmission of power from the state to the soviets. Such a transmission of power would threaten the Provisional Government and the forces of parliamentary democracy, hence the soviets functioned as insurrectionary cells of destabilisation. After the October Revolution, Lenin completely changed his opinion on the role of the soviets, and now argued, 'For us the soviets have no importance as a form; what we care about is which classes the soviets represent' (qtd in Anweiler 1974: 165). The crucial importance of this short evaluation is not to be underestimated. To Bakunin, Kropotkin and Marx, the importance of the Paris Commune lay in its political *form*. Famously, Marx (1996a: 187; emphasis added) claimed that the Commune was 'the *form* at last discovered' for the emancipation of labour. What mattered to Marx was that the Commune was a *formalisation* of democratic power, making the in*formal* force of revolution *form*able. This is crucial, as political thought from ancient Greece onwards has been preoccupied with political *forms*, arguing that different regime forms disclose certain guiding principles. What Marx thought he witnessed in the Paris Commune was precisely a novel political *form* disclosing the principles of self-government, popular participation, and manageable and controllable delegates. As the Bolsheviks had ascended to power, Lenin took no interest in the *form* of the council itself, only in whether it adequately served Bolshevik purposes. Because the soviet did not in Lenin's understanding express working-class interests *per se*, as the influence of Mensheviks and Socialist Revolutionaries in the soviets made clear, the soviets had to be subordinated to the party, as only the party truly represented the interests of the working class. 'Depending on the program and leadership' of the councils, 'they can serve various purposes. The program will be given to the soviets by the party', Lenin argued (qtd in Anweiler 1974: 165).

Evaluating the revolutionary period in Russia and the role of the soviets, Lenin concluded that 'the total experience of the 1905 and 1917 revolutions and all Bolshevik resolutions . . . signifies that the soviet exists only as an organ of insurrection, as an instrument of revolutionary power' (qtd in Anweiler 1974: 188). Other major Bolshevik leaders, such as Joseph Stalin and Leon Trotsky, voiced conceptions similar to Lenin's new position on the soviets. According to Stalin, the Bolshevik Party 'is, of course, in favour of those soviets in which it commands a majority. The heart of the matter is not the *institution* [i.e. the form], but which class will prevail in the institution' (qtd in Anweiler 1974: 171; emphasis added). Trotsky, who had served as Chairman in the 1905 St Petersburg Soviet and had been a great proponent of the council form, also warmly welcomed the bolshevisation of the soviets, as 'the slogan "Power to the soviets" was not removed from the agenda a second time, but it was given a new meaning: all power to the *Bolshevik* soviets' (qtd in Anweiler 1974: 176). These quotations entail a purely instrumental understanding of the councils. The council form is nothing in itself if not guided by the right class-consciousness and political aspirations of the delegates. The intrinsic value of the council form as a mode of economic self-management of factories, as a way of holding delegates accountable, ensuring that a split between 'the people' and its institutions does not occur, has little value for Lenin and the Bolsheviks in the end. In Anweiler's apt phrasing:

> For the Bolsheviks the soviets were never a question of 'doctrine' or 'principle', but expediency. Lenin's theory of the soviets as a radical form of democracy [i.e. his 1917 conception] is irrevocably tied to the soviets' practical role as leadership instruments of the Bolshevik party ... Plainly, to him [Lenin] the soviets were only pawns and had no intrinsic value as a superior form of government. (Anweiler 1974: 165, 170)

The council system in Lenin's late evaluation, hence, loses the key component of anti-statism and becomes a tactical instrument in the struggle for state power. The moment the soviets lose their instrumental value, they become unimportant for Lenin. In the years after the Bolshevik takeover of power and pacification of the soviets, a critique of the Bolsheviks emanated from the left, that is, from communists, who were initially in favour of the Russian revolutions, but were disappointed with the development of Bolshevik dictatorship from above instead of an expansion of the council system's power from below. These critics were mostly German radicals who had somehow been involved in the council movement of the German Revolution. In the famous pamphlet written against these critics of Bolshevism, *'Left-Wing' Communism: An Infantile Disorder* ([1920] 1940), Lenin launched an unforgiving critique of those 'left-wing communists' who sought to drive a wedge between the working masses and the Party. 'All talk about "from above" *or* "from below", about the dictatorship of leaders *or* the dictatorship of the masses, etc.', Lenin argued, 'cannot but appear as ridiculous and childish nonsense, something like discussing whether the left leg or the right arm is more useful to a man' ([1920] 1940: 33). What mattered to a revolutionary communist, according to Lenin, had nothing to do with the trifles of whether political power would spring from below or from above, or whether society would be self-governing or whether party leaders would be in control. For Lenin, the primary question was how to conquer state power and hold on to it:

> Let the 'Lefts' put themselves to a practical test on a national and international scale . . . let them try to prepare for (and then implement) the dictatorship of the proletariat, without a rigorously centralised party with iron discipline, without the ability to become masters of every sphere, every branch, and every variety of political and cultural work. Practical experience will soon teach them. (Lenin [1920] 1940: 78)

In conclusion, Lenin changes the expected political function of the councils as well as their counter-concepts. Instead of permanent self-government, the Leninist councils are expected to function as temporary fighting organisations, subordinated to the party. Instead of being in opposition to the state and parliamentary democracy, the primary counter-concept to Lenin's second conceptualisation of the council, is that of radical council self-government as expressed by Marx and by Lenin himself in his 1917 analysis. Through these conceptual innovations, Lenin completely turned the council concept on its head and exercised a lasting influence on the intellectual tradition of council democracy.

Council Communism in the Interwar Period

With Lenin's new theory of the councils, the scene was set for a new political struggle over the councils. The theoretical tendency known as *council communism*, which emerged in the 1920s as a critique of both Bolshevism and parliamentary social democracy, argued that both the means of the revolution against capitalism and the end goal of that struggle would be in the format of councils. Council communists thus argued that prior instruments of working-class struggle such as trade unions, parties and the parliamentary system belonged to the dustbin of history, and that the council form was appropriate for the new phase of history (Schecter 1994: 78). Council communists were critical of replacements for autonomous working-class action and relied on the council form as an expression of the genuine self-emancipation of the workers.

The historical experiences of the councils show that this political form has two rival political systems, which have defeated and succeeded the councils: multiparty parliamentarianism and communist one-party dictatorship. From the anarchists through Marx and to Lenin's 1917 conception of the soviets, only the first of these historical enemies was theorised as a counter-concept to the council system. For these writers, the councils disclose the positive form of a socialist democracy beyond bourgeois parliamentarianism embedded in the state. With Lenin's second, instrumental concept of the councils and the subordination of the councils to the Bolshevik Party, along with the developments of the Russian Revolution, which led to further centralisation of power, the stage was set for council thinkers to elaborate on the difference between the councils and their second historical enemy – the Bolshevik party (Lucardie 2014: 82–3).

Consequently, in the years after the historical councils lost their impetus, a diverse group of *council* communists developed a vision of communism in direct opposition to *party* communism (Gombin 1975: 78; 1978: 103–18). German–Dutch political activists such as Anton Pannekoek, Herman Gorter, Otto Rühle, Karl Korsch and Rosa Luxemburg, as well as Antonio Gramsci in Italy, all sought to develop a vision of council democracy which deliberately distanced the councils from their fate in Russia (Rachleff 1976; van der Linden 2004; Shipway 1987). Meanwhile, the council communists also combatted the reformist socialists and social democrats, who sought to realise the goals of socialism through parliamentarianism and hierarchical institutions such as parties and unions. Against such reformist socialists, the council communists stressed the self-emancipation of the working class through mass strikes, self-established organs and other autonomous forms of politics (Luxemburg 1906). Hence, it was in the 1920s – after the historical experience of the councils had played its part in the revolutionary transformations after World War I – that council democracy was theorised as an alternative to both parliamentary democracy and Leninist vanguardism.

Council Communism against Leninism

The theory of council democracy that council communists developed in opposition to Leninism was advanced through a series of disappointments with political developments in Russia. Thinkers and activists such as Luxemburg, Pannekoek, Rühle, Gorter and Korsch had all been in favour of the Russian Revolution – also the Bolshevik October Revolution – but had grown weary of the developments in the country, especially after the repression of the Kronstadt rebellion in 1921. Rosa Luxemburg was among those who expressed dissatisfaction with the developments in Russia, as she saw an evolving dictatorship exercising its power over a lethargic population. She argued:

> Lenin and Trotsky have presented the soviets as the only true representation of the working masses . . . But with the nationwide suppression of political activity, soviet activity must also diminish . . . Public life gradually goes to sleep, a few dozen party leaders of inexhaustible energy and boundless idealism control and rule, a dozen outstanding minds among them are in charge, and an elite from among the workers are occasionally

bidden to conventions to applaud the leaders' speeches, unanimously to approve resolutions put before them – at the bottom, therefore, government by clique. True, a dictatorship; but not the dictatorship of the proletariat, rather the dictatorship of a handful of politicians – dictatorship in the bourgeois sense, in the sense of Jacobin rule. (Luxemburg qtd in Anweiler 1974: 243–4)

These disappointments with the Russian Revolution led the council communists to theorise the councils as providing an answer to the central question: who is to emancipate the working masses? Their answer was clear: the workers would have to do it themselves, through the council form. As a response to Lenin's scornful pamphlet on the infantile disorder of left-wing communism (i.e. council communism), Herman Gorter wrote his famous *Open Letter to Comrade Lenin* (1920). In it, Gorter argued that the conditions of revolution in Western Europe were completely different from those of Russia. In Russia, the proletariat had a natural ally in the peasantry, but in Western Europe the peasantry was so influenced by bourgeois ideology that collaboration seemed impossible (Gorter 1920). At the same time, the Western European workers faced a well-developed bourgeois propaganda machine, which required that the struggle should focus on developing a strong working-class consciousness (Gorter 1920).

By driving a wedge between the Russian Revolution and the conditions of Western Europe, the Russian experience was desacralised (Shipway 1987: 107). Until 1921, the council communists – primarily organised in the Communist Workers' Party of Germany – had been members of the Bolshevik-controlled Third International, but they broke away in 1921 and established the Fourth International. Gorter wrote the manifesto of the new International, which argued that the Russian Revolution had in fact been a *dual* revolution: a working-class revolution against capitalism in the metropolitan areas, and a bourgeois-style revolution against feudalism in the rural areas. According to Gorter, the bourgeois component of the revolution became dominant with the introduction of the New Economic Policy in 1921 (Shipway 1987: 107). Other council communists went even further than Gorter's assessment of the dual character of the Russian Revolution. Pannekoek (2003: 76–82), for example, argued that the Russian Revolution was simply a bourgeois revolution in the tradition of the French Revolution, and Otto Rühle agreed that the Russian Revolution was 'the last in the line of the great bourgeois

revolutions of Europe' (Rühle 1924). Instead of a communist society founded upon the self-management of the workers through the
councils, Russia had become a system of state capitalism and statist
domination of the individual worker, as 'the soviets gradually were
eliminated as organs of self-rule and reduced to subordinate organs
of the government apparatus. The name of Soviet-republic, however,
was preserved as camouflage' (Pannekoek 2003: 78).

Having dethroned the unique proletarian nature of the Russian
Revolution, the council communists argued that the future revolution had to be conducted only by the working class itself, and
that the political form through which this leaderless struggle had
to be advanced was to be the council form. Although Pannekoek in
around 1920 still believed in some kind of revolutionary leadership,
even if this was only to educate and inspire, he later advanced the
argument reminiscent of Marx's that the council was both an instrument of revolutionary struggle and a germ of post-revolutionary
society: 'The workers' councils growing up as organs of fight will
at the same time be organs of reconstruction' (2003: 51). With the
emphasis on the double expected function of the councils, as both
organs of insurrection and organs of public authority, the council
communists often argued that the working masses needed no guidance from parties or leaders, because the workers would spontaneously invent the political forms they needed, when they needed
them. The chief difference between the vision of council democracy,
which the interwar council communists advanced, and the Leninist
vision (the non-1917 conception) is hence that Lenin comes to disregard the councils as a germ for a new society or as a political form
with a value in itself. Rühle succinctly summarised the critique of
Leninism which many council communists advanced:

> The revolution is a party affair. The dictatorship is a party affair. Social-
> ism is a party affair. And in addition: Party is discipline. Party is iron
> discipline. Party is leadership. Party is the strictest centralism. Party is
> militarism. Party is the most strict, most iron, most absolute militarism.
> Concretely formulated, this schema means: Above the leaders; below
> the masses. Above: Authority. Bureaucratism. Personality cult. Leader
> dictatorship. Power of command. Below: Slavish obedience. Subordina-
> tion. (Rühle 1920a)

In distancing themselves from the Bolsheviks, the council communists
oscillated between understanding the council as a determinate political form with certain positive characteristics, which makes it suitable

for working-class self-government, and understanding the council as the process through which revolutionary transformations are made (Korsch 1929). In doing so, their difference from and critique of Leninism is clear. By subordinating the soviets to the Bolshevik party and arguing for the superiority of the party vanguard, Lenin would accept neither the intrinsic value of the political form of council democracy nor the image of the council form as a leaderless, egalitarian and anti-hierarchical mode of revolutionary transformation.

Council Communism against Parliamentary Democracy

While council communists criticised Lenin's instrumental theory of the councils, they did not accept parliamentary politics as a mode of working-class struggle. Many council communists thought that parliamentarianism, parties and unions were organisational forms of struggle that predated World War I, when the proletariat was more atomised, less numerous and without advanced class-consciousness (Gorter 1920; Gombin 1978: 106). As the proletariat grew in number, parties and unions developed into bureaucratic organs that more or less fused with the state. When most of the European social democratic parties declared themselves on the side of war in 1914, and when they helped to dissolve the councils in Germany and Austria in 1918–19, council communists came to disregard parties and unions as appropriate forms of working-class struggle (Rachleff 1976: 188–206). New forms of revolutionary organisation such as councils, the council communists argued, had superseded parties and unions. According to Pannekoek, to continue to work within the confines of parliamentarianism would only strengthen the bourgeois consciousness of the workers, whereas direct action and self-management through councils would help create a new form of proletarian consciousness (Schecter 1994: 83–6). As Antonio Gramsci phrased it during the height of the council movement in Turin: 'The workshop commissions are organs of worker democracy which must be freed from the constraints imposed on them by the bosses and infused with new life and energy' (1994c: 98). Because of these arguments, council communists very often opposed any participation in parliamentary elections.

On a theoretical level, the case against parliamentarianism and the party form was advanced through a critique of leadership and hierarchy not unlike the critique of Bolshevism. In a pamphlet from 1920, Pannekoek argued that the most basic element of parliamentarianism 'is dependence upon leaders, whom the masses leave to determine general questions and to manage their class affairs. *Parliamentarianism inevitably tends to inhibit the autonomous activity by the masses that is necessary for revolution*' (Pannekoek 1920; original emphasis). Rühle expressed the same distrust in parliamentarianism, as the party 'leaders have the first word. They speak, they promise, they seduce, they command' (1920). In the *Open Letter*, Gorter also argued that parliament was an old form of organisation, which relied on separation between leaders and masses, and that councils and others forms of autonomous working-class activity suited the new era. The council communists thus agreed with Marx's dictum that the working class cannot take hold of the state apparatus and its parliament, because these are basically class institutions which uphold the power of the bourgeoisie. Parliamentary democracy, hence, is a deficient form of democracy, because of its division of executive and legislative powers, its checks and balances, and its huge unelected and unaccountable bureaucracy, which turns parliaments into mere talking-shops. Gramsci aptly expresses the council thinkers' dissatisfaction with parliamentary democracy: 'The workers feel that "their" organization has become such an enormous apparatus . . . they feel that their will to power is not being expressed, in any clear way, by the existing hierarchies' (1994b: 115).

The council communists' idea of council democracy was hence developed as a counter-concept to parliamentarianism: a council democracy signified the direct power of the people in the government of the polity. The mechanisms for such a direct power of the people were drawn from the experiences of the historical councils, as well as from the established council discourse (Marx's communal analysis and Lenin's 1917 conception of the soviet). Relations between local committees and council delegates were to be regulated by imperative mandate and instant recall in order for the local committees to retain power. Moreover, the council communists also argued that a federation of councils would ultimately supersede the state, as a variety of councils, assemblies, committees and organs would coordinate and collaborate, and power would be dispersed throughout society. In this way, the council communists developed their theories of council democracy in a conceptual war on two fronts: both Bolshevik communists and parliamentary Social Democrats were violating the core principle of council communism, namely workers' self-emancipation. The councils were theorised as a political form, which could achieve these aims due to their spontaneous emergence from the actions of the workers themselves, and due to the internal structures of the council form such as local self-management, instant recall and imperative mandate. Councils were thus expected by council communists to perform the task of revolutionary struggle, while also being the embryos of a future society.

Conclusion: The Council System and Constituent Power

As an alternative to both parliamentarianism and Leninism, the theory of council democracy is essentially a contribution to democratic theory. The basic idea of council democracy is somewhat simple: local people meet in local councils to decide on local matters and afterwards delegate individuals to participate in higher councils. This process is repeated at multiple different levels in order for decision-makers to be delegated by citizens, who interact with them directly. The delegates can at any time be recalled and are given a mandate from the delegating councils. This idea is oppositional to the structure of political authority in parliamentary democracy, where representatives are put forward by party organisations, excluding the citizenry at large from the exercise of power, and primarily accountable to their own conscience between elections. According to such a theory of council democracy, parliamentarianism is yet another way to institute the age-old division of society into governors and governed. A genuine democracy, according to advocates of the councils, needs to supersede the confines of liberal democracy, which leaves economic exploitation unchallenged (through private property) and distorts the popular will through its manifold divisions and separations. Council democracy, instead, revolts not merely against bourgeois governors, but against the very division between governors and governed. For this reason, the project of the councils becomes the project of democracy in its most basic sense: self-government.

The method of procuring a self-governing society is to overcome the conceptual pair of *separation* and *domination*: in the economic realm, the separation between ownership and labour is to be replaced with self-managing producers; in the political realm, the separation between governors and governed is to be replaced by a self-governing *demos*. The larger project of council democracy is hence to eliminate hierarchical relations of command and obedience, and instead democratise those relations of power. The effect is that the state itself – the ultimate agent of separation and domination – is replaced with a political form founded upon self-government and self-management. The aim of council democracy, hence, is to transform passive and obedient subjects into active and autonomous citizens – from *animal laborans* to *zoon politikon*.

Before I turn to the theories of council democracy by Cornelius Castoriadis, Hannah Arendt and Claude Lefort, I want to begin the discussion of the constituent power's relationship to the council system on the basis of the discussions in the first two chapters of this book. The European council movements were absolutely central during the uprisings from 1917 to 1919 that brought the three European empires to an end, but nowhere did the councils stay in power for any significant span of time. Everywhere, the council movements were challenged either by liberal parliamentarianism, as for example in Germany and Austria, or by communist one-party rule, as in Russia and Hungary. In the cases where the forces of parliamentarianism destroyed the councils, it was often argued that the councils took their revolutionary ambitions too far, and that the councils operated through lawless insurrection, which needed to be substituted with the rule of law. The forces of parliamentarianism wanted to terminate the revolutionary situation, introduce a liberal constitution with the safeguarding of individual liberties and introduce a capitalist economy. In short, the forces of parliamentarianism wanted to terminate the constituent power exercised by the councils. They were content with the results of this constituent power, namely the abdication of tsars, emperors and monarchs, but they wanted to reduce the constituent power to a momentary experience, which was to be completely exhausted in the newly established constitutional regimes – the so-called 'juridical containment thesis'. The representatives of the people in parliament, not the workers, soldiers and sailors assembled in the councils, were to govern after the revolution. Hence, the *historical* struggle between parliamentarianism and the council system can be translated into the *theoretical* conflict between constituent power and constitutional form. The forces of parliamentarianism therefore evaluated the council system as a *formless* power, which introduced extra-legality, lawlessness, too much flux and too many new, unworthy faces into politics (workers, soldiers, sailors). Their response was to counter the perceived formlessness of the councils' constituent power with the stability and rigidity of *form*, that is, with a liberal constitution that was to limit popular power, thereby privileging constituted politics over constituent politics.

In contrast, the critique of the council system advanced by Bolsheviks was that the soviets did not go far enough. In a speech at the First All-Russian Congress of Soviets in June 1917, Lenin argued that in revolutionary times, 'the question is one of advance or retreat. No one can stand still during a revolution' (Lenin 1917d). Either, the Bolsheviks argued, the council system would relinquish its power to the Provisional Government, that is, the forces of parliamentarianism, and hence the revolution would retreat, or the Bolsheviks, who would advance the revolution to its next stage, would control the soviets. As a political *form* in itself, the soviets did not interest the Bolsheviks; the importance of the soviets was dependent on who held the power within the soviets, and hence which classes the soviets represented. According to Lenin, crucially, 'For us the soviets have no importance as a *form*; what we care about is which classes the soviets represent' (qtd in Anweiler 1974: 165; emphasis added). Whereas the liberal forces understood the councils as too in*formal* and exercising a *form*less power, the Bolsheviks evaluated the councils as being too *form*alistic. For them, revolutionary power was indifferent to form, as it was itself formless and groundless. On the evening before the Bolsheviks took power in Petrograd, Lenin sent a letter to the members of the Central Committee of the Party. In that letter, Lenin argued that it would be 'a sheer *formality*' to wait for the *formal* authorisation of the takeover of power from the Second All-Russian Congress of Soviets, which would open the day after. In revolutionary times, Lenin argued,

> we are confronted by problems which are not to be solved by conferences or congresses (even congresses of Soviets), but exclusively by peoples, by the masses, by the struggle of the armed people . . . the people have the right and are in duty bound to decide such questions not by a vote, but by force; in critical moments of revolution. (Lenin 1917a)

Constituent power is, according to Lenin, antithetical to form; it cannot be exercised 'by conferences or congresses (even congresses of Soviets)' but must be carried out 'not by a vote, but by force'. As soon as any kind of formalisation of constituent power takes place, its radical and creative potentialities are exhausted in its *formalisation* and institutionalisation. Constituent power, according to Lenin, cannot be legalised; it functions only in a state of nature and is by definition arbitrary and violent. For this reason, Lenin prioritised constituent power in the tradition of Sieyès and Robespierre, and reformulated in the twentieth century by Carl Schmitt, over constituted politics. As such, the communist one-party dictatorship also saw a stark opposition between political form and constituent formlessness, and opted for the formlessness of permanent revolution instead of what they perceived to be the rigidity of the council form.

Consequently, the historical experiences with the councils and their defeat by either parliamentarianism or Leninism can be translated into a conflict between constituent power and constitutional form. In this interpretation, constituent power is regarded by both forces as equated with formlessness, extra-legality, insurrection and violence, and constitutional form is equated with the lack of direct popular power, procedural rigidity, instituted legality and representation – that is, as a clear-cut division between form and formlessness, constituted and constituent politics. In one interpretation, the council system is equated with the formless force of insurrection (by liberals); in another interpretation, the council system is equated with 'sheer formality' and the obsession with form (by the Bolsheviks). Hence, the council system can historically be understood as *either* form *or* formlessness, as *either* constituted politics *or* an expression of constituent power.

Moreover, within the theory of council democracy there exists a basic distinction between the councils as temporary instruments of insurrection and as permanent forms of self-government. Like the historical experiences with council politics, it is possible to translate this dichotomy into a question of constituent power. In the first conceptualisation, the councils are viewed as instruments of revolt; their defining mark is the spontaneity of their emergence, as the council in Trotsky's words is 'an organization that could be created within twenty-four hours' (1907). The council is an organisation for extraordinary politics, appearing in states of emergency, and hence not an organisational form fit for normal politics. '[T]he workers have realised that in revolutionary times they need *not only* ordinary, but an entirely different organisation', Lenin argued (1917b; original emphasis). The definite aims of the councils are those of tearing down and abolishing the old regime. In the language of constituent power, the Leninist critique of the council system regards the councils as only temporary, *constituent* organs, which are needed for eradicating the state and capitalism, but which must surrender power to the vanguard party after the revolution. 'The soviet exists only as an organ of insurrection, as an instrument of revolutionary power', Lenin states (qtd in Anweiler 1974: 188). The power exercised by the councils is not disciplined enough compared with the iron discipline of the party officials; it is too volatile and unpredictable and hence in need of guidance by the professional revolutionaries. As a temporary, insurrectionary power, the councils are too *formless* to govern society on a permanent basis. The constituent power of the councils can only be exercised momentarily, and then it has to be exhausted in the constituted institutions under the firm control of the Leninist vanguard party.

In contrast, some council thinkers argued that the council system is indeed a model prefiguring a post-revolutionary society. Gramsci states, 'the Factory Council is the model for the proletarian State. All the problems that are inherent to the organization of the proletarian State are also inherent in the organization of the Council' (1994b: 118). In this conceptualisation, the council system specifies a political *form*, which due to the *specificities* of the form itself is a model to be replicated – it is 'the *form* at last discovered', in Marx's famous formulation (1996a: 187; emphasis added). The council in this conceptualisation, hence, is in no way merely a formless, negating force; instead, it is a positive political form, a form of government on par with other forms of government, and which aspires to the permanent and formalised self-government of the working masses.

Just as the historical experiences of council politics can be interpreted as fluctuating between constituted form and constituent power, so can the theoretical interpretations. One of the primary contributions to council theory made by Castoriadis, Lefort and Arendt, as we shall see in the next three chapters, is to take advantage of this ambiguity and conceptualise the councils as *both* form and formlessness as a way to recuperate the revolutionary energy of the constituent power, but without its arbitrary and violent elements.

In the brilliant essay 'Revolutionary Commune' (1929), Karl Korsch reinterprets Marx's analysis of the Paris Commune in the language of political form and constituent formlessness. Korsch argues that despite Marx's enumeration of the specificity of the communal form,

> there remains still an unbalanced *contradiction* between on one hand Marx's characterization of the Paris Commune as the finally discovered '*political form*' for accomplishing the economic and social self-liberation of the working class and, on the other hand, his emphasis at the same time that the suitability of the commune for this purpose rests mainly on its *formlessness*; that is, on its indeterminateness and openness to multiple interpretations. (Korsch 1929; original emphasis)

Korsch argues that Marx might *not* mean that the communal form could emancipate the working class only due to the specificities of the form itself (imperative mandate, instant recall, federalism, local self-management). The fact that the commune embodies a formless force of self-transformation also plays a role. In this interpretation, the commune is 'the form at last discovered' not only due to the specificities of the form itself, but also due to its capacity of reconstitution. Marx himself also characterised the commune as 'a thoroughly *expansive political form*, while all previous political forms of government had been emphatically repressive' (1996a: 187; emphasis added). The expansiveness of the political form of the commune/council means that it retains elements of the constituent power in a constituted form, whereas other forms of government exhaust the constituent power in constituted reality, as they are 'emphatically repressive'. As Korsch mentions, 'every historical form turns at a certain point of its development from a *developing form* of revolutionary forces of production, revolutionary action, and developing consciousness into the *shackles* of that developing form' (1929; original emphasis). If unaltered, therefore, political institutions, although created for nurturing progressive development, will turn into the shackles of that development – that is, human political institutions will start confronting their creators as dominating forces. This process, according to Korsch, will also take place in the council form if it is not imbued with a dose of 'formless activity', since the final goal 'is not anyone [sic] *state*, however "democratic," "communal," or even "council-like"', but instead to establish political institutions that are '*relatively undeveloped and indeterminate*' and hence open for self-alteration (Korsch 1929; original emphasis).

To sum up, the historical experiences with council politics as well as the theoretical interpretations of council democracy point to the fact that the council system can be understood as both too formalised to express the revolutionary energy of the masses and too formless to provide a stable institution of government. The councils can be understood as both temporary organs capable of negating and abolishing, but not of governing, and as permanent political forms of proletarian self-government. In this way, the question of constituent power, form and formlessness that we shall encounter in the interpretations of Castoriadis, Lefort and Arendt in the following chapters is already apparent in the historical and theoretical evaluations of the councils.

Chapter 3
Institutionalising the Instituting Power? Castoriadis and the Councils

As fascism began to rise in 1930s Europe, and as the experiences with workers' councils faded in the memory of political thinkers, workers and citizens, discussions on council democracy started to live a marginal life within minor theoretical tendencies. After World War II, the council system's two major political enemies – representative democracy and one-party communism – ossified into a clear-cut dichotomy. After the war, many political thinkers were occupied with understanding totalitarianism in Germany, Italy and Russia and displayed little ambition of finding the seeds of alternative models in a Western tradition whose rationalism, bureaucratism, materialism, consumerism and nationalism were thought to be the natural breeding ground for totalitarian ideologies. This gloomy evaluation of Western society changed to some degree with the Hungarian Revolution of 1956, when the Hungarians and their workers' councils began the first major uprising against Russian oppression. The events in Hungary sparked at least a reinvigorated theoretical concern with the council system and theories of council democracy.

The three pre-eminent council thinkers in the second half of the twentieth century, Castoriadis, Lefort and Arendt, all encountered the council system at close range during the months of popular upheaval in Hungary. In the case of Castoriadis, the experience of the Hungarian Revolution became the starting point for his lifelong exploration of the main concept of his thinking, namely *autonomy*; that is, the practice of the deliberate self-creation of society's laws and institutions. At the time of the Hungarian Revolution, though, Castoriadis still called the idea of autonomy as deliberate self-creation *socialism*. The analysis of council democracy in the political thought of Castoriadis, Lefort and Arendt thus begins with Castoriadis, because he most forcefully throughout his writings exemplifies the transposition of the council tradition from Marxism to (radical) democracy.

Arendt, on the one hand, was never a Marxist, as she was almost something like an anti-Marxist, and Lefort, on the other hand, had already left *Socialisme ou Barbarie* – the influential Marxist journal, where he and Castoriadis were the animating actors – in 1958 because he perceived it to be an essentially Leninist organisational form (Lefort 1975). Moreover, with Castoriadis we encounter the strongest appraisal of the councils' constituent nature, whereas both Lefort and Arendt are more critical of the councils' constituent power, inasmuch as Lefort goes as far as to abandon the language of constituent power in his analysis of the councils and develops a theory of the council system as a thoroughly constituted power, while Arendt draws out elements from both Castoriadis and Lefort, as she sees in the councils a strong sense of order and stability along with their constituent capabilities. In other words, of the three thinkers analysed in this book, Castoriadis most clearly inaugurates a post-Marxist, radical democratic mode of interpreting the council system, which Lefort and Arendt will discuss, critique and nuance.

The main part of Castoriadis's thought is devoted to interrogating what *autonomy* means and how it relates to democracy. Castoriadis does not think of autonomy in relation to collective decision-making in a Rousseauian register or in relation to moral law in a Kantian fashion, but instead as a way of reflectively relating to society's institutions, laws, values and structures as created by human beings rather than naturally prescribed or God-given. Autonomy, for Castoriadis, is instead the deliberate self-creation of society's institutions and laws, as well as the self-reflective awareness of the contingent character of such creations. Autonomy stands in opposition to *heteronomy*, which Castoriadis understands as the concealment of the contingent character of institutions, law and hierarchies. The dichotomy between autonomy and heteronomy is the organising principle of Castoriadis's political thought, as historical movements, strains of thought and contemporary actors can be understood according to this dichotomy. The dichotomy between autonomy and heteronomy is complemented by another crucial distinction in Castoriadis's work, namely the distinction between instituting power and instituted reality – somewhat similar to the distinction between constituent power and constituted form. The instituting power designates society's ability to create and transform its institutions, whereas instituted reality refers to institutions as already created. Autonomy for Castoriadis is hence to participate in the deliberate self-institution of society (Castoriadis 1997a: 4). It is Castoriadis's contribution to the tradition of council democracy that he stresses their character as institutions, where individuals can experience autonomy and participate equally in exercising the instituting power.

Although Castoriadis has written extensively on the council system, his writings on the subject have received little attention.[1] One reason is the strong divide between 'the early' and 'the late' Castoriadis in the reception of his work. Together with Lefort, Castoriadis was the most prominent member of the left-wing group *Socialisme ou Barbarie* and from this platform, during the 1950s and 1960s, he launched a stern critique of Soviet communism and Western capitalism through the concept of 'bureaucratic domination'. In this period, Castoriadis theorised the council system as 'the positive content of socialism', as a socialist form of government, insofar as he stipulated as concretely as possible the institutional conditions for a self-managing counter-regime to bureaucratic domination. Castoriadis's self-proclaimed break with Marxism in 1964–5 altered his conceptual vocabulary altogether, as he developed his theory of autonomy, the radical imaginary and the instituting power in critical dialogue with certain traits of scientism in the Marxist tradition, which denied human beings their instituting capabilities (Castoriadis 1987: 41). In this period, from the mid-1960s onwards, Castoriadis seldom discussed the councils in their own right but instead as historical exemplars of democratic autonomy. Instead of understanding the councils as a concrete political form with certain positive institutional features, which principally secures self-management in perpetuity, as Castoriadis had earlier argued, the councils become paradigmatic for a practice of democratic autonomy, where the creative, instituting and constituent dimension of politics is emphasised.

In the reception of Castoriadis's work, the latter, post-Marxist period has received by far the greatest attention. Whereas it is commonplace to distinguish between the 'early' and the 'late' Castoriadis, between the Castoriadis of *Socialisme ou Barbarie* and the post-*Socialisme ou Barbarie* period, little work has engaged with the first period, let alone tried to bridge the two periods. The interpretive approach most often applied to Castoriadis's work is to regard the period from 1949 (the publication of the first volume of *Socialisme ou Barbarie*) to 1975 (the publication of *The Imaginary*

Institution of Society) as a relatively unimportant precursor to his project of autonomy and the instituting power. As a result, most discussions on Castoriadis fail to historicise 'the later' Castoriadis and are unsuccessful in demonstrating the fundamental relationship between Castoriadis's early critique of bureaucracy, his positive evaluation of the council system, and his later project of autonomy and the instituting power.[2] The interpretation of Castoriadis advanced in this chapter covers both periods and stresses the continuing engagement with the council tradition. Instead of positing an ultimate break between the two periods, I emphasise the continuities as well as the changes in his evaluation of the councils. The primary argument will be the following: Castoriadis's analysis of the councils shifts from an understanding of the councils as a concrete, socialist form of government, a modern update of Marx's *communal constitution* so to speak, to an institutionalised form of human creativity and instituting power, through which the people can exercise their autonomy. Hence, the council system is transferred from a discourse of socialism to a discourse of democracy. Such transposition, though, is not a complete break in Castoriadis's own evaluation. As he states, 'what was intended by the term "socialist society" we henceforth call autonomous society' (1993b: 317). Instead, Castoriadis's theory of council democracy combines concrete form (the councils as the content of socialism) with instituting formlessness (human creativity and novelty) in order to achieve an 'institutionalised instituting' power. One could object that such a combination of instituting power and instituted form undermines Castoriadis's central distinction between autonomy and heteronomy, as complete autonomy through the exercise of a pure instituting power becomes problematic. Hence, one could argue that via his interpretation of the council system, Castoriadis acknowledges that the project of autonomy is a burdensome, maybe even impossible, project to realise completely. This objection has some merit, and Castoriadis (2007b: 123) acknowledges this himself, as he deems democracy an essentially *tragic* regime, where autonomy is always potentially undermined, and the instituting power always potentially exhausted. But this does not mean that the opposition between autonomy and heteronomy, instituting power and instituted reality, needs to be abandoned. Castoriadis's council democracy is not an argument for the annihilation of instituted society as such, but instead for a combination of instituting power and instituted society, where the former has priority over the latter. Hence, the politics of the councils in Castoriadis's own evaluation is not one of *complete* popular control and democratic autonomy, but instead a politics which continually reasserts the priority of autonomy over heteronomy in the face of new forms of domination and alienation.

The Councils as 'the Content of Socialism': Castoriadis's Early Theory of Council Democracy

In formulating his early theory of council democracy and his theory of bureaucratic domination, which council democracy was to counter, Castoriadis engaged in critical dialogue with other council communists such as Anton Pannekoek, Tony Cliff and the so-called Johnson–Forest tendency. In an exchange of letters with Pannekoek in 1953, Castoriadis argued – contrary to Pannekoek – that the Russian Revolution, although it did overthrow a monarchical regime, was not the latest bourgeois revolution in line with the American and French Revolutions, but was characterised by the advent of a truly novel governing class: the bureaucracy. Whereas theory had predicted that the transformation of the ownership of production would terminate the alienation of the workers, the reality in Russia was the opposite, as the fundamental opposition between capital and labour, which characterised capitalism, was only replaced with a new opposition between bureaucracy and labour:

> As traditional forms of property and the bourgeoisie of the classical period are pushed aside by State property and by the bureaucracy, the main conflict within society gradually ceases to be the old one between owners of wealth and those without property and is replaced by the conflict between directors and executants in the process of production. (Castoriadis 1988d: 79)

Hence, the hierarchy characteristic of capitalism was not abandoned in Soviet communism, as the communist bureaucracy directed production and the workers executed the orders; and from their vantage point, the communist revolution had changed nothing in relation to the hierarchical system of production (Castoriadis 1988d: 82–3). From this fundamental similarity, Castoriadis argues that the central conflict of modern society is between *directors* and *executants*, as both capitalism and Soviet communism divide society 'into a narrow stratum of directors (whose function is to decide and organize every-thing) and the vast majority of the population, who are reduced to carrying out (executing) the decisions made by these directors' (1988a: 93). In this account of bureaucratic domination, Castoriadis shares certain characteristics with the council communists. Castoriadis similarly criticises both representative democracy and Bolshevik one-party rule for its hierarchical, elitist structure; and just as the council communists deemed the self-management of the councils an alternative to both these systems of government, so did Castoriadis, when he first experienced the formation of councils during the Hungarian Revolution of 1956.

Castoriadis's early theory of council democracy ought to be reconstructed from the background of this critique of bureaucracy, as well as from the workers' councils of the Hungarian Revolution of 1956. Before the Hungarian Revolution, Castoriadis had only delivered a very limited positive account of politics, therefore the council system as it developed during the Hungarian Revolution signifies for Castoriadis nothing less than a possible solution to the fundamental political problem in the capitalist West and the communist East. Through the workers' self-management of society from below in the council system, the bureaucratic distinction between directors and executants can be transcended. In other words, 'the content of socialism' for Castoriadis becomes the masses' self-management of society through the council system. In this way, Castoriadis reiterates the argumentative structure of the interwar council communist: by joining together capitalist, representative democracy and communist one-party rule under the concept of bureaucratic domination, Castoriadis similarly points to an alternative political system beyond this dichotomy, namely a political system founded upon self-managing councils. In an article published in *Socialisme ou Barbarie* only a couple of months after the Hungarian Revolution, Castoriadis argues that

> Through this revolution, through its heroic example – whatever may be its subsequent fate – it overturns existing political classifications, it creates a new line of demarcation both within the workers' movement as well as within society at large . . . For years to come, *all questions that count* can be summed up as follows: Are you for or against the action and the program of the Hungarian workers? Are you for or against the constitution of workers' councils in all sectors of national life and workers' management of production? (Castoriadis 1988d: 61–2; original emphasis)

For years to follow, to be sure, Castoriadis's main theoretical concern was to theorise the experiences of the workers' councils in Hungary during the last months of 1956. The initial significance of these experiences is the amount of hope they sparked for a different kind of politics than bureaucratic domination. In short, the Hungarian councils pose for Castoriadis the foundational political question of who is to rule: the few or the many?:

> Either the real social life of society, in all its aspects, will become identical with a single network of institutions, the councils, or else the traditional institutions – Party, State, the management of the economy and the factories – separated from the mass of people and thereby from their real life as well, will rise up anew above society. (Castoriadis 1988d: 85)

Decisions are taken either by bureaucrats, or by the citizenry organised through the 'real social life of society'. Similarly, to Marx's argument on the Paris Commune, the separation of an independent stratum of decision-makers equals the dominance of this stratum, that is, the state's domination over society as well as society's depoliticisation. The Hungarian councils testify to the possibility of politicising society by redistributing power and eliminating the two oppositional spheres of decision-making and executing. 'For the workers, "democracy" has never signified and will never signify anything but this: the right to organize themselves as they want to, to be able to meet together and to express themselves freely' (Castoriadis 1988d: 77). In this manner, the councils in Castoriadis's interpretation not only reduce social hierarchy and increase the power of the workers, but also provide the germs of a new form of government, as the ruling class and its party, along with the state apparatus, crumble when confronted with the organised power of the Hungarian workers.

From Castoriadis's early analysis of the Hungarian councils, we can identify certain key traits from the political theory of council democracy, as identified in Chapter 2. The council system – like Marx's commune – functions as a working body combining legislation and execution, which helps to overcome the separation of state and society, as well as the former's dominance over the latter. Instead, the council system embodies an anti-statist logic, which transcends the distinction between state and society through society's self-management These insights taken from the Hungarian councils animate Castoriadis in his subsequent theorisation of the councils as concrete forms of socialist government.

From Practice to Theory: Councils and Socialism

The previous chapter demonstrated how the councils have been understood both as a permanent political form, what Marx called 'the form at last discovered', and as temporary organs of insurrection, primarily in the Leninist interpretation. In Castoriadis's early council theory, he is thinking in the former, formal direction, insofar as he believes that self-management is a completely realisable political goal through the development of the correct political form. Castoriadis provides this positive evaluation of council democracy in a tripartite series of articles, 'On the Content of Socialism, I–III', appearing in *Socialisme ou Barbarie* in 1955, 1957 and 1958. As the insurrection of the Hungarian workers was the first full-blown popular uprising against bureaucratic communism, the content of socialism stood in need of a 'revision' emanating from the 'raw materials' found in the 'vast experience of . . . the Hungarian workers' councils, their actions and their program' (Castoriadis 1988d: 90). Ultimately, for Castoriadis, such a change can be initiated only by the restructuring of '*all of political theory* around the principles embodied in the soviets and the councils' (1988e: 214; emphasis added). According to Castoriadis, 'the Russian factory committees of 1917, the German workers' councils of 1919, the Hungarian councils of 1956 all sought to express (whatever their name) the same original, organic, and characteristic working-class pattern of organization' (1988d: 95). The reason for joining these historical situations together into a tradition of working-class action is that the different organisations all aim, according to Castoriadis, at the elimination of the bureaucratic distinction between directors and executants. This implies that socialism as an alternative to both capitalism and bureaucratic communism is equal to the 'people's self-organization of every aspect of their social activities' (Castoriadis 1988d: 95). Socialism is thus quite simply the collective's self-management of its own affairs. Moreover, the councils resist the crystallisation of an internal bureaucratic layer of management. Essentially, the council system is a type of institution, which governs itself *without* instituting a hierarchical distinction between rulers and ruled. According to Castoriadis, though, 'we should condemn any fetishism for the "soviet" or "council" organization', as 'the council is not a *miraculous* institution' (1988d: 95, 96; original emphasis). Instead, the council is a structure that makes it possible, but not *per se* secures, that popular self-management can come to the fore at all. On the contrary, 'parliament is designed so that it *never* fulfils this function', as it is 'founded on a radical separation between the people, "consulted" from time to time, and those, who are supposed to "represent" them, but who are in fact uncontrollable and irremovable' (Castoriadis 1988d: 96; original emphasis). Democracy, therefore, 'means to decide for oneself', Castoriadis asserts, but representative democracy 'inevitably contains a kernel of political alienation, namely the separation of representatives from those they represent', and consequently, 'to decide who is to decide is already not quite deciding for oneself' (1988d: 98, 144, 98).

How does Castoriadis envision the council form – in contrast to capitalism, bureaucracy and representative democracy – as enabling self-management? It is important to remember that Castoriadis at this point understands the councils as a concrete political form. Hence, 'to define the socialist organization of society in concrete terms', Castoriadis contends, 'is to draw all the possible conclusions from two basic ideas: workers' management of production and the rule of the councils' (1988d: 95). He provides the following institutional sketch for a self-managing society, consisting of three core elements, which is more or less equivalent to Marx's *communal constitution*: *firstly*, at the most basic level, socialist society is to be composed of local, self-managing collectivities (factory, mine, office, farm, plant, neighbourhood, etc.). This means that the communities that form the basic surroundings around people's lives will manage their internal affairs sovereignly and democratically. At the most elementary level, this is the method for abolishing the distinction between directors and executants.

The *second* important characteristic is the mechanisms of imperative mandate (*ex ante* instruction) and instant recall (*ex post* control). These mechanisms appeared already in the Paris Commune, in the Russian soviets of 1905 and 1917, the German workers' councils of 1918–19 and the Hungarian councils in 1956. As Castoriadis explains,

> factory councils (or councils based on any other place of work such as a plant, building site, mine, railway yard, office etc.) will be composed of delegates who are elected by the workers, responsible for reporting to them at regular intervals, and revocable at any time. (Castoriadis 1988d: 95)

In theory, instant recall and imperative mandate will ensure, according to Castoriadis, that the collectivity as a whole retains control over its representative organs and delegates, and forecloses the possibility that a permanent managerial stratum might develop.

In short, in contrast to representation, delegation implies – at least theoretically – neither the alienation of power nor the unity of *the* people. Some might argue that this proposition set the bar too high; that it requires too much of the collectivity, and that full autonomy and control cannot be achieved in politics, as too many alien forces influence and exert power over the collectivity. As Castoriadis shifts his analysis of the councils from an emphasis on political form to an emphasis on instituting power, he acknowledges that the project of autonomy is not concerned with establishing the right or just institutions once and for all, but instead with continually renewing and reinstituting them in the face of new challenges and forces of alienation.

Thirdly, the council system, as it developed historically, cannot be adequately understood only in terms of the internal structures of the individual self-managing unit. The reorganisation of society in its entirety is the most abstract element of the council system and can most adequately be understood as a process of upward *federalisation* between the individual self-managing units. In order to coordinate between the different units and resist a degree of fragmentation unsuitable for a modern, complex society, the council of every unit delegates – again under imperative mandate and instant recall – councilmen to regional soviets, that is, geographically based assemblies consisting of delegates from the producing units (Castoriadis 1988d: 137). Through an iterative process, these regional soviets federate into a central general council. This federalisation of the polity henceforth combines decentralisation and centralisation in a novel way, ensuring – according to Castoriadis – both direct democracy and relatively effective decision-making power:

> Direct democracy gives an idea of the amount of *decentralization* that socialist society will be able to achieve. But this democratic society will have to find a means of democratically *integrating* these basic units into the social fabric as a whole as well as achieving the necessary degree of *centralization*, without which the life of a modern nation would collapse. (Castoriadis 1988d: 99; original emphasis)

Instead of being discouraged by any talk of centralisation, 'socialist society therefore will have to provide a socialist solution to the problem of centralization', which is entailed in the exercise of 'power by a federation of workers' councils' as a 'real and identifiable centre, controlled from below' (Castoriadis 1988d: 100). In Castoriadis's early formulation of council democracy, these three institutional characteristics of the councils are the specific and positive content of socialism. Formulated crudely, if these institutional mechanisms are established, socialism is created.

After Castoriadis's break with Marxism, he began to develop a theory of autonomy and the instituting power. The central reason why Castoriadis decided to break with Marxism was the deterministic understanding of history and the human power of creation in parts of this tradition. In his newfound theoretical vocabulary, Castoriadis instead argues that historical developments are initiated by the radical imaginary, society's instituting power and the human power of creation; a fact which parts of Marxism had occluded by its emphasis on a law-like, deterministic understanding of historical and societal development (Castoriadis 1988a: 25–9). After the break with Marxism, Castoriadis now reformulated his vision of council democracy from a specific political form to a 'formless form', a 'process-form', which combines political action and political institutionalisation in novel ways. In order to understand this unusual formulation of council democracy, I engage with Castoriadis's theory of autonomy below.

Democratic Autonomy and the Instituting Power

Autonomy is the key concept in Castoriadis's political thought, and he devoted the second half of his career to elucidating the meaning and historical origins of autonomy. For Castoriadis, a society becomes autonomous when it begins to have a *specific relation* towards itself; when it starts to evaluate its institutions, laws and customs as *creations* brought into the world by itself, which are therefore changeable by society itself. This might seem banal, but that is most certainly not the case. According to Castoriadis, most societies throughout history and most contemporary societies have denied the very fundamental fact that they themselves create their institutions,[3] and they continually conceal that their structures are established by the activity of human beings. They are, in Castoriadis's vocabulary, in a condition of *heteronomy*, as they attribute the social order to 'an extrasocial source of *nomos*' (1991b: 162). Whether this is God, nature, the forces of history, the inevitable process of progress, the workings of the invisible hand or the politics of necessity, most societies have sought to explicate their order, hierarchies and structures by pointing towards forces outside of their own control. When societies relate to their institutions in this heteronomous manner, they come to understand them as unalterable, and politics consequently becomes merely the game of power *within* these established institutions, never the question of how society as such ought to be structured. Or, in fact, politics ceases to exist in a heteronomous society, as such societies seal off the possibility of conscious self-alteration and self-criticism. Another way to phrase it is that heteronomous societies deny the functioning of the constituent power, that is, the power to alter and transform the basic coordinates of political life, and associate themselves exclusively with constituted politics.

Behind these notions of autonomy or heteronomy lies Castoriadis's basic argument that society is always *instituted*. Society always consists of self-created values, structures and traditions; every society constitutes for itself a 'world' of meaning through which subjectivity, human relations, social status and political power come into being. According to Castoriadis,

> Each and every society creates within what must be called its cognitive closure – or, even better, its *closure of meaning* – its own world . . . our fountains are inhabited by Nymphs, our stars are palaces for our gods, only a young virgin woman may honorably marry, and so on. (Castoriadis 1991b: 37; original emphasis)

Out of the fundamental chaos of being, the cosmos is created by a closure of meaning. The difference between how societies constitute a 'world' of meaning for themselves speaks to the fact that society's institutions, values and hierarchies cannot be explained with reference to pre-existing laws, such as functionalism, structuralism or historical materialism have argued. Instead, human beings *institute* these values and hierarchies, therefore every society, whether it conceals this fact or not, is *instituted* by itself – by what Castoriadis calls the *instituting* society. Society's horizon of meaning, its evaluations of just and unjust, its assessment of death, its notion of truth, its modes of acquiring fame and glory, its hierarchies and priorities – all the elements that make a society *this particular* society cannot be attributed to functionality, to trans-historical structures, or to inevitable historical progress. Differences between societies cannot be logically deduced, because they are created *ex nihilo* (Castoriadis 1987: 172–3). This means that the institution of society is accomplished by society itself, albeit in a different capacity, namely by society as instituting power. To quote from *The Imaginary Institution of Society*: 'That which in the social-historical is positing, creating, bringing into being we call social imaginary in the primary sense of the term, or *instituting society*' (Castoriadis 1987: 396; emphasis added). What lies beyond every particular institution of society, that is, *instituted* society, is thus society as *instituting*: 'What escapes it [instituted society] as well is the very being of society as instituting, that is to say, ultimately, society as the source and origin of otherness or perpetual self-alteration' (Castoriadis 1987: 371).

In order to explicate further the crucial idea that society is always instituted, we can say that the 'social-historical' manifests itself in two modes: as instituted society, that is, as a more or less stable 'world' organised by hierarchies and structures; and as instituting society, that is, as the source of its own transformation. One could think of this duality in perhaps more well-known terms. Think, for example, of Bruce Ackerman's (1988) distinction between constitutional and normal politics: constitutional politics is a mode of politics which transforms the basic coordinates of political life and creates the framework for normal politics, which adheres to the confines established by constitutional politics. In one mode of politics, the general laws are created (society's instituting power); in another mode of politics, citizens live by these already established laws (instituted society). During revolutions, society's form of government is transformed by the constituent power of the people, whereas during normal politics, the constituted powers and the people's representatives govern. Whereas Castoriadis's instituting power is certainly broader in scope compared with what in political theory is called 'constituent power' – as Castoriadis's instituting power designates the creative force which brings temporary order to the fundamental chaos of being (1991a: 103–4) – it is indeed pertinent to use the two concepts interchangeably in political terms, as both designate the creative process through which society's laws are created and transformed.[4]

The question worth posing, hence, is what kind of relationship exists between the distinction of instituting and instituted society and the project of autonomy. The project of autonomy fundamentally consists in recognising that society itself is the source of its own institution, that society itself carries its instituting power. As Castoriadis aptly puts it,

> To be able to decide, however, is not only to be able to decide about 'current affairs', to participate in a state of affairs considered sacrosanct. Autonomy signifies giving one's own law . . . To participate in power is to participate in *instituting power*. (Castoriadis 1993b: 321; original emphasis)

Most societies throughout history and most major systems of thought have concealed this fact. Instead, the project of autonomy that began with the ancient Greeks' dual invention of philosophy and democracy has waxed and waned throughout history, and has only reappeared in Western modernity with the advent of the workers' movement and the establishment of councils (Castoriadis 1991b: 169). From the discussion already provided, we can see why the Greek invention of philosophy and democracy inaugurates the project of autonomy, that is, the project of rendering explicit society's *instituting dimension*. Through philosophy's questioning into the grounds of justice, the legitimacy of the laws, the sources of the good life and the nature of the community, the naturalness of the inherited laws of the gods (or of nature, of reason, of science) are denaturalised (Castoriadis 1991b: 163). In addition, through democracy's deliberate questioning and transformation of the laws of the community, an autonomous reinstitution of society becomes possible:

> Autonomy does not consist in acting according to a law discovered in an immutable Reason and given once and for all. It is the unlimited self-questioning about the law and its foundations as well as the capacity, in light of this interrogation, *to make*, *to do* and *to institute* (therefore also, *to say*). Autonomy is the reflective activity of a reason creating itself in an endless movement. (Castoriadis 1991b: 164; original emphasis)

Importantly, then, the project of autonomy begins with the awareness that the present constellation of meaning and the established order is *nothing but* a contingent, human creation. Autonomy is firstly the process of making the self-creation of society explicit; and secondly, the process of creating institutions, where all citizens can participate in the instituting process of creation. Moreover, the project of autonomy emerges within society as *instituted*; it disrupts its core meanings and institutions, which means that the project of autonomy is fundamentally *revolutionary*, as 'the instituted society is always subject to the subterranean pressure of instituting society. Beneath the established order, the flow of the radical imaginary continues steadily' (Castoriadis 1991b: 152–3). The project of autonomy thus contains a revolutionary kernel, because it implies the human ability to institute new forms of life; to alter and abolish instituted reality and its social and political hierarchies. In addition, institutions of direct democracy are an integral part of autonomous society because such a society requires that everyone partake in the conscious creation of society itself. It requires that specific institutions are made accessible for people to participate in society's self-alteration. Democracy as collective autonomy is hence simply another name for politics: 'Politics is a project of autonomy. Politics is the reflective and lucid collective activity that aims at the overall institution of society' (Castoriadis 1991b: 169).

Castoriadis's theory of autonomy and instituting power has received various criticisms. I briefly engage with the critique by Jürgen Habermas and Claude Lefort (whose vision of council democracy will be examined in Chapter 4), because Castoriadis's later theory of council democracy, which I reconstruct below, provides a privileged vantage point to nuance these criticisms. Habermas's critique of Castoriadis concerns his fundamental distinction between instituted and instituting society, and the value Castoriadis ascribes to the instituting elements of politics. According to Habermas (1987a: 327–35), Castoriadis envisions an irreducible gap between politics as exceptional and instituting and politics as ordinary and instituted, and he locates moments of freedom, autonomy and democracy *only* in the process of instituting society; that is, Castoriadis advances a vision of politics as *solely* extraordinary, revolutionary and constituent. Consequently, Habermas (1987a: 330) considers Castoriadis's concept of institution to be problematic because it lacks a normative foundation which can guide the institution of society. Because Castoriadis, according to Habermas, advances a conception of human creation *ex nihilo*, he conceptualises the gap between the instituting power and instituted reality as irreducible. In this way, Castoriadis has been accused of advancing a Schmittian theory of decisionism (Breckman 1998: 40). Another way to phrase Habermas's critique is that Castoriadis has no regard for ordinary politics. Hence, Castoriadis's privileging of extraordinary politics, according to Habermas, has the consequence that he denigrates representative government and thinks popular sovereignty in the tradition of Rousseau, Sieyès and Schmitt, namely as 'the people' above all law, unrepresentable, mute and indivisible.

Castoriadis's former *Socialisme ou Barbarie* comrade Lefort has voiced another critique, which is directed at their diverging notions of autonomy and different understandings of the council system. Castoriadis and Lefort initially shared critical views on Bolshevism, as well as on important events throughout the 1950s such as the uprising in East Berlin in 1953, and the insurrections in Poland and Hungary in 1956 (Lefort 1975: 177). Lefort left *Socialisme ou Barbarie* in 1958 and partly ascribed his break to the inspiration he took from the French philosopher Maurice Merleau-Ponty: 'I had adopted his critique of any claim to absolute knowledge', which sparked for Lefort 'the desire to break with the Bolshevik mythology of which *Socialisme ou Barbarie* seemed an offshoot' (1975: 176, 179). Instead, Lefort began to develop his theory of democracy as an 'empty place' of power (Lefort 1988b), which refers to the fact that power has become disincorporated in modern democracy, meaning that no determinate figure – like the monarch, the tribal leader or the divine prophet – can claim full legitimacy over political decisions. Not even 'the people' can, as it always consists of a plurality of conflicting interests. The conflict characteristic of modern democracy, according to Lefort, thus revolves around diverse claims to speak momentarily with the voice of the people. As a consequence, any attempt to fully realise self-government through the institutional complex of the council system, which was Castoriadis's ambition in his early theory of council democracy, is redundant for Lefort (1975: 80). The very problem of advocating for a specific set of institutions is, according to Lefort, that one thereby understands society as a homogenous totality, which *can* actually master its own affairs successfully. Describing the council system as the 'content of socialism', and specifying in detail the institutional structures of a council democracy is, according to Lefort, to place oneself in a position of absolute knowledge and to view society as a transparent totality. Hence, Lefort argues that the domination and hierarchy which the council system is to counter in Castoriadis's early analysis are actually reintroduced in Castoriadis's detailed sketch of the institutional structures of the council system:

> After all, what does the pyramid model of the councils signify? It assumes a hierarchy of responsibilities and the circulation of information both downward and upward, so that the will from the bottom clears a path to the top . . . But could I have admitted that the functions of the executive recreate the conditions for a division between dominators and dominated under the pretext of the selection according to ability, or under the guise of the power of speech, in spite of the principle of permanent revocability of those delegated with power? (Lefort 1975: 180)

In order to keep the place of power empty, and not reintroduce a logic sovereignty and homogeneity, Lefort argued for a pluralisation of political forms within a mixed regime, where parties, unions and councils collaborate.

Below, I argue, firstly, that Castoriadis, *pace* Habermas, provides a theory of council democracy in which constituent power and political form – extraordinary and ordinary politics – are entangled in order for autonomy to become accessible to the many on a regular basis. Secondly, I argue that Castoriadis's later theory of council democracy, *pace* Lefort, does not envision the council system as realising a static form of autonomy, wherein society is fully mastered, but instead – by understanding the councils as institutional expressions of the instituting power – Castoriadis understands council democracy as a political form, which can continually combat heteronomy by its privileged access to the constituent power.

Although I will seek to nuance these criticisms of Castoriadis below, I agree with Lefort that Castoriadis's early formulation of council democracy is problematic due to its excessive focus on concrete institutional set-up. It also becomes problematic when looked at from the perspective of Castoriadis's own theory of autonomy and the instituting power. If autonomy is the key political and democratic value, it means that only by partaking in the institution of new forms of political life can autonomy and democracy be experienced. But Castoriadis's early, detailed description of the institutional mechanisms of self-managing councils contains an *already instituted society*, where fixed structures create certain outcomes (namely the avoidance of bureaucratic domination). These structures ought not to be reinstituted, therefore, because they already express a socialist form of government in the first place – the council form is 'the form at last discovered', as Marx said – and hence there is no need to reactivate the instituting power of society. The experience of participating in exercising the instituting power has no independent value if the councils are solely associated with a fixed form. But as Castoriadis makes clear, instituted society is always under potential pressure from the instituting power; no political form can obtain pure fixation in an autonomous society. Hence, Castoriadis's concept of autonomy, I argue, should not be understood as a fixed state, as something that can be realised once and for all through clever institutional design. Instead, autonomy is equal to 'becoming-autonomous', that is, a process through which the forces of heteronomy are continually confronted. Castoriadis, hence, cannot hold on to his concrete description of the council system after the development of the project of autonomy. Consequently, his analysis of the council system changes considerably in his later writings. The best way to grasp the consequences of this change is by engaging with Castoriadis's second interpretation of the Hungarian Revolution in the article 'The Hungarian Source' published in 1976 (Castoriadis 1993a).

The Councils as Moments of Autonomy: Castoriadis's Late Theory of Council Democracy

With Castoriadis's later development of a theory of council democracy, the council system is transferred from a discourse of Marxism with an emphasis on political form to a discourse of democracy with an emphasis on constituent power and continual reinstitution. On the one hand, this transfer could be understood as a decontextualisation of certain key categories in Castoriadis's vocabulary. What was previously called bureaucracy is now known as the general category of heteronomy; what was known as socialism and self-management is now called autonomy and self-creation. Castoriadis also acknowledged this continuity, as he argued that although historically the project of autonomy began in ancient Greece, he himself discovered it in the contemporary workers' movement and their establishment of councils.[5] But on the other hand, as I shall argue, a vital change in the interpretation of the council system is acquired through Castoriadis's new conceptual language – most visible in Castoriadis's late reinterpretation of the Hungarian Revolution.

In his 1956 article on the Hungarian Revolution, Castoriadis asserted that for years to come, all important political questions could be boiled down to whether one was for or against the Hungarian workers' councils. By 1976, in his second article on the revolution, 'The Hungarian Source', Castoriadis uses this proclamation as the epigraph and adds that 'twenty years later, I stand by these lines – more firmly, and more savagely, if possible, than when I wrote them' (1993a: 250). Certain elements of the analysis had not changed during those twenty years: the Hungarian Revolution is still evaluated as the first revolution against bureaucracy and points towards the creation of a self-managing society. Castoriadis still holds that the council form will not *guarantee* self-management, but that at least, in contrast to representative democracy, it *enables* it. Moreover, he still mentions the mechanisms of instant recall and imperative mandate and argues that a federation of councils would be a negation of the state (Castoriadis 1993a: 261, 260, 267, 263). But alongside these familiar elements, a new conceptual language is also employed to understand the workers' councils. In the Hungarian Revolution we now not only find the source of the abolition of the bureaucratic division of society, as in the earlier article; in addition, 'we find a new departure, a new source, which forces us to reflect anew the problem of *politics*' (Castoriadis 1993a: 254; original emphasis). The problem of politics amounts to, as we know, the 'institution of society' as such (Castoriadis 1993a: 254). The emergence of councils forces us to reflect on the instituting dimension of society, insofar as the councils transgress the already established order of things (the instituted society) and signify the positing of something new:

> The positive content of workers' councils, the demands for self-man-agement and abolition of work norms, etc. was not a deduction, infer-ence, choice of 'the only alternative' etc. It was an elaboration that *transcended* the given (and all that is given with the given, implied or contained in it) and posited something new. (Castoriadis 1993a: 259; original emphasis)

The spontaneous emergence of councils and their transgression of the existing order show for Castoriadis the opposition between the instituting power and instituted reality, insofar as the councils did not emerge as a form of 'repetition, neither *strictu sensu* nor in the sense of a "variant" of the already given, but positing of new forms and figures and of new meanings – that is, *self-institution*' (1993a: 257; original emphasis). Entailed in the practice of council democracy is thus a deliberate process of self-institution. The councils – by emerg-ing within societies which were completely dominated by bureaucratic power – did not respect the present institution of society and sought to establish a new institution of society. It is through these arguments that Castoriadis connects the councils' deliberate practice of institut-ing society anew with the project of autonomy. 'When I speak about autonomous organs of the masses, I do not call them autonomous only because, for example, they do not "obey" given individuals or parties or the "government"', Castoriadis asserts; instead

> I call them autonomous because and insofar as *they do not accept the established institution of society*. This means in particular, first, that they do not accept, outside themselves, any other source of legitimate power; and, second, that they abolish, within themselves, the division between those who direct and those who execute. (Castoriadis 1993a: 263; original emphasis)

In sum, this means that the councils as 'autonomous organs posit themselves as the only legitimate source of decisions, rules, norms and law' (Castoriadis 1993a: 263). Autonomy, as Castoriadis now formulates it in relation to the Hungarian councils, means that the collectivity does not accept a law posited by external agents, and in addition, that when the group posits its own laws, it does so collectively without splitting itself into directors and executants. The collectivity is autonomous once it demands that it *itself* is the *only* source of the institution of society.

From this analysis of the Hungarian councils two vital changes in Castoriadis's theory of council democracy are achieved, which together signify the aforementioned shift from understanding the council system through a discourse of Marxism to a discourse of democracy. The *first* shift has to do with political subjectivity and implies a change from a proletarian subject located in the terrain of economic production to a popular subject without any specific location. As the experiments with council organisation point toward the problem of the institution of society as such, 'their exemplary character does *not* stem from being *workers'* councils; it is not linked to their "proletarian composition", to their springing from "productive enterprises", or even to the external aspects of the council "form" as such' (Castoriadis 1993a: 260; original emphasis). This is very important. In Castoriadis's early analysis of the councils, their hallmark was precisely their 'proletarian composition', 'the council "form" as such', that their specific institutional mechanisms equalled the positive content of socialism. But as a consequence of Castoriadis's theory of autonomy and the councils' intimate relation to the institution of society, the council form is no longer tied to the economic sphere, but instead to the collectivity as an instituting agent. Hence, it is not the council form itself which accounts for its exemplarity, but its ability of trans*form*ation, that is, it is a form which is able to change itself. As such, the exemplary character of the councils is democratic and constituent, not socialist, in nature:

> Their decisive importance lies in (a) the establishment of *direct democracy* – in other terms, of *true political equality* (equality as to power); (b) their rootedness in existing concrete collectivities (which need not be the 'factories'); and (c) their demands relative to *self-management* . . . Implied in these points is a striving toward the abolition of the established *division* of society and of the *essential separation* between main spheres of collective activity. Involved here are not only the division between 'classes', but the division between the 'rulers' and the 'ruled' (including the division between 'representatives' and 'represented'). (Castoriadis 1993a: 260; original emphasis)

The significance of the council system, once it is connected to the concept of autonomy, is that it is now freed from its socialist origins and its economic roots and becomes a political project with the main aim of politicising society and restoring the 'rulers' and the 'ruled' into one combined figure: the autonomous people.

The *second*, crucial shift is – as Castoriadis suggests in the above – that the councils cease to be important merely because of their specific form, but instead are important as moments of the instituting power in action. It is not only their form (local self-management, imperative mandate, instant recall, federalism) which makes them democratic institutions, but also the fact that they render possible the control of the instituting power over its instituted reality. Now, this presents us with a paradox, which Castoriadis will not try to solve because the paradox is what makes the council a unique political institution. It goes as follows: the ambition of democratic, Castoriadian politics is to ensure that the instituting power takes precedence over instituted powers, as this is the condition for living autonomously. This generally implies that every institution is subordinate to society's instituting power. The paradoxical element of Castoriadis's second formulation of council democracy is that although the instituting power stands above instituted reality, although the people is superior to its institutions, they need institutional ways of expressing their autonomy and exercising their instituting power. The councils thus mediate between a pure instituting power which creates new forms *ex nihilo* and the heteronomy of instituted reality, that is, the alienation of the instituting power implied in the power of institutions over individuals (i.e. bureaucratic domination). Castoriadis's re-evaluation of the councils through the theory of autonomy thus amounts to an understanding of the councils as *institutionalised* spaces for exercising the *instituting* power, as they combine the creative formlessness of the instituting power with the stability of the instituted form.

Institutionalising the Instituting Power

We can further explicate the idea of the council system as an 'institutionalised instituting power' by relating it to the criticisms by Habermas and Lefort. The crux of Habermas's critique was that Castoriadis tends to exclusively valorise exceptional politics without properly appreciating the importance of the quotidian practices of ordinary politics. Habermas suggests that Castoriadis argues for a pure instituting society, a free flow of creations, which will never ground itself in instituted reality due to the constant reactivation of the instituting power, as this is the only way autonomy can be realised. Politically this would be akin to a *permanent revolution* – politics in an exclusively constitutional key with clear references to Rousseauian, Sièyesian and Schmittian versions of popular sovereignty. Moreover, according to Lefort, Castoriadis covers up democracy's inherent emptiness by formulating a vision of council democracy which – in Lefort's analysis – seeks to realise complete autonomy through concrete institutional design. This ambition, says Lefort, departs with the plurality, ambiguity and conflictual nature of modern democracy.

Castoriadis's second theorisation of council democracy is partly at odds with these criticisms. The principle of autonomy which can be realised through the council system neither amounts to a permanent revolution, constantly negating every instituted reality, as Habermas argued, nor does it signify a static state of complete mastery without conflict, as argued by Lefort. The council movement, for Castoriadis, is not an attempt to exercise a pure revolutionary power, not an aspiration to eliminate all institutional structures and let loose an uncontaminated and instituting power. 'To abolish heteronomy', Castoriadis argues, 'does not signify abolishing the difference between instituting society and instituted society – which, in any case, would be impossible – but to abolish the *enslavement* of the former to the latter' (1993a: 330; original emphasis). What happens in the councils, rather, in Castoriadis's analysis, is the realisation that if 'the people' wants to live autonomously, institutions, laws and traditions should not dominate it. The project of council democracy is that *we* should dominate *our* institutions, because they have been *created* by us:

> The collectivity will give itself its rules, knowing that *it itself* is giving them *to itself*, that these rules are or will always become at some point inadequate, that it can change them – and that they bind it so long as it has not changed them in a *regular way*. (Castoriadis 1993a: 330; original emphasis)

The regularity stressed by Castoriadis signifies that council democracy is not an attempt to go beyond instituted reality, but that instituted society should always be subordinated to society as instituting. No institution should be able to enslave its instituting origin; no law should achieve status as sacrosanct. The council system is an *institutional expression* of this hierarchical relation between instituted and instituting society. In this analysis, the council system is therefore crucial because it is an institution which makes society's *instituting* power accessible and open to mass participation. As such, the council system in Castoriadis's analysis is a political space which provides the grounds for society's self-transformation. According to Castoriadis, this combination of form and trans*form*ability, of instituting power and institutionalisation, has always been at the centre of the council tradition:

> The Commune of 1871, the soviets of 1905 and 1917, the factory committees in Russia in 1917–1918, the factory councils in Germany in 1919–20, and the workers' councils in Hungary in 1956 were organizations formed to combat the ruling class and its state [i.e. expressions of the instituting power] *and at the same time* new forms of human organization based on principles radically opposed to those of bourgeois society [i.e. political forms] . . . it shows that the proletariat has the need and at the same time the ability to argue the question of social organization as such not simply during a revolutionary explosion, but systematically and permanently. (Castoriadis 1988b: 198–9; emphasis added)

Through the councils, Castoriadis suggests, the collectivity can partake in the instituting power *both* 'during a revolutionary explosion' *and* 'systematically and permanently'. The unbridgeable gap between extraordinary and ordinary politics, which Habermas criticised Castoriadis for reproducing, is simply difficult to square with his theory of council democracy. In the council system, the extraordinary and the ordinary fuse because of Castoriadis's repeated stress on the need for *continual* institutional renewal. As Jay Bernstein has also argued, Castoriadis 'poses the being of the social-historical as neither act nor product, neither instituting nor instituted, but as the continual passage from one and the other without rest and resolution' (1989: 119). Consequently, Lefort's interpretation of Castoriadis's council system as a fixed state with perfect autonomy is also at odds with Castoriadis's second formulation of council democracy. The heart of the matter is that autonomous institutions cannot be given once and for all, and hence that democratic institutions need to have mechanisms of self-alteration inscribed in them. In this way, crucially, autonomous society

> can be neither the absurdity of a society without institutions nor one of good institutions given once and for all, since every set of institutions, once established, necessarily tends to become autonomous and

to enslave society anew to its underlying imaginary significations. The content of the revolutionary project can only be the aim of a society that has become capable of perpetual renewal of its institutions. Post-revolutionary society will not simply be a self-managed society; it will be a society that self-institutes itself explicitly, not once and for all, but continuously. (Castoriadis 1988a: 31)

At the most general level, the instituting power is always activated *in* an instituted reality because it is impossible to stand outside society and history, but not all forms of instituted reality allow for self-alteration, as whether a society has access to its self-altering powers is an institutional question, insofar as we remember that Castoriadis's concept of 'institution' covers thought, religion, language and politics. The collectivity is autonomous not once it is outside all political forms, but once it has institutions that are reflexively trans*form*able by themselves. Castoriadis's prioritisation of the instituting dimension of politics is not a disdain for ordinary politics. We cannot escape instituted reality, as we are social and historical beings, but we can relate to instituted reality more or less autonomously. It is not a matter of either–or, extraordinary or ordinary politics, but of infusing ordinary, institutional politics with the spirit of the instituting power such that such institutions should aim at 'bringing to light society's instituting power' (Castoriadis 1991b: 174). This means, in my interpretation, that the political environment of the councils, for Castoriadis, fosters the *recognition* of society's instituted character and thus of its transformability, and in addition, it provides the *ability* to institute new laws collectively and without hierarchy. The council system is the institution within modernity which most successfully has been able to put a distance between society as instituted and society as instituting, with the consequence that instituted society must be rendered contingent and temporary, as it is a creation of society as instituting. The council system is thus an institutionalisation of society's self-instituting power and equals the constitution of a political space through which 'the many' can participate equally in the exercising of this power.

'This is the new meaning that must be given to the much sullied term "politics"', Castoriadis argues:

Politics is not a struggle for power within given institutions, nor is it simply a struggle for the transformations of institutions called 'political', or of certain institutions or even of all institutions. Henceforth politics is the struggle for the transformation of the *relation* of society to its institutions, for the instauration of a state of affairs in which man as a social being is able and willing to regard the institutions that rule his life as his own collective creations, and hence is willing to transform them each time he has the need or the desire. (Castoriadis 1988a: 31; original emphasis)

Castoriadis does not think of autonomy and heteronomy as fixed states or as a clear-cut distinction. As the last sentence reveals, the collectivity will continually need to transform its institutions because they begin a process of alienation. Since every historical situation is characterised by *both* autonomy *and* heteronomy, human creations always have the possibility of making themselves independent and dominating, according to Castoriadis. Autonomy means that individuals have the mental capability to realise the possibilities of alienation, and that the collectivity has the political resources for transforming such alienation into momentary control.

Conclusion

The primary ambition of this chapter has been to interpret Cornelius Castoriadis's theory of council democracy. The main argument is that Castoriadis develops not one formulation of council democracy, but two distinct formulations. As the early formulation gives way to the later one, the council system is transferred from a discourse of Marxism with an emphasis on political form to a discourse of democracy with an emphasis on constituent power and the council as a 'formless form'. Castoriadis's early formulation of council democracy is developed against his notion of bureaucratic domination, which equally characterises representative democracy and Soviet communism. The council system expresses a refutation of bureaucracy, insofar as it constitutes a self-governing political system. The councils as 'creations of the proletariat were a practical refutation of the ideas that have dominated man's political organizations for centuries' (Castoriadis 1988e: 198). This status as self-governing organs is achieved by a host of concrete institutional mechanisms, such as local self-management, instant recall, imperative mandate and federalism. In this interpretation, the council system is the concrete 'content of socialism' and a specific proletarian form of government.

As Castoriadis develops the theory of autonomy and the instituting power, his analysis of the council system changes respectively.

Instead of identifying the councils with a specific set of institutional mechanisms, he now understands the councils as institutionalised spaces for the self-alteration of society. They are institutions where questioning and renewal can take place, not for the sake of finding the right institutions once and for all, but with the ambition of the continual reinstitution of the polity. Accordingly, the councils foster an awareness of the instituted character of human creations and express an institutionalised version of the ideal that the people ought to control its institutions and not the other way around. With this vision of council democracy, the socialist connotations of the system as a proletarian government originating in the sphere of production give way to the democratic idea of how a collectivity can control its institutions by continually recreating them, as new forms of alienation and domination arise.

Although the key aspect of council democracy in Castoriadis's late analysis is to evaluate the council system as an institutionalisation of the instituting power – that is, as an attempt to combine constituent power and political form – it is important to notice that for Castoriadis, the threat to autonomy comes *only* from instituted reality, from constituted powers. In other words, depoliticisation, routinisation, representation and bureaucracy, *heteronomy* in short, are the chief dangers in Castoriadis's thinking. The councils' combination of constituent power and political form is thus more of a logical necessity than a deliberate attempt to limit and constrain the constituent power, insofar as something like a pure constituent or instituting power in a state of nature is logical nonsense for Castoriadis, because human beings are social, historical actors which cannot step outside time and space. This one-sided relation between constituent power and council democracy in Castoriadis's thought, where only depoliticisation (constituted power) and not total politicisation (constituent power) poses a threat to democratic autonomy, is, in my interpretation, the primary issue of conflict between Castoriadis and Lefort, as well as Arendt's main point of intervention.

Chapter 4
Self-Limitation and Democracy
Lefort's Model of Council Democracy

Claude Lefort's political thinking is best known for the analysis of democracy as an 'empty place' of power (Lefort 1988b: 9–20). Lefort's central idea is that modern democracy is characterised by a form of emptiness, namely the condition that no one can speak authoritatively with the *true* voice of the people, because the people is always plural, divided and in conflict. No group or individual can fully and permanently incarnate the people, and therefore the place of power becomes empty (Lefort 1988b: 7–8). When Lefort introduces the idea of the empty place of power, he notes how 'there is no need to dwell on the details of the institutional apparatus' producing democracy's emptiness (1988b: 7). Hence, although Lefort's abstract theorisation of democracy is appealing due to the inherent open-endedness and pluralism of democracy, it is difficult to imagine the specificities of such a democratic regime. What is this 'empty place'? How it is created and maintained?

This ambiguity is reproduced when evaluating Lefort's political position. Can his political thinking best be associated with liberal democracy or radical democracy? In one reading, Lefort is a critic of revolutionary politics, and by starkly contrasting democracy and totalitarianism and rejecting Marxism, Lefort could be said to foster a reorientation (in French political thought) from radical transformation to liberal constitutionalism and human rights (Christofferson 2004). In another reading, Lefort's idea of democracy as an empty place signifies how democracy is always at odds with its specific, present institutionalisation. This idea of an irreducible gap between the principle of democracy and its institutionalisation has inspired theories of democracy as a radical and transformative project (Laclau and Mouffe 1985; Nancy and Lacoue-Labarthe 1997; Abensour 2011a, 2011b). Lefort's political thinking, as James

Ingram (2006) has aptly argued, does indeed contain the resources for both such political positions.

Another way to pose the question of Lefort's oscillation between liberal and radical democracy is the following: is Lefort radicalising liberal democracy or liberalising radical democracy? Lefort's thinking again provides at least two possible answers: on the one hand, Lefort demonstrates the sometimes neglected, radical nature of standard elements of liberal democracy such as representation and elections, as the vacated parliament on election day is the best symbol of democracy's emptiness. Furthermore, the principle of political representation ensures the distance between the principle of democracy (the government of the people) and its institutional realisation (the government by the representatives of the people) (Weymans 2005; Marchart 2007). Liberal democracy and its key components of political representation and periodic elections, Lefort could be taken to argue, deserves to be understood as the radical regime that cut off the monarch's head and replaced it with the multi-headed people. On the other hand, Lefort can be taken to infuse the revolutionary tradition with a dose of libertarianism.[1] Whereas the revolutionary tradition has insisted on versions of organicism and homogeneity in, for example, Jean-Jacques Rousseau's general will, Karl Marx's communist revolution or Lenin's proletarian state, Lefort also led the call to deepen democracy, but without sacrificing pluralism, internal conflict and difference. On this reading, when democracy is coupled with libertarianism, Lefort's thinking acquires an almost anarchical bend, where democratic action is never able to stabilise itself, as it is hostile to any form of fixation and institutionalisation (Abensour 2011b: 102–25).

This chapter evaluates these questions through Lefort's writings on the council system. When discussing the council tradition, Lefort notes how the councils form the basis of a *socialist* democracy 'infinitely more extensive than bourgeois democracy has ever been' (1976b: 209; my translation), but simultaneously upholding the pluralist and conflictual nature of the people, which strong versions of democracy and popular sovereignty often relinquish. Lefort's idea of a socialist democracy is built on an interpretation of the council system that stresses their self-limiting and power-dispersing qualities. In the programmes of the Hungarian councils, Lefort detects a self-limiting ambition of creating a society where councils, parties and unions coexist in institutionalised conflict. Instead of imagining a republic exclusively consisting of councils, as Castoriadis and earlier council thinkers ultimately do, Lefort stresses that only by combining uneven and conflicting sources of power can freedom be secured and totalitarian tendencies held in check. In the light of this analysis, Lefort can neither be understood as a liberal nor as a radical democrat. On the one hand, Lefort's socialist council democracy offers a more widespread democratisation of the economy and civil society than that available within liberal democracy. On the other hand, such democratisation is achieved through the institutionalisation of democratic politics within parties, councils and unions, rather than through episodic and insurgent forms of politics occurring at the margins of a political system as with certain varieties of radical democracy.[2]

Lefort's engagement with the council tradition and his novel conception of councils, parties and unions working together in a mixed regime is neglected in the literature in a double sense. On the one hand, general accounts of council communism in the interwar years frequently mention how Lefort and Castoriadis are notable heirs to this tradition, but they fail to mention that Lefort welcomes a division of power between councils, parties and unions, whereas Castoriadis argues for the sovereignty of councils (Schecter 1994: 102–3; Gombin 1975: 102–3). In these general accounts, the specificities of the different council concepts are blurred, which is a pity, as these differences also reflect different political projects. On the other hand, in the English-speaking reception of Lefort's thinking, his analyses of the council system are almost completely absent. Despite some very few remarks by Andrew Arato (2013: 116–17) and my own earlier intervention (Popp-Madsen 2018), one will hardly find any theoretical engagement with this theme.[3] This chapter remedies this lack of engagement with Lefort's writings on the council tradition and reconstructs his idea of a socialist democracy of self-limiting councils and discusses its consequences for Lefort's theory of the empty place of power more generally.

Like Castoriadis, Lefort interpreted the Hungarian councils both before and after the development of his theory of democracy, and like Castoriadis, Lefort's view on the councils changes dramatically throughout his writings. In developing the idea of democracy as an empty place of power, that is, a pluralistic form of government always in internal conflict, he also becomes critical of the constituent power, hereby delivering an analysis of council democracy which is markedly different from that of Castoriadis. In order to appreciate this difference, I need to briefly engage with Lefort's early analysis of the council system. Lefort published his first analysis of the Hungarian councils in the article 'The Hungarian Insurrection' in *Socialisme ou Barbarie* in December 1956, shortly after the events in Hungary. In Lefort's early analysis, he is very close to Castoriadis's 1956 analysis of the Hungarian councils. In an interview in 1975, Lefort stated:

> in the face of the major events (French politics, East Berlin, de-Stalinization, Poland, Hungary and Algeria), Castoriadis and I found ourselves so close that the texts published by either of us were also in large part the product of the other. (Lefort 1975: 177)

Lefort later dismissed his early interpretation of the council system on the grounds of his theory of democracy as an empty place of power. Lefort thus takes a different route than Castoriadis: because of his analysis of the democratic experience and its haunting spectre of totalitarianism, he rejects the account of the council system as being in fundamental opposition to parliamentarianism, rather than affirming it, as Castoriadis ultimately does. This difference not only relates to different interpretations of the councils, but testifies to deeper differences in political theory as such. According to Lefort, the role of the councils is *instrumental*, as they primarily have a part to play in a constitutional matrix with the object of mixing different forms of power. The councils are not an end in themselves for Lefort, as Castoriadis and Arendt will later argue, but are instrumental for upholding a 'form of society' where the place of power is empty. Another way to phrase this is that for Castoriadis (and for Arendt, as we shall see), the councils are intimately related to a theory of politics as instituting/constituting; for Lefort, I argue, because he has no theory of action, but is a thinker of political forms, the councils are to be understood as instruments, whose consequences have to be evaluated at the level of the polity, namely whether they contribute to upholding a political system with differential and conflicting logics.

The political theory of Lefort is hence more modest than that of Castoriadis, as the councils contribute to the Machiavellian ambition of not being dominated, whereas Castoriadis as well as Arendt see the councils as part of a more ambitious political project of autonomy and freedom. This means that in Lefort's vision of council democracy, we are left with a choice between an ambitious political project with the inherent possibility of failure (the position of Castoriadis) or a more modest project, where the spectre of totalitarianism is so haunting that power dispersion and self-limitation become the primary goals that democracy is able to achieve. The reason for engaging with Lefort directly after the chapter on Castoriadis is thus to bring out the differences in their vision of council democracy and general political theory as clearly as possible.

Conforming to Tradition: Lefort's Early Analysis of the Council System

Socialisme ou Barbarie published a special issue on the Hungarian Revolution only a few months after its end. The issue featured analyses of the events by several pseudonym writers, including Castoriadis and Lefort. Lefort's article is a meticulous examination of the events in Hungary giving special attention to the formation of councils and their political demands. Although Lefort provides insights into the demands and proclamations issued by different local councils, he nonetheless examines the council movement in Hungary as a whole, arguing that the revolutionaries 'demanded the constitution of councils in all factories. This proves that the workers saw in their autonomous bodies a power that had universal meaning . . . they were tending toward a sort of republic of councils' (Lefort 1956: 201–23). This simple evaluation is very important for the argument I provide in this chapter. From this description we can recognise the contours of earlier interpretations of the council system: firstly, the councils originate in the production sphere, but their primary significance lies outside this milieu due to their universal meaning. Secondly, the councils are autonomous; they are products of the organisational qualities of the workers themselves. Finally, and very importantly, from the dispersed and localised struggles emerges a *republic* of councils, meaning that some kind of integration takes place – traditionally understood as federalisation. Such integration of the dispersed councils into a republic implies the creation of a new sovereign council regime, that is, the eradication or subordination of all other political forms. This final point is important because it demonstrates that Lefort in this early interpretation of the councils, before he elaborated on the project of democracy as an empty place of power, understood them as being in conflict with other forms of political power and with the ambition of eradicating these other forms. In a republic of councils there is no place for parliamentarianism, as Castoriadis would also argue. It is precisely this evaluation that changes when Lefort's political thinking progresses.

In the early article, Lefort also provides the, for the council tradition, classic choice on how post-revolutionary society should be organised. Lefort argues that if the Russian oppressors had been defeated, the Hungarians would have been faced with a fundamental choice of government, 'as the insurrection bore within itself the seeds of two absolutely different regimes' (1956: 223). Either the Hungarians would have started 'a process leading to the rebuilding of a separate state apparatus opposed to the Councils, of a parliamentary "democracy"', or they would have accepted 'the victory of workers' democracy, the takeover of factories by the Councils' (Lefort 1956: 223, 222). According to Lefort – and this point is crucial in relation to his later reinterpretation of the councils – 'it would have been necessary for one solution to win out brutally at the expense of the other and for a bourgeois-type parliament *or* the Councils . . . to win out' (1956: 223). The two regimes – party system and council system – are absolutely different political systems and are both entailed embryonically in the insurrection. This description is of special importance, as Lefort twenty years later labelled the councils' call for the coexistence of councils, parties and unions as the real and unregistered novelty of the Hungarian councils. The argument is thus that in his initial encounter with the councils, Lefort reproduces the central tenets of the council tradition as it had been developed before him. He highlights the spontaneity of the councils' emergence, their impulse to federate, their negation of the existing political powers, their demands for self-government, their expression of true proletarian power and their fundamental opposition to parliamentary democracy. All these elements have been central to the various analyses of council democracy from the Paris Commune onwards.

For the reader familiar with Lefort's democratic theory of the empty place of power, the language of Lefort's analysis of the Hungarian councils seems peculiar. How can a thinker of the constitutive division of society speak of a 'true expression' of proletarian power? How can a thinker, who is most famously known for understanding democracy as an 'empty place' due to the 'disincarnation of power', let a substantive category such as 'the proletariat' and a positive institutional form such as the council system fully occupy the place of power? What these series of questions imply is that Lefort decisively changes his political thinking after his break with *Socialisme ou Barbarie* in 1958. Due to his fundamental re-evaluation of democracy, Lefort's assessment of the council system evidently changes as well.

The Democratic Experience: Emptying the Place of Power

In order to grasp Lefort's later re-evaluation of council democracy, it is necessary to engage with his democratic theory and democracy's counter-regime, totalitarianism, in some detail. Lefort mentions in various places that democracy and totalitarianism need to be understood together (1988a: 301; 1988b: 12), as both regimes are the result of the major transformations of society taking place with the break between premodernity and modernity. For Lefort, modern democracy emerges from this radical break, and totalitarianism is a revolt against the democratic experience. Hence, Lefort's democratic theory can be said to revolve around a tripartite typology of regime forms: the *ancien régime*, democracy and totalitarianism.

Before discussing the three regimes, it is necessary to understand what Lefort means by a 'place of power'. Lefort contends that every society is organised around a place of power, which gives it its unity and stability (1988b: 11–12). This symbolic pole is a place of identification for the members of society, which ensures that society does not disintegrate. This unity is strictly symbolic, but nonetheless structures and forms reality (Lefort 1988a: 225; Flynn 2005: 131). As Lefort contends,

> the fact that this space is organized as *one* space despite (or because of) its multiple division and that it is organized as *the same* in all its multiple dimensions implies a reference to a place from which it can be seen, read and named . . . it manifests society's self-externality, and ensures that society can achieve a quasi-representation of itself. (Lefort 1988b: 225; original emphasis)

In every society there exists a gap between society's self-representation and the factual reality of its everyday conflicts (Lefort 1988a: 225–6). Every society – except for modern democracy, and this is the radical element of democracy – has sought to conceal this gap by fully occupying the symbolic place with a determinate figure.

The Ancien Régime

With the transition from the *ancien régime* to modern democracy the symbolic place does not disappear, but the place of political power is altered from an *incorporated* power to a *disincorporated* power. Premodern society, which mainly for Lefort means the monarchical societies of Europe, is unified in the figure of the king. Lefort follows the influential medieval scholar Ernst Kantorowicz, who had argued that in monarchical societies, unity was created by reference to the dual body of the king: 'we thus have to recognize [in the king] a *twin person*, one descending from nature, the other from grace . . . concerning one personality, he was, by nature, an individual man: concerning his other personality, he was, by grace, a *Christus*, that is, a God-man' (Kantorowicz 1957: 46; original emphasis). Besides the individual, corporeal, finite body of the king, which eventually dies and is replaced by another sovereign, the monarch also has *another* body – a sacral, infinite, collective body, which represents society at large.[4] The body politic is unified and incorporated in the sacral body of the king, which makes it possible for society to transcend its differences and conflicts. Ultimately, the eternal and sacral body of the king is an earthly representative – in the European context – of the body of Christ. This means that premodern society grounds its order and unity in *another* and *fully occupied place*. 'Nevertheless', Lefort argues, 'it turns out in every case that the origin of the discourse about the order of the world and the order of the social is conceived from *elsewhere*' (1986b: 199; original emphasis). Hence, the figure of the king occupies the place of power, creating a symbolic unity which transcends differences and disagreements. 'For thousands of years', Lefort concludes, 'societies have represented their institutions as grounded in another place and have only welcomed the new . . . by inscribing it in a mythical or religious discourse' (1975: 185).

Democratic Disincorporation

The radical break which is created by modern democracy is not that the place of power disappears, or the symbolic dimension of power vanishes. Instead, modern democracy is the regime in which power cannot be incorporated in a body – in a determinate figure or external absolute. Power resides in the people, but the people can never be totally present and can never speak with one voice. Power becomes *disincorporated*: 'The modern democratic revolution is best recognized in this mutation: there is no power linked to a body' (Lefort 1988a: 303). Modern democracy is the only regime which openly acknowledges the gap between the symbolic and the real, as modern democratic regimes recognise that the place of power is empty, meaning that order, unity and legitimacy are only tendentially and periodically achieved and only partly justified

(Lefort 1988a: 303). Because there is no determinate figure of power, there is no final determination of society's foundations. 'If we bear in mind the monarchical model of the Ancien Regime', Lefort argues, 'the meaning of the transformation can be summarized as follows: democratic society is instituted without a body, as a society which undermines the representation of an organic totality' (1988b: 18). The conflicts which dominate every society are not concealed by the symbolic operation of power; instead, modern democracy welcomes disagreement and conflict. A very peculiar force thus holds the democratic regime together: democracy is unified around *nothing*, a void, an empty place. This means that perpetual questioning, doubt, indeterminacy, uncertainty and ambiguity are constitutive parts of the democratic experience.

This analysis of the break between premodern and modern society is initially developed in Lefort's monumental dissertation on Machiavelli. According to Lefort, Machiavelli is the first to register the symbolic mutations in the functioning of power, which is fully exposed with the democratic revolutions of the eighteenth century. Moreover, in Machiavelli Lefort finds a principle which he takes to be absolutely central to the democratic experience: the centrality of *conflict*, or what Lefort calls the 'original division of the social'. Lefort highlights how Machiavelli asserts that every republic is fundamentally split between two orders, the patricians and the plebeians, the wealthy and the poor, the elite and the people (Lefort 2012: 139–40). Famously, Machiavelli reasoned that these two orders have completely different desires: 'For in every city these two diverse humors are found, which arises from this: that the people desire neither to be commanded nor oppressed by the great, and the great desire to command and oppress the people' (Machiavelli [1517] 2003: 39). In every republic, the elite desires to govern the many, whereas the many desire to live freely; they simply wish not to be dominated. Not only is society fundamentally divided between those who want to rule and those who desire not to be dominated, but the very *freedom* of the republic is dependent on the appropriate institutionalisation of the conflict between the few and the many. 'To me', Machiavelli argues,

> those who condemn the quarrels between the nobles and the plebs, seem to be cavilling at the very things that were the primary cause of Rome's retaining her freedom, and that they pay more attention to the voice and clamour resulting from such commotions than to what resulted from them, i.e. to the good effects which they produced. (Machiavelli [1517] 2003: 113)

In short, for Machiavelli, the conflict between the nobles and the plebs produces good effects; most importantly, it secures the freedom of the polity. According to Lefort, it is precisely the association of freedom with conflict that empties the place of power and effaces the corporeal figure of power. 'Disunion, we are to understand', asserts Lefort, 'has not only preserved the independence of Rome; it has established freedom within it, that is, it has established a regime such that the power can be taken over neither by a man, nor by a faction' (2012: 227–8). Because conflict is constitutive of freedom, a free polity is one that keeps the question of unity open and undecided: 'there is no order that can be established on the elimination of disorder, unless at the cost of a degradation of law and liberty' (Lefort 2012: 229).

It is instructive to highlight the different usages of Machiavelli and Roman republicanism by Lefort and Arendt. According to Lefort, Machiavelli highlights how freedom is a *good effect* of a specific constitutional matrix, which institutionalises society's constitutive conflict between the elite and the people. According to Arendt, as I shall explain more thoroughly in the next chapter, Machiavelli highlights how freedom is a form of *action*, which is intimately connected to the augmentation of the constitution. For Lefort, neither the patricians nor the plebs *act* freely when they engage in institutionalised conflict, but instead freedom is a systemic effect at the level of the polity because of this conflict. For Arendt, the polity is characterised by freedom once it allows for continual action and recreation. In contrast, freedom for Lefort is a *consequence*, not a mode of acting. One outcome for the analysis of the councils is that Lefort conceptualises the councils as an instrument for producing freedom at the level of the polity, whereas Arendt and Castoriadis conceptualise the councils as ends in themselves, because they disclose the principle of action and freedom and express relations of autonomy.

Crucially for Lefort, Machiavelli's analysis of the conflict between the nobles and the plebs is not exhausted in the historical situation of the Roman Republic. Instead, the analysis by Machiavelli is, according to Lefort, characteristic of every society. Conflict, disunion, disagreement are constitutive for every society. Whereas premodern society conceals this fact through the figure of the Other, which fully occupies the place of power, modern democracy acknowledges it and makes conflict central to its functioning. For Lefort, it is not the case that social and political conflict can at some point be eradicated, as in Marx's classless society, in Rawlsian ideas of 'overlapping consensus' or in Habermasian ideas of 'communicative rationality'. Rather, conflict is a fundamental, ineradicable part of social life – the division of the social, to speak in Lefortian terms, is *original* and *constitutive*. Lefort aptly discusses the fundamental nature of conflict as he universalises Machiavelli's perspectives on Rome:

> As long as one imagines society as the place in which all things tend to rest in the fullness of a natural form, the unstable, the moving and the discord are signs of a degradation of Being. But Being, we are to understand, only allows itself to be grasped in relation to what happens, in the interconnectedness of appearances, in the movement that prevents appearances from becoming fixed. (Lefort 2012: 180–1)

The moment institutions become fixed, the moment perfect harmony exists, we are dealing with the concealment of conflict. Because of the permanence of conflict, the democratic experience 'passes through the experience of a void that no politics will ever fill – through the recognition of the impossibility of the state's reducing society to a unity' (Lefort 2012: 140). Because the democratic regime leaves the place of power open and inserts ambiguity as to its own foundations, the 'unifying' experience of democracy is that of indeterminacy. Democracy is, then, the regime that openly acknowledges the originary division of the social and hence its own ultimate indeterminacy towards its foundation. Nowhere does Lefort express it more programmatically than in the following:

> Power appears as an empty place and those who exercise it as mere mortals who occupy it only temporarily . . . there is no law that can be fixed, whose articles cannot be contested, whose foundations are susceptible of being called into question. Lastly, there is no representation of a centre and of the contours of society: unity cannot now efface social division. Democracy inaugurates the experience of an ungraspable, uncontrollable society in which the people will be said to be sovereign, of course, but whose identity will constantly be open to question, whose identity will remain latent. (Lefort 1988a: 303–4)

As a way to further elucidate this important paragraph, as well as Lefort's understanding of democracy in general, it might be valuable to introduce Lefort's idea of 'savage democracy', which is only very rudimentarily discussed in the English-speaking literature.[5] The notion of 'savage democracy' is itself rather enigmatic, and Lefort neither defines it clearly nor discusses it very often. Lefort most often uses the term 'savage democracy' to describe events such as May 1968 or the initial phase of the French Revolution, where spontaneous political activities emerged in open confrontation with established political institutions. Lefort uses the qualifier 'savage' in order to elucidate democracy as a type of political practice that cannot be mastered and domesticated by political form. In other words, 'savage democracy' is Lefort's version of the uneasy relation between constituent power and political form. As Abensour picturesquely describes it, savage democracy is 'like an impetuous river that incessantly overflows its bed, cannot "go back home" and submit to the established order' (2011b: 107). Such an excessive and disobedient mode of action 'may only be an element of revolutions', Lefort argues in the context of May 1968,

> but it is extraordinary enough to warrant our interest. For a period of time that can be longer or shorter, its gives form to *savage democracy*, the trace of which can be lost, or is always lost, yet it reveals certain specific aspirations of the modern world. (Lefort 2007: 592; emphasis added)

Interestingly, this depiction of savage democracy as an element of revolution which appears suddenly, is destined to disappear again yet reveals something fundamental about political modernity, is very much akin to Arendt's description of the council system as the lost treasure of revolution which has appeared and disappeared time and time again under the most varied circumstances since the modern revolutions. The term 'savage democracy' is thus used by Lefort to highlight his fundamental contention that modern democracy inaugurates the experience of division, uncontrollability and permanent contestation. Democracy is savage because of its unending and by definition unsuccessful search for legitimacy, foundations and order. As Lefort argues,

> It is true that, in a certain sense, no one holds the formula for democracy and that it is most profoundly itself by being savage democracy. Perhaps this is what constitutes its essence; as soon as there is no ultimate reference on the basis of which the social order might conceived and determined, this order is constantly on the quest for foundations, in search of its own legitimacy. (Lefort 1979: 10–11)

With this description, Lefort's idea of savage democracy comes close to Castoriadis's instituting power, Arendt's new beginnings, and hence, to the constituent power, as the savage essence of democracy lies in its creative, transformatory and constituent nature. As Abensour aptly argues,

> 'savage democracy' evokes, rather, the idea of a wildcat strike (*grève sauvage*), that is, a strike that arises spontaneously, that begins with itself and unfolds in an 'anarchic' fashion, independent of any principle (*arche*), of any authority – as well as of any established rules and institutions – and strikes in such a way that it cannot be mastered. (Abensour 2011b: 106)

Lefort's discussion of savage democracy as a form of constituent, uncontrollable politics unlimited by established forms and procedures is clearly a part of the anarchical, radical democratic strain of his thought most thoroughly explored by Abensour. Savage democracy comes close to what Rancière simply calls *politics* (as opposed to *police*), what Wolin calls *democratic constitutionalism* (as opposed to *constitutional democracy*), or what Negri calls *constituent power*; or more surprisingly, it resembles the classic formulations of constituent power by Sieyès and Schmitt, thereby going well beyond Castoriadis's evaluation of council democracy as a combination of instituting power and institutional form.

But Lefort's savage democracy does not fit well with the argument I make in this chapter, namely that Lefort abandons the constituent power due to its affinities with totalitarianism, insofar as he continually cautions against popular political projects that seek a revolutionary transformation of society. What is certainly the case, as demonstrated below, is that the idea of 'savage democracy' is never used to explain the nature of the council system, and that Lefort goes to great lengths to disassociate the council system from constituent power, thereby also distancing himself from Castoriadis. While savage democracy is indeed an extremely interesting concept, it plays a minor role in Lefort's oeuvre, and the spectre of totalitarianism that visibly haunts his political thinking. Moreover, Lefort's understanding of democracy as a 'form of society' is difficult to reconcile with the idea of savage democracy.

Totalitarianism as a Revolt against the Emptiness of Democracy

As mentioned above, Lefort argues that democracy and totalitarianism ought to be understood together. The totalitarian society regards the democratic experience as scandalous and cannot accept ambiguity towards its own foundations (Lefort 1988b: 12–13). 'The people', who in the democratic discourse is an object of contestation, whose identity cannot be determined in empirical reality, is understood as a realisable object in the totalitarian discourse. Power, which as a result of society's constitutive division became disincorporated in the modern, democratic period, is in totalitarianism again represented as a determined figure:

> A logic of identification is set in motion, and is governed by the representation of power as embodiment. The proletariat and the people are one; the party and the proletariat are one; the politbureau and, ultimately, the *egocrat*, and the party are one. Whilst there develops a representation of a homogenous and self-transparent society, of a People-as-One, social division, in all its modes, is denied, and at the same time all signs of differences of opinion, belief and mores are condemned. (Lefort 1988b: 13; original emphasis)

In addition, totalitarianism cannot assent to the constitutive character of conflict; for the totalitarian society, unity is always threatened by conflict, by the intrusion of the Other (the Jews, the kulaks, the bourgeoisie, etc.) and must be overcome at all costs. Totalitarianism therefore seeks to resurrect the premodern, fully incorporated figure of power in the figure of the *Führer* or party leader, who will substantially occupy the place of power left open by the democratic revolution. Totalitarian society seeks to be fully visible to itself and in complete harmony with itself, and the fiction of the People-as-One lives on in totalitarian society, as the gap between the symbolic referent of 'the people' and empirical people is denied.

Another way to characterise totalitarianism is through political theology and what Lefort investigates as the possibility of 'the permanence of the theologico-political' during modern times. A theological element is present in every political project that alludes to forms of unity (Lefort 1988a: 233–6). This means, according to Lefort, that versions of popular sovereignty that allude to the People-as-One also reproduce a theological element apparent in totalitarianism. Lefort's countermove to the possibility of a permanent theological feature of modern democracy is the strategy of pluralisation: to pluralise demands, claims, interests, positions and values is the best way to avoid a recurrence of theological elements of unity and one-ness because fixation will always be postponed. It is instructive to compare this idea with Castoriadis's and Arendt's theories of political action. According to both Castoriadis and Arendt, action is groundless, as it cannot be legitimised by extra-human absolutes (the theological element for Lefort). For Castoriadis and Arendt, the lack of extra-human absolutes is what makes political action an expression of human freedom, but also what makes action potentially dangerous – hence, what makes politics potentially tragic. Where action and transformation are possible, defeat and tragedy are inherent risks. By advocating for the strategy of pluralisation, though, Lefort is not willing to take the risk of acting. Hence, he does not affirm a project of autonomy or freedom, but instead a project of pluralisation of different logics. That is, Lefort takes the systemic position, as logics of autonomy and action need to be countered by logics of self-limitation and power-dispersion. Freedom, as already argued, is not a quality of action, but the systemic effect of pluralisation and conflict.

With Lefort's tripartite typology of regime forms at hand, it is possible to analyse the reasons why he changes his analysis of the council system and discards the constituent power. In Lefort's early analysis of the council system he argued, similarly to Castoriadis, that the council system was an expression of a self-governing society, through which the people could regain control over its institutions. When taking Lefort's democratic theory of the empty place into account, no such thing as complete autonomy or self-government can be achieved because full autonomy would be the end of conflict. Moreover, 'the people' cannot, according to Lefort, fully control its institutions simply because the people is always internally scattered. Hence, the 1956 analysis of the Hungarian councils, where Lefort praised the emergence of a sovereign republic of councils, he would now – equipped with his theory of democracy as an empty place of power – evaluate as an attempt to overcome conflict and division through rational design, and as an effort to stop the play of indeterminacy with an institutional blueprint. As Lefort himself said in an interview in 1975: 'I would have perceived the fact that my attachment to the idea of a society of workers' councils was itself no less ambiguous than the one that I denounced with my critique of the revolutionary Party' (1975: 177).

Self-Limitation and the Mixed Constitution: Lefort's Late Theory of Council Democracy

In the article 'The Age of Novelty' (1976a), Lefort once again takes issue with the political proclamations of the Hungarian councils; only this time he highlights very different aspects of their programmes than in 1956. Whereas in his 1956 analysis Lefort situated councils and parties in stark opposition, he now saw in the proposals of the councils a mixed polity, where conflict between council system and party system, as well as trade unions, would be productively institutionalised. The differences between Lefort's first analysis of the Hungarian Revolution in 1956 and his second analysis in 1976 are difficult to overlook. In 1956, Lefort stressed, in accordance with the council tradition, the councils' aspirations of complete sovereignty and their fundamental opposition to the state, the parties and the unions. By 1976, Lefort argues that this analysis, which has affinities with the one that Castoriadis delivers, fails to see what is *genuinely new* in the efforts of the Hungarian revolutionaries. 'In adopting this language', Lefort argues, 'one could still allow part of the novelty to escape' (1976a: 34). The novelty that Lefort detects in the Hungarian councils is their recognition of the hazards of constituting a new polity.

Actually, Lefort goes as far as abandoning the constituting dimension of politics, inasmuch as he has no theory of action, and instead applies a systemic view as an interpreter of 'forms of societies'. According to Lefort, the Hungarian revolutionaries realised the inherent perils of instituting a new sovereign power; they knew of 'the danger that was posed by a power . . . that concentrated all the decisions affecting the fate of society' (1976a: 34). The revolutionaries thus exhibited a significant degree of reflexivity, as 'they showed new insight into the danger which issued from the development of their own power' (Lefort 1976a: 34). In essence, the consequence of this insight is that 'the idea of a new revolutionary power totally in the workers' hands was condemned because it would have a totalitarian bend' (Lefort 1976a: 35). Instead of aspiring to a total takeover of power through the councils, Lefort argued that the workers' councils themselves knew that such an aspiration could end in totalitarianism, and thus they refrained from it. Instead, the programmes issued by the Hungarian councils advocated for the establishment of councils as a *limited* political power existing side by side with parties and unions. Consequently, the experiences with totalitarianism made the Hungarian councils support a *self-limited* democracy.

Which examples does Lefort provide? In the first place, he points to a crucial discussion in the most powerful council, the Budapest Council, where the participants renounced the idea of setting up a national council with delegates from local and regional councils, that is, the classic pyramidal model of council organisation which

Marx, council communists and Castoriadis favoured. The Budapest Council, according to Lefort, rejected such creation because
they were 'haunted by the problem of their own representativity'
and clearly 'opposed the criterion of efficacy to that of democracy'
(1976a: 34). Although it might be more effective to have a central
council assembling delegates from the entire country, it could not
be the mandate of the Budapest Council – in their own self-understanding – to create such a council republic. Therefore, according to
Lefort, the councils deliberately placed themselves between responsibility and limitation. Emerging from a totalitarian society with a
power totally occupying the place of power, the Hungarian councils
wanted to assume power and responsibility, but in a *limited* fashion.

Crucially, Lefort highlights three central demands issued by the
Budapest Council. According to the Budapest Council, three different institutions ought to constitute the polity after the revolution:
firstly, workers' councils should direct the economy, and decide on
national investment, salaries, production norms and general conditions of working life. As an important site of domination, the economy would be democratised. Secondly, a multiparty system with
free, general and secret elections to parliament would complement
the councils' direction of the economy. Thirdly, new trade unions
would be established to ensure the right of the individual worker to
strike (Lefort 1976a: 35). This division of the polity into three distinct institutions recognises, according to Lefort, that society cannot
eradicate conflict, because 'the worker is caught in at least three different webs of socialisation' and hence 'the fiction of unity must be
realized' (1976a: 35). In terms of production, the councils represent
the worker; in terms of the individual as a citizen, he is represented
in parliament; in terms of local working conditions, the so-called
'worker-unionist-potential striker' (Lefort 1976a: 35) is represented
by the trade unions. The fact that the Hungarian councils argued
for both councils and unions to represent the workers testifies for
Lefort their awareness of the potential conflict between the aims
of the economy in general, directed by the councils, and the individual worker, whose interests are handled by the unions, and thus
shows 'the difference at the heart of the same individual', and how
'the councils themselves do not constitute the entire working class'
(Lefort 1976a: 35).

Lefort's novel vision of council democracy is to support this principle of coexisting but conflicting powers. Lefort aptly summarises
his position as the attempt to ensure that the state does not dominate

civil society, which has been the general object for council democratic thinkers from Marx onwards:

> A new and very remarkable fact is the search for a new political model combining several types of power, which would in effect forbid a state apparatus to solidify and detach itself from civil society. We want a parliament elected by universal suffrage (whose effectiveness would be guaranteed by the existence of multiple parties in competition), a government elected by it and remaining under its control; we want a federation of workers' councils that governs national economic affairs – which obviously gives the councils a political role – and we also want democratic trade unions that defend the specific interests of workers. (Lefort 1976b: 211; my translation)

The mixing of institutions into a divided polity is for Lefort 'the formula for a *socialist democracy*, infinitely more extensive than bourgeois democracy has ever been' (1976b: 211; my translation; emphasis added). This Lefortian socialist democracy grounded upon the self-limiting and power-dispersing proposals of the Hungarian councils is indeed a different conceptualisation of the council system than what we get from Marx onwards as well as from Lefort's contemporaries, Arendt and Castoriadis. As Andrew Arato, who is one of the sole interpreters of Lefort to even mention this issue, argues,

> By postulating the self-limitation of the council movement itself, the Hungarian Revolution, though involving councils, went beyond, according to Lefort, the famous counciliar model developed by Marx and reintegrated as such by his younger self [Lefort], as well as by Arendt and Castoriadis. It would have been as wrong for the councils to claim all power as it would for the old party. (Arato 2013: 116)

The crucial difference is this: the situation of *dual power* that historically existed between the Petrograd Soviet and the Provisional Government after the Russian February Revolution, that is, between the council system and the party system, and which for other council thinkers was a period to be transcended due to the aspiration of achieving a sovereign, council republic, is for Lefort a situation to be upheld and further developed. In their self-understanding, according to Lefort, the Hungarian councils rejected the idea that they incarnated the will of the people, or, in a more general manner, that any single institution could ever do so. As the councils deliberately argued for giving themselves only limited power, they 'were outlining a new model for a division of power' that is 'unknown in bourgeois democratic systems', and which 'alone would make socialism possible' (Lefort 1976a: 35). Lefort immediately acknowledges that this new model of political division did not exist long enough to thoroughly evaluate its viability, but, as he puts it, 'it is impossible to misconstrue its impulse', which consists in the idea 'to combine authorities whose sources are openly recognized as dissimilar' (Lefort 1976a: 35). The result of such a deliberate combination of dissimilar sources of power 'presupposes that there cannot exist a society in accord with itself, delivered once and for all from internal antagonisms' (Lefort 1976a: 35). By drawing power from different springs, adherence to society's fundamental division is upheld.

Here we can recognise Lefort's general strategy of pluralisation in order to overcome the theological element of discourses of unity and harmony. Because the Hungarian councils emerge from the background of totalitarian society, they recognise the dangers of *one* source of power, be it from the People-as-One (popular sovereignty), the race (Nazism) or from history itself (communism). For other council thinkers, the idea of combining councils, parties and unions would be desperately confused. It would signify a confused mixture of bureaucratic and self-governing elements (Castoriadis), a muddled combination of institutions of action and representation (Arendt), or a chaotic blend of revolutionary and counter-revolutionary forces (the Marxist tradition in general). As Lefort devotes only a couple of pages to this proposal of a self-limiting democracy, it is indeed difficult to understand thoroughly his proposal. Lefort says nothing in detail on the specificities of the relation between the three institutions, how conflict between them is adjudicated, or who decides on the division of tasks. Therefore, it is necessary to supplement the analysis with a discussion of the concepts of the *mixed constitution* and *self-limitation* in order to understand Lefort's proposal in more detail.

The Mixed Constitution

One concept through which Lefort's notion of an internally divided socialist democracy can heuristically be understood is that of the mixed constitution. By drawing a vision of society from the proposals of the Hungarian councils, where conflicting modes of power and institutional complexes mix with each other, Lefort can be said to reinterpret the classical concept of the mixed constitution. The idea of a mixed constitution takes its starting point in the well-known typologies of pure constitutions developed in Greek antiquity. According to such typologies, political regimes can be distinguished by who governs (the one, the few or the many), and whether or not they govern according to the common good of the city. The result is three good forms of government – monarchy, aristocracy and democracy – and three vicious forms – tyranny, oligarchy and mob-rule.[6] The theory of the mixed constitution argues that the ideally best form of government is established by combining monarchy, aristocracy and democracy into a mixed polity (Hansen 2010: 522–3).

In the classical theory – in Polybius' analysis of the constitutional structures of the Roman Republic for example – legislative, executive and judiciary power are divided between different institutions in order for each institution to perform all functions of government to some degree. In Rome, for instance, the two Consuls constituted the monarchical element. The aristocratic element was the Senate, which consisted of elected members from the upper classes. Finally, the democratic element resided in the popular assemblies, which passed much law, and ratified decisions on war, peace and alliances as well as judging in matters punishable by death. Obviously, the mixed constitution of ancient Rome and Lefort's proposed division between councils, parties and unions are miles apart. But when the perceived benefits of the mixed constitution as well as its historical successor – the theory of unitary sovereignty – are taken into consideration, it is possible to see the adequacy of the concept of the mixed constitution for the discussion of Lefort's council theory.

In the classical argument, the reason for mixing the pure forms of government was to ensure that no individual or group would impose their will on the whole of society. The pure regime forms will always be corrupted because power is undivided and springs from one source, but by mixing them, one can ensure that the institutions will not alienate themselves from the people and dominate them (Pettit 2012: 220–5). No class of society will be able to govern society sovereignly, but by situating different institutions in conflict, collaboration, struggle and negotiation are necessary for political decision-making. Lefort had already engaged with the tradition of the mixed constitution in his work on Machiavelli, where the division between nobles and plebs produced the good effect of Roman freedom, and these reasons for mixing institutional forms fit well with Lefort's descriptions of the self-limiting ambitions of the Hungarian councils. Remember that for Lefort, the Hungarian councils favoured a mixed regime without the establishment of a firm locus of sovereignty because of their experiences with a regime form which favoured unity over conflict and homogeneity over division. The councils were afraid of every power, even their own, in its pure form, and the reasons they gave were somewhat similar to the reasons the classical political philosophers of the mixed constitution gave: the Hungarian revolutionaries were afraid that a sovereign council system, even with the mechanisms of instant recall and imperative mandate, would become an alien and dominating power. As Arato has aptly phrased it,

> this project had to and did involve the renunciation of the utopia of revolution in the sense of the dream of a single, imposed model of the good society that breaks completely with the present, that is beyond conflict and division. (Arato 1990: 26)

One could maybe object that the self-limiting proposals of the Hungarian councils arose solely due to the fact that they rebelled against a totalitarian society, and hence that the mixed constitution in the Lefortian register has little relevance outside this historical context. Another detour through the history of the mixed constitution might help us to detect the general significance of Lefort's interpretation. While the concept of the mixed constitution was repeated by many major political thinkers up till the Enlightenment, it gradually went out of fashion as theories of sovereignty were formulated by absolutist thinkers such as Jean Bodin and Thomas Hobbes in the sixteenth and seventeenth centuries.

As theories of absolutist sovereignty gave way to theories of popular sovereignty with Sieyès, Rousseau and the American Federalists, another device for the division of powers was developed. Starting with Montesquieu, every true republic needed to divide its power into three distinct branches of government – legislative, executive and judicial power – and ensure that no person exercised more than one form of power (Hansen 2010: 510). Hence, the theory of the mixed constitution gave way firstly to the theory of absolutist sovereignty, and secondly, to the theory of the popular sovereignty of the unitary subject of the people. Importantly, theories of sovereignty both in their absolutist and popular variants were directly developed against the mixed constitution (Pettit 2012: 220–5). For both Bodin and Hobbes, something like a mixed constitution was a problem, as logically there had to be one place in the polity, which was sovereign, otherwise – politically – anarchy would emerge. Rousseau, Kant and Hegel voiced similar arguments.

There are many reasons why the mixed constitution fell out of favour, one being that the rising individualism and nationalism discredited the essentially estate-based notion of politics which was entailed in the mixed constitution (McCormick 2007: 107–9). Viewed against its historical successor (the theory of unitary sovereignty), the mixed constitution essentially entails another understanding of politics than the unitary, sovereign model, namely a *pluralistic* form of politics. In the model of unitary sovereignty, the foundation of new political regimes is the result of the constituent power by the unitary people in a normative, legal and political state of nature. In the *interregnum* between two systems of legality, the People-as-One emerges with a revolutionary programme and a constituent will. This is the classical notion of the constituent power from Sieyès to Schmitt, which is firmly located within the revolutionary tradition of the French Revolution. According to Sieyès, the constituent power of the unitary people 'exists prior to anything; it is the origin of everything. Its will is always legal. It is law itself' (2003: 136), and for Schmitt, 'the constitution-making power is unified and indivisible . . . it is the comprehensive foundation of all other "powers" and "division of powers"' ([1928] 2008: 126).

What Lefort detects in the proposals of the Hungarian councils is instead another model of politics, which shifts the emphasis from monism and unity to pluralism and difference. A number of differences between the models immediately come to mind: firstly, whereas the unitary model of sovereignty and the constituent power is intimately linked to the state, Lefort's pluralist model prioritises civil society (Blokker 2009: 282–5). Accordingly, the proposals of the Hungarian councils do not revolve around how to constitute themselves as new organs of state power, but instead are occupied with creating a self-democratising civil society with a host of institutions, associations and groups. Secondly, by building on and radicalising already existing institutions, it can be argued that Lefort envisioned a pluralistic form of power which never found itself in the normative and legal state of nature. The novelty of the proposals of the Hungarian councils was the recognition of a plurality of constituting actors and of their fundamental different interests. Hence, in a way, the crux of Lefort's analysis is that the councils argued for a reconstitution of the polity through already constituted powers, not through the mythical fiction of constituting people outside legality.

As I shall explore in depth in the coming chapter, Lefort's vision of council democracy through the concept of the mixed constitution and its pluralistic mode of politics definitely has affinities with Arendt's analysis of the revolutionary tradition of France and America. Arendt's ambition is also to develop an alternative to politics as unitary and homogenous, and the reason why she travels to the American, federal tradition is also that civil society and already constituted institutions were prioritised over statism and constituent power in a legal void. But Lefort's proposal of mixing councils, parties and unions displays clear differences from Arendt's vision of council democracy. Firstly, because Lefort's proposal has the status of a mixed regime, it involves less self-government than Arendt's council system, as other logics blend with that of action. Secondly, in Lefort's conceptualisation, the principle of self-government is coupled with the principle of difference. Arendt imagined that the federal nature of the council system would reflect the condition of plurality, which she thought was constitutive of political action. But whereas plurality for Arendt is a condition of action, which the federal structure of the council system mirrors, pluralisation and difference for Lefort are not qualities of action, but systemic qualities at the level of society. According to Lefort, the proposals of the Hungarian councils show a way in which self-government can be combined with pluralism, as Lefort in the Hungarian councils

> sees a democratic will affirmed very deliberately according to two poles which could not, in effect, be disassociated without being annihilated: the pole of collective organization [i.e. self-management in the councils] . . . and the pole of social differentiation which presupposes the recognition of the specificity of the domain of politics, economic, law, pedagogy, science, aesthetics etc. (Lefort 1976a: 37)

The politics that the councils proposed was 'not only owing to the mobilization and the near-fusion of collective energies, but also owing to a new experience and an authentic desire for difference' (Lefort 1976a: 38). The dynamic which the mixed constitution and the pluralistic mode of politics inaugurate can be thematised by Lefort's concept of a *plural revolution*, which he uses to describe the Hungarian Revolution. The concept of the plural revolution is precisely meant to differentiate the proposals of the Hungarian councils from the notion of the singular revolution in the French tradition.

A plural revolution takes place in many different parts of society at once and changes parts of society in different ways according to different logics. The result of a plural revolution is social and political differentiation through the rejection of one logic governing all spheres of society. The Hungarian Revolution

> is a *plural* revolution that passes through multiple locations; it grows in factories, in the university, in the cultural and informational sectors, it sees the proliferation of committees in local factories and of soviets, of various associations, political parties, and popular assemblies. This wild process resembles the experiences in the first quarter of the century [i.e. the formation of workers' councils across Europe]. The forms of organization and the methods of struggle particular to the workers' movement are spontaneously 'rediscovered'. (Lefort 1976b: 211; my translation; original emphasis)

According to Lefort, the plural revolution is characteristic of all the council movements in the twentieth century. The result is similar to the benefits of the mixed constitution as developed by classical political philosophers: different modalities of power are created, and different, even opposing, political institutions are established. The multiparty system, the democratically managed economy through the workers' councils and the trade unions coexist side by side due to the pluralistic nature of the Hungarian Revolution. In this way no *one* institution can claim to speak with the voice of the people.

Self-Limitation

According to Lefort, it is the self-limiting attitude of the councils that creates the conditions for a mixed constitution. Self-limitation, hence, is a normative principle, which can be institutionally expressed by the mixed constitution. Lefort does not directly use the notion of a self-limited revolution. Instead, the concept is provided by Eastern European intellectuals such as Adam Michnik and other members of the Polish Solidarity movement, which played an essential role in the velvet revolutions of 1989. Arato (2013) has also associated the Hungarian Revolution in 1956 and Lefort's analysis of the event with the notion of a self-limiting revolution. To understand Lefort's council democracy through the concept of self-limitation provides an option to see how Lefort differentiates himself from the council tradition, as well as from Castoriadis, and how the idea of democracy as an empty place of power influences his evaluation of the councils. The notion of self-limitation can be understood as the refusal to impose fundamentalist projects on the rest of society, and therefore, as 'a revolution against the revolution' (Arato 2013: 116). By proposing a mixed regime, the councils engaged in self-limitation and sought to reject foundationalism. Hence, the self-limiting revolution is a revolution against 'the metaphysics of the Jacobin–Bolshevik type of revolutions' (Blokker 2009: 281), which seek to appropriate state power through a violent break with the former regime and a totalising vision of the future.

In discussing the concept of self-limitation, Arato and Blokker highlight a crucial theme which sets Lefort in direct conversation with Castoriadis. Blokker mentions how the self-limiting revolution is a 'third way' between 'liberal constitutionalism' and 'permanent, totalizing revolution' (2009: 280). In a similar vein, Arato argues that the difference between a self-limited and an unlimited revolution is 'the survival of its spirit beyond institutionalization', that is, 'how to save something of the spirit of revolutionary public freedom in settled constitutions' (1990: 30). These observations take us to the heart of our discussions of the council tradition. In the Marxist discourse, the council system was precisely understood as an alternative beyond the dichotomy of parliamentarianism and communist one-party rule; and Castoriadis argued that one of the primary ambitions of the councils was to preserve the constituent power in some de-revolutionised form in constituted politics. Castoriadis wanted to preserve some revolutionary energy beyond the revolutionary moment, that is, to make autonomy an everyday practice. With the idea of self-limitation, Lefort shares Castoriadis's ambition of going beyond both liberal democracy and permanent revolution. But Lefort's insistence on self-limitation gives the impression that this task is way more difficult than Castoriadis perceived it. In a sense, Lefort is more attuned to the intricate workings of power and the perils of constitutionalising the revolution, but as I shall argue below, this awareness is also paralysing in such a way that social transformation and the affirmation of popular projects become problematic. While Castoriadis seeks to make one logic govern society – autonomy, or self-rule for the council tradition in general – Lefort is determined to inject society with conflicting logics. Hence, freedom for Lefort is not associated with a form of action, but is instead a systemic effect of the pluralisation of conflicting logics. In this way, the council system is not an end in itself for Lefort, but an instrument in a constitutional matrix which employ other logics as well.

Surprisingly, when viewed from the vantage point of the mixed constitution and self-limitation, it could be argued that Castoriadis's evaluation of the council system has certain affinities with the tradition of sovereignty, from which he otherwise tried to distance himself. Although Castoriadis does distance himself from the unitary subject due to the federalism of his council system, he wants to eradicate the multiplicity of differential logics of power that any mixed regime incorporates. Even though Castoriadis's project is anti-statist and advances an anti-unitary conception of political subjectivity, he nonetheless wants the council system to become the sole system of government within the polity. According to Arato, in Lefort's analysis of the Hungarian councils he had learned 'the Tocquevillian lesson' not 'to impose the logic of democratic coordination on all spheres' because 'it is this outcome that leads to the collapse of the forms of self-organization that in many cases were the major carriers of the revolutionary process: revolutionary societies, associations, clubs, councils, movements' (Arato 1990: 26).

In this way, Lefort's self-limiting council system might serve as an alternative to Castoriadis's essentially tragic understanding of politics. For Castoriadis, and for Arendt as we shall see, the tragedy of modernity is that autonomy or public freedom seldom survives for longer periods of time, as even the council system has not continually been able to stabilise itself in the face of representative government and permanent revolution. Lefort might have a proposal as to why that is. The way to pause the tragic oscillation between constituent politics and constituted politics that characterises modernity for Castoriadis and Arendt is to carry the conflicting demands and interests which exist in any moment of revolution into constituted politics. This is what self-limitation means. In other words, the 'preservation of heterogeneity has priority over the construction of a unified discourse framework' of a pure council democracy (Priban 2002: 50). This is essentially where Lefort differs from the council tradition and from Castoriadis. For Lefort, it is key to institutionalise the historical situation of dual power, and hence to combine the strengths and check the weaknesses of different forms of democracy (parliamentary and councilist) (Arato 1984: 3–6). According to Arato, 'paradoxically then the self-limitation of the actors of a self-organizing society allows the continuation of their social role and influence beyond the foundation of a new form of power' (1990: 26). It is therefore the self-limited nature of the revolutionary actors which makes the revolutionary energy survive in constituted politics.

With this idea, Lefort can be said to reorient the discourse of the council system from political society to civil society, that is, from an ambition of combining civil society and the functions of the state into one unified political society to an ambition of upholding the divide between civil society and the state, albeit further democratising both. One of the basic analytical tropes in the council tradition – starting with Marx's description of the state as a parasite and going all the way to Castoriadis's equation of the state with bureaucratic domination, and Arendt's understanding of state sovereignty as pre-political relations of domination and obedience – is the ambition to eradicate the division between state and society because this distance is equal to alienation and domination. In the liberal tradition, which the council tradition sees itself as a critic of, this divide meant that politics was located firmly in the state, and that in civil society individuals could pursue economic interests and cultural aspirations, partake in voluntary associations and enjoy family life. For council thinkers before Lefort, this divide masked the state's domination of society due to the liberal conceptualisation of society as an unco-erced space of individual liberty and the state as inhabited solely by citizens with equal rights. Instead, by destroying the state and politicising society, council thinkers imagined the council system as an expression of a fully democratised society, and hence a society with the institutional mechanisms to counter the ever-recurrent domination through the retained constituent power of the councils. The main ambition was to overcome a separation of society into distinctly *political* and *non-political* spheres, including a separation between rulers and ruled, since these forms of separation enabled domination. Hence, previous council thinkers conceptualised the council system as unifying the dispersed functions, tasks and activities of liberal society into *one* unified and self-managing system.

Lefort's conceptualisation of the mixed regime through the idea of self-limitation upholds the division between the state and civil society. Obviously, civil society is democratised through the workers' councils and the trade unions, but it is not reduced solely to a political society governed exclusively by the logic of self-management. In this way, we are back at Lefort's idea of democracy as an empty place of power. The reason why Lefort appraises the proposals of the Hungarian councils – and why he decisively changes his analysis from the one he provided in 1956 – is exactly that they constitute democracy as an empty place. By upholding the difference between the state and civil society, by refusing to replace conflict with one governing logic, by revolting against the unitary subject of the tradition of sovereignty, as well as the unitary voice of the popular sovereign of the Jacobin tradition, the councils seek a society of competing logics, conflicting institutions and a heterogeneity of demands and interests. These characteristics are those of a regime which is founded upon what Lefort understands as emptiness.

Conclusion

Lefort's thinking, according to two dominant interpretations, can be associated with both a liberal democratic project that cautions against unitary forms of popular sovereignty, and a radical democratic project which stresses the inherent hostility of (savage) democracy to institutionalisation. Because Lefort does not spell out the institutional structures producing and maintaining democracy's emptiness, his thinking is open to a multiplicity of interpretations. In Lefort's analysis of the councils, he argues that the self-limiting proposals for a mixed regime of councils, parties and unions constitute the basis for a *socialist democracy*, which can be subsumed under neither liberal nor radical democracy. Lefort's mixed regime of socialist democracy is, on the one hand, more democratic than liberal democracy because of its democratisation of the economy through the councils as well as its flourishing civil society, in which individuals can participate through unions and other voluntary associations. On the other hand, it is less politicised and more institutionalised than most versions of radical democracy. Consequently, Lefort's vision of the mixed regime of socialist democracy is a pertinent way to understand how a society founded upon an empty place would look. For this argument, it is not absolutely central that the institutions that are mixed are councils, parties and unions. Instead, the important point is that for a society to be democratic in the Lefortian register, it is not enough that representation and elections divide the principle of democracy from its actualisation (the liberal interpretation), or that democracy is hostile to institutionalisation (the radical interpretation), but instead that a host of conflicting institutions are established in institutionalised conflict.

Socialist democracy as institutionalised conflict between councils, parties and unions runs counter to both the liberal and the radical interpretations of Lefort. Contrary to the liberal interpretation of Lefort, which highlights democracy's emptiness as primarily a result of the mechanism of representation, Lefort's socialist democracy includes a much wider democratisation of society along with self-management of economic production through the councils. In opposition to the radical democratic reading of Lefort, which interprets democracy's emptiness as emerging through an inherent hostility towards institutionalisation as such, Lefort's socialist democracy reveals that it is the conflict *between* institutions, not the *absence* of them, which continually produces and secures democracy's empty place of power.

Discussions of what the 'empty place' is, and how it is maintained, might fruitfully turn to Lefort's discussion of the councils and their self-limiting proposal of a mixed regime. When looking at this proposal, it can be argued that it is not the *emptiness* of the place of power that secures the disincarnation of power so essential to the democratic experience for Lefort. Is the place of power in the mixed regime of socialist democracy not more *crowded* than empty? Is it not because too many voices, too many claims, too many interests and too many institutions want to speak with the voice of the people that no one can do it authoritatively and sovereignly? It might be a question of semantics whether the place of power is empty or crowded, but my argument is that it is *institutions*, not the lack of them, that secure the democratic disincarnation of power. This is the crucial insight into Lefort's political thinking which his writings on the council system provide.

Lefort's analysis of the council system could be interpreted as a reaction to Castoriadis. Although Lefort shares many of the ambitions of the Marxist council thinkers – such as the desire for political institutions not to dominate the people and to de-hierarchise spheres of domination – and although he shares Castoriadis's ambition of developing an alternative to the concept of revolution in the Jacobin tradition, Lefort's proposals for doing this are markedly different. The chief difference resides precisely in the idea of mixing conflicting modes of power into a divided whole. For all other council thinkers, the historical situation of *dual power*, which has existed in every revolution involving council-like formations, is one to be transcended, hopefully with the councils' victory over the *ancien régime* and the party system. By advocating for a council republic, council thinkers such as Marx and Castoriadis are arguing for the sovereignty of the council system and hence for the logic of self-government to pervade all spheres of society. The novel vision of the council system which we get from Lefort is the idea that the aspiration of the council system to be a sovereign political form makes it potentially undemocratic, if not quasi-totalitarian. This is because every sovereign political form envisions society as a totality which can be governed according to one logic. The novelty of Lefort's interpretation is thus to *appreciate* the situation of dual power, to institutionalise it through the mixed regime of councils, parties and unions. The essence of Lefort's self-limited council system is the awareness that to stipulate the sovereignty of the council system is to partake in a tradition of foundationalism, which believes that conflict and division are temporary obstacles on the road to perfect autonomy and freedom. Hence, the Lefortian council system is one where self-government, social conflict and pluralism are combined into a conglomerated polity through the plural revolution of society and its institutions.

The basic difference in this regard between Castoriadis and Lefort is the extent to which they imagine opposing political forms as integral parts of a council democracy. While Castoriadis imagines that other institutional forms can coexist with the council system, he is not willing to let directly conflicting forces exist on equal footing with the councils. He agrees with Marx, Lenin of 1917 and most interwar council communists when they argue that the councils emerge in opposition to the state, capitalism, bureaucracy and parliamentarianism. Hence, Castoriadis argues for the intertwinement of state and society into a political society governed to the widest possible extent by the logic of self-rule. Consequently, a separate system of parliamentarianism has no place in Castoriadis's council democracy. This does not mean, as argued, that the council system for Castoriadis is a fixed state of being characterised by perfect autonomy, as the council system does not amount to the end of history in a communist, classless society. On the contrary, for Castoriadis, the council system welcomes the effects of history, meaning that every political form has the potential for bureaucratisation; or maybe formulated more strongly, every political form *will* eventually bureaucratise and alienate itself from its constitutors. Hence, there are lots of other, conflicting logics than self-government in Castoriadis's council systems, but these conflicting logics do not originate in institutions *created* for this very purpose, like Lefort's self-limiting model of the councils.

Whereas for Castoriadis representation is a mode of domination, it is for Lefort a crucial feature of a society with the ambition of keeping power disincarnated, which in turn means that Lefort wants to uphold a separation between state and society, the political and the economic spheres, parliamentary representatives and their constituencies. Through the mixed polity, Lefort proposes the strategy of pluralisation in order to keep the totalitarian threat of incarnation at bay. This strategy entails a grave suspicion towards political movements that formulate their ambitions in strong, popular terms. Instead, Lefort values political projects with the impulse of compromise inscribed at their core because various self-limited projects will create a status of freedom at the level of the polity.

This vision of council democracy also highlights how Lefort's evaluation of constituent power is completely different to that of Castoriadis. If we bracket Lefort's marginal notion of 'savage democracy', which does not feature in any of Lefort's programmatic statements of his theory of democracy or in his writings on the councils, Lefort, contrary to Castoriadis, has no theory of action, and in turn the constituent dimension of politics has little place in this theory of democracy. He is instead a systemic thinker of 'forms of societies', for whom movements and actors ought to be evaluated for the effects they produce at the level of the polity, not for their actions in and of themselves. As Lefort argued via Machiavelli, the conflict between the nobles and the plebs should be evaluated for its good effect, namely that of the freedom of the republic. This mode of evaluation is also characteristic of Lefort's evaluation of the councils. The councils are instruments for producing good effects at the level of the polity because of their aspiration of self-limitation and power-dispersion, but they have little intrinsic value. Although in most respects Lefort could not be further away from Lenin, as he is highly critical of every political project of unity and vanguardism, both Lenin and Lefort evaluate the councils due to the *effects* they have, not as ends in themselves or as displaying valuable principles of autonomy and freedom.

The consequence of this systemic view upon 'forms of societies' is that Lefort becomes suspicious of popular demands and transformative projects because his thinking is so definitively marked by the trace of totalitarianism. Therefore, Lefort applauds the strategies of pluralisation, self-limitation and the mixed regime. But has he not in the councils seen a strategy of the division of powers which essentially strips them of their politico-historical specificity? For Lefort, the experience of freedom is *not* situated at the level of the citizen or at the level of the collectivity. Instead, freedom is a systemic quality characteristic of the polity, once it embodies conflicting logics. The political experiences available to real, existing citizens or collectivities in a Lefortian democracy are those of indeterminacy, contingency, emptiness and uncertainty, and such experiences are very difficult to use as points of orientation, if not as values of mobilisation. Hence, Lefort's project is one of moderation because – one may ask – how can a positive project of political transformation be articulated within Lefort's theory, if any movement needs to limit itself, and if, at the level of the polity, such project needs to be countered by a conflicting logic? Hence, Lefort's theoretical project makes sense at the level of institutional design, at the level of constituted power or political form, but is nonsensical to the actors involved, as they never experience the freedom which Lefort – as a political thinker looking at society in its totality – is able to detect at the level of the polity.

Contrary to Castoriadis, Lefort is not a tragic thinker, as tragedy deliberately needs actors. The tragedy inherent in politics is, according to Castoriadis, that we cannot know in advance the results of our actions. By acting we set something in motion, the outcome of which we cannot know in advance. But politics is intimately related to action, Castoriadis (and later Arendt) would argue, because action is the precondition for the creation of new forms of political community and new modes of participation. This also means that in order to make the instituting dimension of society or the constituent power a *human* capacity, which is the project of Castoriadis, human beings must be able to reconstitute the polity and transform their political existence, even though this activity involves great perils. Hence, whereas Castoriadis situated his project of council democracy only in direct relation to totalitarianism in his early encounter with the councils, for Lefort the totalitarian threat is so omnipresent that it forever haunts the democratic experience. For Castoriadis, the councils are a way to begin to think about modernity as entailing a positivity of politics beyond totalitarianism, but for Lefort, the mixed regime of self-limiting councils is merely a way of keeping the totalitarian threat at bay. For Lefort, the primary goal of (council) democracy is to counter totalitarianism, to continually keep the place of power empty and prevent forms of incarnated power from arising. In other words, Lefort's project is a negative one, whereas Castoriadis's project is positively formulated. Hence, Lefort, in line with a liberal conception of politics, imagines the division of powers as a safeguard against incarnated modes of power.

By failing to provide a theory of action and instead situating his thinking at the level of the polity as such – that is, at the level of constituted power – Lefort actually violates some of his own political principles. Remember that Lefort cautioned against understanding society as a self-enclosed totality which can be fully elucidated, because this would imply an external subject with absolute knowledge. These arguments are his reasons for leaving *Socialisme ou Barbarie* and discarding the revolutionary project. But as an interpreter of 'forms of societies' and their governing principles, Lefort is close to conceptualising the council system as an enclosed totality, where the chief danger of incarnated power can be held at bay through the strategy of pluralisation. By providing an understanding of freedom at the level of the polity that does not make sense to its citizens, but which is recognisable to the political theorist, Lefort approximates the external subject which he otherwise seeks to abandon. In this way, Lefort is a thinker of political forms and a *critic* of constituent power. Lefort, in conclusion, would not allow the constituent power into his democratic structure, and consequently, he is a thinker of political forms rather than a thinker of the sources of their trans*form*ation.

Chapter 5
Between Liberal Constitutionalism and Permanent Revolution
Arendt's Republic of Councils

To find Hannah Arendt among the most influential interpreters of council democracy in the twentieth century is somewhat surprising. On the one hand, her investigation of the council tradition is different from other interpretations of the councils, as she disregards the working-class character of the council system. In some instances, Arendt even argues that the failure of the council system to stay in existence for longer periods of time was due to the councils' emergence within the economic sphere of production ([1958] 1998: 212–20; [1963] 2006: 265–7). Hence, capitalism, economic exploitation and the emancipation of the working class play no significant role in Arendt's vision of council democracy. But on the other hand, Arendt shares many elements of prior conceptualisations of council democracy, especially the councils' opposition to parliamentarianism, as well as the celebration of the degree of popular participation in the councils. The similarities with Castoriadis's understanding of the councils are also striking, as Arendt likewise provides a conceptualisation of the councils as 'formless forms', what she describes as the councils being 'organs of order as much as organs of action' ([1963] 2006: 255). To an even further degree than Castoriadis, Arendt unshackles the council system from Marxism and instead provides a republican interpretation of the council system that centres on the its ability to institutionalise a form of constituent politics which makes the founding of the polity a recurring event through the continual augmentation of the constitution. In a manner similar to Castoriadis's conceptualisation of the council system as an institutionalised version of society's instituting dimension, Arendt understood the council system as combining important elements from otherwise opposing models of constitution-making, with the purpose of keeping the revolutionary spirit alive after the moment of foundation.

But Arendt's council analysis also differs from that of Castoriadis in important ways. Whereas a pure constituent power is for Castoriadis a logical absurdity, as human beings cannot step out of history, Arendt is well aware that both political thinkers (through the 'state of nature' figure in Hobbes, Rousseau, Sieyès and Schmitt, for example) and revolutionary movements (such as French Jacobins and Russian Bolsheviks) have actually tried to do so – with catastrophic consequences. Arendt, in contrast to Castoriadis, is as critical of pure constituent power as she is of pure constituted politics; overpoliticisation and depoliticisation are equal vices in her political thinking. Arendt could thus be said to provide a third vision of council democracy beyond the dichotomy between Castoriadis and Lefort. Whereas Castoriadis ends by celebrating the instituting power of the councils, and whereas constituent politics is completely abandoned in Lefort's mixed regime of councils, parties and unions, Arendt – much like the revolutionaries in John Reed's narration of the storming of the Winter Palace – sees in the councils an ambition to combine constituent power and political form, and she is well aware of the potentialities as well as the pitfalls of both.

Arendt's interpretation of the council tradition was for a time a neglected theme in the ever-growing secondary literature on her work, but this is no longer the case. What is the case, though, is that her council analysis has often received negative treatment.[1] Many of Arendt's interpreters have regarded her appraisal of the council tradition as an immature attempt to translate her cherished principles of action, freedom, promise-making and new beginnings into institutional reality. The critique of Arendt's analysis of the council tradition has either tried to rescue Arendt from the council tradition, stressing that the affinity with such a political tradition seriously undermines the credibility of her insights into politics; or, on the contrary, has sought to rescue the council tradition from Arendt, arguing that she misrepresents the tradition. Margaret Canovan, for example, argues that Arendt's engagement with the council system is 'something of an embarrassment', as her model of council democracy is 'fatally damaged' because of its 'lack of realism' due to Arendt's normatively questionable 'distrust of the mass of ordinary voters' (1992: 237–8). It remains 'baffling' why Arendt considered such a 'wildly utopian' system to be 'obviously preferable to the system of representative democracy' (Canovan 1978: 20, 19).[2] Generally, Arendt's proposal for a council democracy is often deemed normatively questionable and politically unrealistic, as it is regarded as a naive attempt to resurrect something like an Athenian *polis*-style democracy under modern conditions (Wolin 2001: 69). Arendt may have provided evidence for this accusation by stating that she had a 'romantic sympathy with the council system', this 'people's utopia' (1979: 327). At other moments, though, she clearly stressed that 'if you ask me now what prospect it has of being realized, then I must say: Very slight, if at all' (Arendt 1969: 233).[3]

The criticisms of Arendt are not without force. Her proposal for council democracy does at times seem without ground in historical reality. Like the critique of Castoriadis that accuses him of lacking a perspective on normal politics due to the distinction between instituting and instituted society, Arendt has been criticised for defending a vision of council democracy that is too utopian, too demanding and without a genuine concern for the normal political questions of ordinary citizens. The origin of this critique might be Arendt's stark distinctions between action, work and labour, the public and the private, freedom and sovereignty, which could be said to privilege the extraordinary moments of politics while denigrating everyday political concerns. Yet, despite the charge of the utopianism of Arendt's council democracy, she *does* in fact engage with an actual political tradition and a type of institutional complex which has emerged in some form or another throughout the twentieth century. To say that a council system is *completely* unrealistic under modern conditions and that any allusion to such system is *complete* utopianism is thus equally historically distorting.

Another critique of Arendt's council system stems from a historical perspective, as she is charged with misunderstanding the historical councils and therefore distorting their principles. Arendt's major diagnosis of modernity, relying on her core distinction between 'the political' and 'the social', is the so-called 'rise of the social' in modern times (Arendt [1958] 1998: 22–78). This means that originally nonpolitical conditions such as poverty, social want and the desire to consume have been elevated to the core of modern politics. The private, economic realm – the Greek *oikos* – has colonised the political sphere, so to speak, which means that the ability to think and act politically has diminished. As we have seen in previous chapters, the historical councils as well as their theoretical interpretations are predominantly a working-class, Marxist tradition. To argue, as Arendt does ([1958] 1998: 212–20; [1963] 2006: 265–7), that the councils' engagement in economic production is the source of their failure, because the management of necessity (economics) is inherently apolitical, is indeed to consciously misrepresent the council tradition. But does that make Arendt's analysis obsolete? Arendt's ambition is not to deliver a historically accurate analysis of the council tradition from the Paris Commune to the Hungarian Revolution, but instead to *reinterpret* this tradition, to put it into dialogue with the questions of her own time, to see whether the council system in her consciously novel reinterpretation could answer some of the problems that she identified with modern society.

In relation to the critique that Arendt's thinking in general has no regard for ordinary politics and privileges politics as extraordinary action, creation and co-institution, the chapter provides the following argument: Arendt is *as* afraid of politics as unbound, groundless creation as she is afraid of depoliticisation and privatisation. In many ways, the secret enemy throughout Arendt's writings was Carl Schmitt and his conception of sovereignty and constituent power (Kalyvas 2008: 187–253; Scheuerman 1998), and Arendt provides severe criticisms of Hobbesian, absolute sovereignty and Rousseauian, popular sovereignty. Throughout Arendt's writings, there is not just a preoccupation with beginnings, novelty and natality, but also an equal focus on stability, limits and boundaries. Rather, her political theory ought to be understood as an attempt to wrest free the category of 'the extraordinary' from the tradition of sovereignty, and to formulate a democratic version of constituent power which seeks to normalise the extraordinary. The council system is a well-suited vantage point to reconstruct such ambitions, as Arendt deliberately wants to recombine the exhilaration of novelty and the care for stability which otherwise have come apart in modern political terminology.

The Hungarian Councils

In order to reconstruct Arendt's novel analysis of the council tradition, I begin by surveying Arendt's early encounter with the councils during the Hungarian Revolution. When Castoriadis witnessed the Hungarian Revolution, he enthusiastically argued that all political questions could be boiled down to whether one was for or against the formation of workers' councils in Hungary. Arendt made a similar evaluation of the Hungarian Revolution in her 1958 article 'Totalitarian Imperialism: Reflections on the Hungarian Revolution': 'Once such an event as the spontaneous uprising in Hungary has happened, every policy, theory and forecast of future possibilities needs re-examination. In its light we must check and enlarge our understanding of the totalitarian form of government' (1958a: 8). Arendt's first encounter with the council system came with the Hungarian councils, therefore.[4] In Arendt's later, much longer interpretation of the council tradition in *On Revolution*, she positioned the council system in contrast to the party system, as the councils and the parties displayed opposing principles of action and representation. Moreover, in *On Revolution* Arendt did not detect the birth of the council system in the working-class revolution in Russia in 1917, but in the bourgeois revolutions in France and America in the late eighteenth century. But in Arendt's first engagement with the councils, it was not representative democracy which was the primary counter-concept, but instead twentieth-century totalitarianism. Like Castoriadis, Arendt had no positive conception of politics before the Hungarian councils in 1956, although she was in the process of developing one, as *The Human Condition* was published in 1958. Hence, it was the political events happening around her which made her first realise the positive potentialities of the council system. In a letter she sent to her publisher, Meridian Books, she argued that

> If we take into account the amazing re-emergence of the council-system during the Hungarian Revolution, then it looks as though we are confronted with two new forms of government in our own time, both of which can be understood only against the bankrupt body politic of the nation-state. The government of total domination certainly corresponds better to the inherent tendencies of a mass society than anything we previously knew. But the council-system clearly has been for a long time the result of the wishes of the people, and not of the masses, and it is just barely possible that it contains the very remedies against mass society and the formation of mass-men for which we look everywhere else in vain. (Arendt 1958b)

This paragraph is revealing. Instead of the emergence of the council system being attributed to the modern revolutions at the end of the eighteenth century as in *On Revolution*, the council system is to be understood in relation to a different political problem, namely against the backdrop of the crisis of the nation-state. Consequently, the 'two new forms of government in our time' are not the council system and the party system, as discussed in *On Revolution* and as also mentioned by various thinkers of the councils at the beginning of the twentieth century, but instead totalitarianism and the council system. According to Arendt, 'it is just barely possible' that the council system is the remedy to the problems of mass society, which have otherwise created the conditions for totalitarianism. Modernity, in this early reflection on the council system, thus entails not only the twin possibility of council and party systems, but also a tripartite typology of totalitarianism, mass society and the council system.

Throughout her reflections on Hungary, Arendt often refers to the relation between totalitarianism and the council system. 'The development and expansion of post-war Soviet totalitarianism', Arendt argues, for example, '*must* be seen in the flaming light of the Hungarian Revolution' (1958a: 33; emphasis added). As the council system also arises as a reaction to the crisis of the nation-state, mass society and mass man, it forces us to realise that modernity cannot be solely identified with tendencies that might crystallise into totalitarianism. Mass society, once it is restructured into self-organising councils, does entail another possibility than the production of isolated individuals ready to be spellbound by totalitarian ideologies. Arendt had earlier designated modern society, the rise of the social sphere and to some extent modern, representative democracy as the sources of the production of the easily manipulated mass man (Arendt 1968: 305–40). But between this manipulated mass man and the manipulating parties, between the corrupted mob and the corrupting bureaucrat, the voice of the people can be heard in the councils, Arendt contends. The distinction between 'the people' and 'the mass' thus rests on whether the population has adequate institutions such as the councils to express their opinions and deliberate together. If so, they constitute a people; if not, they degenerate into a mass ready to be spellbound by ideology and propaganda. In Hungary, Arendt argues,

> as in all other instances, when for the shortest moment the voice of the people has been heard, unaltered by the shouts of the mob and unstifled by the bureaucracies of the parties, we can do no more than draw a very sketchy picture of the potentialities and physiognomy of the only democratic system in Europe . . . The rise of the councils, not the restoration of parties, was the clear sign of a true upsurge of democracy against dictatorship, of freedom against tyranny. (Arendt 1958a: 32)

That the council system is one possible answer to the same problems of modernity that also sparked totalitarianism into being, shows that the council system was not only a 'romantic utopia', as Arendt's critics confidently asserted. Instead, the importance of the council system for Arendt in this early rendition lies in the fact that it emerged as the first uprising against totalitarianism, that it could possibly transform 'a mass' into 'the people', and hence that this political system could remedy the innermost problems of modernity. Like Castoriadis's early analysis of the councils as the concrete 'content of socialism', Arendt interprets the council system as a specific political form on par with other political forms such as totalitarianism and mass democracy. Although, Arendt argues, 'the councils have always been undoubtedly democratic, but in a sense never seen before and never thought about', and as such, 'under modern conditions, the councils are the only democratic alternative we know' (1958a: 30), she was only able to formulate clearly the way in which the council system is 'the only democratic alternative we know' owing to the novel account of action, freedom and new beginnings which she developed in *The Human Condition* and onwards in *On Revolution*. Consequently, the shift that is visible in Castoriadis's interpretation of council democracy, from a distinct political form to an attempt at institutionalising the constituent power, is also detectable in Arendt's thinking. The difference is, as we shall see, that Arendt is substantially more critical than Castoriadis of the potential pitfalls of the constituent power.

Action, Freedom and New Constitutional Beginnings

The difference between Arendt's earlier analysis of the Hungarian councils and her later *longue durée* interpretation of the councils implies a shift in orientation from totalitarianism as the primary counter-concept to understanding the council system through the lens of the concepts of freedom and constitution-making. Her later interpretation of the council tradition in *On Revolution* was influenced by her ideas of action, freedom and new constitutional beginnings developed in *The Human Condition*, in subsequent essays, such as 'What is Freedom?', and in *On Revolution*.

Castoriadis wanted to theorise politics as post-foundational, as he took all systems of law and forms of government to be products of human creation. The only regime form that fully recognises its groundlessness and its self-instituted status is democracy, which consequently is the historical regime *par excellence* (Castoriadis 1997a). Arendt's political thinking starts in a similar place. Of the phenomenological categories which constitute the *viva activa* – labour, work and action – only action is an exclusively human activity and hence political. Politics is artificial in Arendt's account, meaning that it is a *human*, not a natural, activity taking place between human beings, grounded in human conditions of plurality and natality and, like Castoriadis, without reference to extra-human absolutes such as God or nature.[5] Whereas the activity of labour is related to the circular reproduction of life, and whereas work is bound up with the production of a stable milieu to inhabit, the truly human capacity for political action is associated with unpredictability, uncertainty and spontaneity (Arendt [1958] 1998: 230–46). The human being itself is a new beginning, a linear temporality inserted in the monotonous time of nature, insofar as human beings 'interrupt the circular movement of daily life in the same sense that a rectilinear *Bios* of mortals interrupts the circular movement of biological life' (Arendt 1961a: 43). 'The constant flux of newcomers who are born into the world as strangers' signifies for Arendt the connection between the unpredicted, the new and political action, 'because the newcomer possesses the capacity of beginning something anew, that is, of acting' ([1958] 1998: 9). Human action is hence conditioned by natality; that we are ourselves newcomers to the world implies that our actions can create novel modes of being and new forms of political life. Arendt argues that

> What makes man a political being is his faculty of action; it enables him to get together with his peers, to act in concert, and to reach out for goals and enterprises that would never enter his mind, let alone the desires of his heart, had he not been given this gift – to embark on something new. (Arendt 1970: 82)

In *The Human Condition*, the faculty of action is primarily an individual quality. It is the capacity to deliberate and decide with one's peers in the public sphere – in short, speech and deed among equals. Action has a self-disclosing component; through action human beings reveal not just what they do, but who they are, and so transcend their private status as a means towards other ends. Whereas the *oikos* is the realm of necessity because it is bound up with the processes of reproduction, as well as the realm of hierarchy, as it is permeated by relations of command and obedience (the household *despot* commands his wife, children and slaves), the public sphere is the realm of freedom and equality. 'To be free meant both not to be subject to the necessities of life or to the command of another *and* not to be in command oneself. It meant neither to rule nor be ruled'

(Arendt [1958] 1998: 32). Politics for Arendt, thus, is not thought in the register of ruling or of sovereignty, but in the register of action. Hence, action as the lack of necessity, equality of speech and deed, and self-disclosure shows how politics is conditioned by plurality, because human beings in the public sphere are different from each other, but equal in this difference (Arendt [1958] 1998: 8). Freedom, hence, is an *individual* experience of distinction, of participating in a public sphere, disclosing oneself and following pursuits different than those of necessity – that is, beginning something new.

But in later writings, most forcefully in *On Revolution*, Arendt shifts from understanding freedom, action and new beginnings as individual capacities to understanding freedom and action as deliberately collective categories. Because, how is the public sphere, where speech, deed and self-disclosure take place, created in the first instance? The process of 'public sphere creation' – what Arendt calls *world-building* – is prior to the action that takes place *in* such a public sphere (Arendt [1963] 2006: 166). 'Freedom itself needed therefore a place where people could come together – the agora, the market-place, or the *polis*, the political space proper' (Arendt [1963] 2006: 21). Hence, Arendt comes to locate the moment of freedom and action in the very process of collectively creating new political forms of life through which equal deliberation and decision-making can take place. By creating new public spheres and novel political institutions, freedom as collective, political action interrupts the established order of things; it provides a distance between the collectivity and their institutions and makes it possible to reconstitute the political structures of the community and create new political beginnings. Freedom, in short, becomes synonymous with the constituent power.[6]

It is no coincidence that Arendt develops this collective, political understanding of freedom in a book devoted to a twin study of modernity's inaugural revolutions. Freedom as the interruptive beginning of something new is politically synonymous with revolution, 'because revolutions are the only political events which confronts us with the problem of beginning' (Arendt [1963] 2006: 11). Now, the concept of revolution ought not, according to Arendt, to be understood only in the negative capacity of destroying old political structures or smashing the state, just as freedom is not exhausted in the act of liberation (Arendt [1963] 2006: 22–3). Revolution is also productive, insofar as it creates new forms of political life, just as freedom is associated with the permanent experience of deliberation and decision-making beyond mere liberation. Hence, according to Arendt, we must 'recognize the truly revolutionary element in constitution-making' ([1963] 2006: 135). Why? Because a constitution in Arendt's understanding is not equal to the liberal idea of *limiting power*; instead, a constitution is the *creation of power*:[7] it is the formalisation of political spaces of deliberation and decision-making. Ultimately, Arendt associates freedom with constitution-making, as constitutions provide the higher laws for the political community: the 'positive notion of freedom . . . was identified with the act of foundation, that is, the framing of a constitution' ([1963] 2006: 226).

Here, it is instructive to compare Arendt and Castoriadis. According to Castoriadis, politics exists in two modes: as instituting and as instituted. The genuine moment of democratic autonomy for Castoriadis is to participate in politics as the reflective self-institution of society as such. Translated into Arendtian terms, we could say that Arendt also conceptualises two different modes of politics. There is one kind of politics, which constitutes public spheres and political institutions, and which can be called *constituent politics*, as Arendt relates it to the collective action of constitution-making. In this understanding of politics, freedom is to partake in the exercise of the constituent power. Then there is a second kind of politics, which takes place inside already constituted institutions, where human beings can enjoy equal deliberation and decision-making, that is, freedom as primarily developed in *The Human Condition*, and which could be called *constituted politics*. Castoriadis's contribution to the theory of council democracy was to conceptualise the councils as a combination of instituting power and instituted politics – as institutionalised spaces for the continual exercise of society's reinstitution in the face of new forms of domination. Arendt also theorised the council system as a political form standing at the crossroads between *constituent* and *constituted* politics. But unlike Castoriadis, Arendt spends more energy on the dangers of both a pure constituent power and pure constituted politics. For Castoriadis, the possibilities of a pure form of instituting power is a logical absurdity because for humans as historical beings, there are no external positions completely outside instituted reality, which is why society as instituting and society as instituted are in perpetual tension and coexistence for Castoriadis. On the contrary, according to Arendt, although a pure constituent power might be a logical absurdity, as it would imply a position outside time and space, she argues that various political movements, as well as various political thinkers, actually thought such a position was a possibility. The theoretical figure of the 'state of nature', as well as the ambitions of the French and Russian revolutionaries, are, according to Arendt, theoretical and political attempts to defy the logical absurdity of a constituent power completely external to established politics. Consequently, although she does not outright disagree with Castoriadis, Arendt develops a more nuanced understanding of the necessity of finding an institutional compromise between constituent and constituted politics. Before I reconstruct Arendt's nuanced position on this matter, I shall analyse in detail the different narratives of *On Revolution*, in which Arendt deems the council system the lost treasure of revolution.

On Revolution: The Lost Treasure of the Revolutionary Tradition

In *On Revolution* Arendt tells the tale of the two modern revolutions: the American and the French. The book conveys at least four important stories. The *first* story is the application of Arendt's concepts of 'the political' and 'the social' to the events in America and France. In this analysis, the French Revolution was essentially misguided because it sought to eradicate poverty and social want, and as such it was motivated by pity (Arendt [1963] 2006: 213). In Arendt's evaluation, such a motivation can never secure the aim of revolution, which is 'the foundation of freedom' (Arendt [1963] 2006: 208), that is, a permanent structure allowing for political participation. Making the social condition of the masses the object of the revolution creates a permanent revolution without any clear end point, as social want cannot be completely eradicated. Instead, the American Revolution, by taking place in a land of abundance and without pre-established class distinctions, did not concern itself with the 'social question', but concentrated on establishing a free republic through covenanting and constitution-making. That the revolutionary tradition from Marx onwards saw the French Revolution as the mother of all revolutions, failed to study the American Revolution and concerned itself explicitly with lifting the masses out of poverty, signifies one of the failures of the revolutionary tradition for Arendt ([1963] 2006: 250).

The *second* story of *On Revolution* is also concerned with the success of the American Revolution and the failure of the French but is instead occupied with the different forms of constitution-making employed by the revolutionaries. As French revolutionaries such as Emmanuel Sieyès and Maximilien Robespierre were essentially inspired by Rousseauian notions of the general will, sovereignty as indivisible and – through Sieyès's transformation of the general will into the national will in 'What is the Third Estate?' (1789) – the supremacy of the nation, they thought of revolution, according to Arendt, as an absolute break with the existing order, as a mode of beginning completely anew. With the attempt to establish such an absolute new beginning, the French revolutionaries only instituted yet another absolute to stand in the place of the God-given monarch, namely the sacredness of the national, indivisible people. Arendt attributes the terror and violence that followed the storming of the Bastille, and which were absent in the American constitutional period, to this attempt at beginning absolutely anew. By making the nation the absolute, sovereign origin of the new republic, the French revolutionaries had placed the nation 'into a perpetual "state of nature"' (Arendt [1963] 2006: 154), which allowed terror against the 'enemies of the nation', as no forms of legality controlled it. Hence, the French revolutionaries drew on the tradition of sovereignty and imagined their endeavour as the transformation of monarchical sovereignty into popular sovereignty.

According to Arendt, sovereignty has conceptual origins in both ancient Greek thought and in the Judeo-Christian tradition, and in both cases, it is antithetical to political freedom. In the Greek imaginary, only the household *despot* was sovereign, as he violently commanded his subjects, whereas equal speech and deed were the mechanisms of the public sphere because

> to force people by violence, to command rather than persuade, were prepolitical ways to deal with people characteristic of life outside the *polis*, of home and family life . . . because absolute, uncontested rule and a political realm properly speaking were mutually exclusive. (Arendt [1958] 1998: 27–8)

In the Judeo-Christian tradition, sovereignty is also hierarchical, as it is bound up with the concept of the will. God's will is absolute and sovereign, it is beyond law, cannot be controlled, be held accountable or be debated with. God's will is equal to his sovereign command, and he is the absolute creator, as he holds a pure, constituent, divine power. According to Arendt, this understanding of God's sovereign will was initially transferred to the paradigm of monarchism, as the sovereign monarch, whose absolute will was law, was the earthly representative of God. This understanding of sovereignty-as-command is characteristic of foundational thinkers of sovereignty like Jean Bodin (1992: 1) and Thomas Hobbes (1994: 177), who both supported their monarchs against popular demands. Later, this understanding of sovereignty was transferred to the deified people as the popular sovereign (Arendt [1963] 2006: 182).

This may be illustrated by a short glance at Rousseau's concept of general will (Rousseau 2002: 170–6). The people's general will, according to Rousseau, is absolute; it is beyond law and by definition uncontrollable by law. It is indivisible and homogenous, it does not tolerate plurality and disagreement, and it is mute and does not deliberate. This discussion is important, as 'the will' is a disputed concept within the Arendtian vocabulary (Jacobetti 1988; Kalyvas 2004). On the one hand, Arendt's political theory in general could be interpreted as an attempt to formulate a theory of politics without recourse to the concept of the will, as politics in the modality of sovereignty stands in stark contrast to Arendt's conception of politics. Instead of command and obedience, Arendt values deliberation and action; instead of indivisibility and homogeneity, Arendt values plurality; instead of absolute beginnings employed by a constituent power or divine creativity outside all laws, Arendt values *relative* beginnings. But on the other hand, some have argued (Kateb 1983: 28–33), Arendt's theory of action as beginning anew, emphasising its miraculous quality of suspending causal chains and natural time, and pointing to the essentially abyssal nature of action and freedom, has affinities with the very concept she sought to refute: the will. Like the concept of the will, Arendt's concept of action as a new beginning cannot be controlled and determined by pre-existing, external principles. Like the concept of the will, Arendt's concept of action is non-institutional, form-giving and could be said to function in a normative void. Hence, critics argue, although Arendt tries to distance herself from the theory of sovereignty and extraordinary politics that Schmitt proposes,[8] she does not do this forcefully enough, which makes her theory of politics closer to decisionism or even totalitarianism than she has ever thought.

Against this criticism I argue throughout this chapter that Arendt was painfully aware of the fact that her theory of new beginnings could be associated with the Schmittian exception and an uncontrollable constituent power, which is why she celebrated the American Revolution and its mode of 'relative beginnings' in contrast to the French beginning anew *ex nihilo*. According to Arendt, 'the greatest American innovation in politics was the consistent abolition of sovereignty within the body politic of the republic, the insight that in the realm of human affairs sovereignty and tyranny are the same' ([1963] 2006: 144). Hence, Arendt argues that the American revolutionaries, while deciding on a common constitution, built on already existing practices of constitution-making. Instead of aspiring to an absolute new beginning, which would have placed them in a violent state of nature, they aimed for a *relative* new beginning, because they already had – since the time of colonialisation – 'widespread experience with self-government' (Arendt [1963] 2006: 148). In order to foreshadow some critiques of Arendt that I discuss later, I argue that her discussion between absolute and relative beginnings contributes to an understanding of politics which stresses both novelty and rupture as well as continuity and regularity. The evaluation of the American Revolution as a relative new beginning, which successfully augmented political practices already existing in the Northern colonies of the British Empire, testifies to an ambition of combining legal change and legal continuity, not of exclusively privileging one or the other.

At a first reading, this *second* story of *On Revolution* seems to tell a stereotypical tale of modernity's two inaugural revolutions: on the one hand, the successful revolution, which aimed at freedom, did not resort to violence and continued existing political practices, but which was unfortunately forgotten by subsequent revolutionaries; and on the other hand, the unsuccessful, corrupt revolution, which sought to eradicate the entire *ancien régime* along with its calendar and units of measurement, which conceptualised 'the people' as a homogenous, sovereign entity outside law, and which – equally unfortunately – has become the model of revolution *per se*.

This opposition between the two revolutions and their sources of success and failure is obviously highly stylised and historically contestable (Hobsbawm 1973: 206). Importantly, the contrast between the two revolutions breaks down even within Arendt's own text. The final chapter of *On Revolution* contains the two last stories of the book – stories 3 and 4 – which are both stories of defeat. The first of these stories of defeat casts the events of the American Revolution in a grim light. Arendt's final evaluation of the American revolutionary period is that, paradoxically, its success was also the source of its failure. The ratification of the constitution, which unified the thirteen states into a federation, also meant the end of the self-government of the individual states, making no room for the local town-hall meetings – 'the original springs of all political activity in the country' (Arendt [1963] 2006: 231). These spaces of freedom, as Arendt calls them, which had made political participation and civic engagement possible prior to the constitution, were given no place in the constitution of post-revolutionary America. As Arendt argues, 'the revolutionary spirit in America began to wither away, and it was the Constitution itself, this greatest achievement of the American people, which eventually cheated them of their proudest possession' ([1963] 2006: 231). The political freedom – which 'means the right "to be a participator in government", or it means nothing' (Arendt [1963] 2006: 210) – that otherwise was available before the constitution, was now, according to Arendt, only available to the people's representatives. In the language of the constituent power, this power became completely exhausted in constituted politics, confirming what Loughlin and Walker (2007) have called the 'juridical containment thesis'.

It is by universalising this American story of defeat that Arendt finally embarks on the *fourth* story of *On Revolution*, namely the story of the council system. Whereas Arendt has criticised almost every aspect of the French Revolution up till this point, she now argues that in order to understand the council system as the lost treasure of revolution, 'we must turn our attention once more to the course of the French Revolution' ([1963] 2006: 231). Arendt argues that from the French Revolution onwards, the germs of a new type of political association – the council system – has appeared in many modern revolutions. The first example of such a germ emerged, in Arendt's evaluation – and here she differs remarkably from other council thinkers – as the forty-eight sections of the first Paris Commune during the French Revolution constituted themselves as local, self-governing bodies and federated into a revolutionary commune, instead of envisioning themselves as electoral districts with the limited task of electing deputies to the newly constituted National Assembly. Instead of staying as constituted electoral districts, as decided by the National Constitutional Assembly, the sections transformed themselves into organs of self-government. Along with these radicalised sections, Arendt mentions the spontaneously emerging *sociétés populaires* as parts of a politicised society where self-government and popular participation were the order of the day ([1963] 2006: 231–2). Amidst the French Revolution these radicalised sections and popular societies inaugurate, according to Arendt, a political tradition of council democracy, which opposes both statism (sovereignty's indivisibility) and the party system (representative government). Instead, 'the societies, each a small power structure of its own, and the self-government of the Communes were clearly a danger for the centralized state power' (Arendt [1963] 2006: 237).

Like the fate of defeat of the American Revolution, the radical sections and societies were also crushed during the revolutionary period in France. Just as the American town halls had no place in the new American constitution, so did the Jacobins destroy the popular organs simply because they were competitors for public power. Even though Robespierre – as a strangely accurate precursor to Lenin's handling of the soviets – had praised the popular sections before coming to power, he took the lead in destroying these popular organs after he ascended to power (Arendt [1963] 2006: 232).

It is only after Arendt's discussion on the Parisian sections and societies that she travels back over the Atlantic to discuss what she takes to be the first *theoretical* engagement with the council system, namely Thomas Jefferson's proposal of a *ward republic* consisting of federated 'elementary republics'. What Jefferson proposed was to subdivide every state, province and county into a number of wards, where actual participation and decision-making would be possible, in order to 'make every citizen an acting member of the government' (Jefferson 1999: 213). Whereas the historical councils in Europe from 1917 to 1921 were most often functionally based, drawing delegates from factories, the army and the navy, Jefferson's ward republic – and by consequence Arendt's council system – is geographically based. The core of Jefferson's proposal is the following:

> Divide the counties into wards of such size that every citizen can attend, when called on, and act in person. Ascribe to them the government of their wards in all things relating to themselves exclusively . . . These wards, called townships in New England, are the vital principles of their governments, and have proved themselves the wisest invention ever devised by the wit of man for the perfect exercise of self-government. (Jefferson 1999: 213–14)

According to Arendt, Jefferson perceived the lack of such participatory wards in the constitutional matrix of the new United States as a 'mortal danger' because 'the Constitution had given all power to the citizens, without giving them the opportunity of *being* republicans and of *acting* as citizens' (Arendt [1963] 2006: 245; original emphasis). Arendt argued that

> the basic assumption of the ward system, whether Jefferson knew it or not, was that no one could be called happy without his share in public happiness, that no one could be called free without his experience in public freedom, and that no one could be called either happy or free without participating, and having a share, in public power. (Arendt [1963] 2006: 247)

With the sections, societies and the federated commune of the French Revolution and Jefferson's proposal for a system of local wards, Arendt sees the inauguration of a political tradition that came to characterise the revolutions throughout modernity. In her evaluation, 'both Jefferson's plan and the French *sociétés révolutionaires* anticipated with an utmost weird precision those councils, *soviets* and *Räte*, which were to make their appearance in every genuine revolution throughout the nineteenth and twentieth centuries' ([1963] 2006: 241). In the face of those accusing Arendt of utopianism, it is necessary to take into account the fact of

> the regular emergence, during the course of revolution of a new form of government that resembled in an amazing fashion Jefferson's ward system and *seemed to repeat, under no matter what circumstances*, the revolutionary societies and municipal councils which had spread all over France after 1789. (Arendt [1963] 2006: 248; emphasis added)

'The main dates of appearance of these organs of action and germs of a new state are the following', Arendt asserts ([1963] 2006: 254): the Paris Commune of 1871, the Russian soviets of 1905 and 1917, the German *Arbeiter- und Soldatenräte* of 1918–19, the short-lived 1919 *Räterepublik* in Munich and the workers' councils of the Hungarian Revolution of 1956. As is evident from this list, Arendt alludes to the same events of revolutionary upheaval as Castoriadis and other council thinkers did.

As Arendt's most sustained analysis of council democracy is located within a book dedicated to a twin study of the first modern revolutions and the subsequent loss of the revolutionary spirit, the council system is, according to Arendt, firstly an alternative to how the concept of 'revolution' has been understood, and secondly, an alternative to a 'post-revolutionary' society dominated exclusively by representative organs. Whereas the concept of revolution became hegemonised throughout the twentieth century by the Marxist tradition, so that revolution was thought to be a planned activity performed by a group of well-trained professional revolutionaries, the councils – according to Arendt – arose spontaneously, without prior planning ([1963] 2006: 254). The councils are thus the exemplar, for Arendt, of an opposition between politics as a spontaneous, popular activity and as a planned and elitist endeavour. In addition, the councils have a different aim with revolutionary transformation than the professional revolutionaries of the Marxist–Leninist tradition, who in Arendt's assessment are 'firmly anchored in the tradition of the nation-state' ([1963] 2006: 248), meaning that they understand revolution as a way to conquer state power and consolidate a monopoly of violence. This has the consequence that revolutionary activity is mainly conceptualised in the capacities to destroy and abolish. These capacities, according to Arendt, amount to *liberation*, which might be the necessary condition for the real objective of revolution, namely the exercising of freedom, but never a sufficient course. As Arendt asserts, the sections, clubs, communes, councils and soviets which appeared during the modern revolutions did not look upon themselves as temporary, insurrectionary organs only to render power to the professional revolutionary elites after the downfall of the *ancien régime* – an attitude towards the councils, which Arendt attributes to revolutionary leaders and thinkers such as Robespierre and Lenin ([1963] 2006: 248–50). Instead, crucially, 'the councils, moreover, were always organs of order as much as organs of action' (Arendt [1963] 2006: 255).

A comparison with theories of council democracy from the early twentieth century is instructive. In Lenin's final formulation, the soviets were only 'organs of action', not 'organs of order', to use Arendt's terminology. The soviets could only be used for insurrection; they were temporary and instrumental, not permanent political forms of self-government, as the government of society in post-revolutionary times was to be handed over to the party. Hence, Lenin deviated from Marx's evaluation of the Paris Commune as 'the form at last discovered', as a political form which, due to its internal structures, would provide self-government for the masses. After Lenin, the interwar council communists developed a council concept which incorporated the idea of councils as organs of both insurrection and permanent self-government. As Pannekoek wrote, resembling Arendt's formulation above, 'the workers' councils growing up as organs of fight will at the same time be organs of reconstruction' (2003: 51). When revolution is understood primarily as negation, the councils become merely temporary fighting organs, which must surrender their power once the monarch or the capitalist has been eradicated; they become organs with no relevance for normal politics. But when the aim of revolution is understood to be the creation of a free republic, the council system could be understood as a permanent, institutional structure for political participation and the experience of freedom:

> The councils, obviously, were spaces of freedom. As such they invariably refused to regard themselves as temporary organs of revolution and, on the contrary, made all attempts at establishing themselves as permanent organs of government. Far from wishing to make the revolution permanent, their explicitly expressed goal was . . . no paradise on earth, no classless society, no dream of socialist or communist fraternity, but the establishment of 'the true republic'. (Arendt [1963] 2006: 256)

This passage is important. Apparently, the ambition of the councils as spaces of freedom in a 'true republic' is different from a 'paradise on earth', a 'classless society' or a 'dream of socialist or communist fraternity'. Why? One interpretation I will pursue below is that 'paradises', 'classless societies' and 'fraternities' are *fixed* states of being, as they exist outside history and hence cannot be disturbed by the effects of history. A paradisiacal state of being is one where human sin has not yet started the flux of history; a classless society is one where the dynamics of history have been transcended and no further transformation is needed; a fraternity is held together by the natural force of blood and heritage unaffected by the shifts in solidarity and commonality due to shared, historical experiences. In contrast to these ahistorical, fixed states of being, Arendt could be taken to argue that the council republic is precisely a regime which welcomes the effects of history and the recurrent needs of transformation. Arendt's council republicanism, as we shall see below, is hence one that stresses renewal and reconstitution instead of permanent revolution or permanent fixation.

Let us return to the shared characteristics which Arendt attributes to the councils. In addition to the spontaneity of the councils' emergence and their attempt to establish themselves as new, permanent organs of government, two other similarities between the enumerated events of council organisation must be mentioned. The first is the opposition between the council system and the party system; the second is the political defeat of all these nascent council systems.

Going back to the council system's inaugural moment during the French Revolution, Arendt detects the birth of two different political systems, namely the council system and the party system. Both these systems are products of the modern revolutionary imaginary and inaugurate two different modes of politics. One kind of politics, taking place in the councils, is founded upon political participation, and another kind of politics, taking place in the parties, is founded upon representation. 'The conflict between the two systems, the parties and the councils', Arendt argues, 'came to the fore in all twentieth-century revolutions. The issue at stake was representation versus action and participation' ([1963] 2006: 265). The various emerging council systems throughout the modern revolutions, therefore, share the fact that they were organs *of* the people, emerging spontaneously through – as Arendt puts it – 'the organizational impulses of the people themselves' ([1963] 2006: 249).

In this way, Arendt shares one of the basic traits of much council theory. Marx, the pro-soviet Lenin of 1917 and the council communists saw in the councils a political system much more democratic than liberal parliamentarianism. The party system was founded upon the party as an organ *separated* and *distinct* from the people, an organ that takes care of the interests of the people without need of their participation. In the same way that Marx conceptualised the state as an agent of domination due to its separation from society, so the party system, according to much council theory, Arendt included, is antithetical to popular self-government because of its distance from the people. All political parties, according to Arendt, from left to right, from revolutionary to conservative, 'agreed that the end of government was the welfare of the people, and that the substance of politics was not action but administration' ([1963] 2006: 265). As such, the different experiences of council politics are united in their disclosure of the principle of *action*, their conflict with the party system and this system's rejection of participation at the expense of representation.

The last major, shared characteristic which Arendt attributes to the councils appearing through the last centuries is their eventual defeat. It is in this sense that the councils for Arendt are the 'lost treasure' of the revolutionary tradition. This treasure is lost in a double way. Most importantly, the council tradition is a tradition of defeat because it – like Jefferson's ward republic – never survived the revolution. Nowhere did the council system become a permanent institutional reality, as political parties, professional revolutionaries or the *ancien régime* crushed the councils during the struggles for power. Moreover, the council system is a lost treasure because it has failed to be remembered. Arendt asserts that the council tradition was 'utterly neglected by statesmen, historians, political theorists, and, most importantly, by the revolutionary tradition itself' ([1963] 2006: 241).[9] Does Arendt's acknowledgement of the continual defeat of the council system make her politics ungraspable and purely episodic, as some critics have argued? Arendt herself admits that the men and women of revolution continually

> lose their treasure. The history of revolutions – from the summer of 1776 in Philadelphia and the summer of 1789 in Paris to the autumn of 1956 in Budapest – which politically spells out the innermost story of the modern age, could be told in parable form as the tale of an age-old treasure which, under the most varied circumstances, appears abruptly, unexpectedly, and disappears again, under mysterious conditions, as though it were a fata morgana. (Arendt 1961b: 5)

This fata morgana is the experience of public freedom, institutionally expressed in the council system, and it does sound as if Arendt understands politics as truly episodic, ephemeral and unpredictable. Even though I do want to advance a reading of Arendt that counters this understanding of politics to some degree, it is also worth emphasising that such a 'fata morgana-esque' understanding of the council system suggests that it is no simple job to establish council democracy. Instead, the loss of the constituent power, which is really what is entailed in the fata morgana of public freedom, is almost inevitable, which is precisely why a project that seeks to recover it, formalise it and make it accessible is important and ambitious.

Through these four stories, Arendt argued that she had discovered a political tradition which expressed many of her political principles and combatted many of her political fears. Instead of sovereignty and the absolutism of the will, the council system was founded upon a plurality of federated organs for deliberation and action; instead of parliamentarianism's reliance on representative elites taking care of the social welfare of the population, the council system functioned through face-to-face interaction as a public sphere allowing speech, deed and self-disclosure. But how is her council republicanism related to her understanding of freedom as constituent power? How does the council system combine constituent power and constituted form?

The Council System between Liberal Constitutionalism and Permanent Revolution

To answer these questions, it is necessary to recall the fundamental distinction between constituent and normal politics. Constituent politics is the kind of politics that creates new constitutions, abolishes the existing constitution or fundamentally amends it. Hence, it is a form of politics associated with a higher form of freedom, according to Arendt. Constituent politics relates to revolution, popular upheaval and constituent assemblies – those forms of politics that institute new forms of legality. Normal politics or *constituted* politics, on the other hand, are those forms of politics which take place through already instituted forms of legality, through formal procedures in everyday politics.

These two modes of politics can be associated with various positive and negative characteristics. A politics that valorises constitution-making would deem normal politics too narrow and legally constrained, too bureaucratic and elitist, insofar as representatives rule on behalf of the people. Such a position argues that the mechanisms of checks and balances and division of powers that dominate normal politics display a fear of popular power. Instead, such a politics locates the genuine political moments in instances of constitution-making, as the participants are here unbound by the past generations, as well as by instituted forms of legality. In this view, genuine politics is the process of *instituting* legality, not living under the rules already *instituted* by the past generations.

On the other hand, a politics that valorises normal law-making deems constituent politics too insecure, arbitrary and violent. As new constitutions are often drafted in a legal void, in the *interregnum* between two legal orders due to popular insurrection, this form of politics can be labelled as nothing more than crude power politics wearing the cloak of constitutionality. The established rules of a constitution, which safeguards the formal negative liberties of the individual, the formal equality among individuals and the formal legality of new laws by established procedural mechanisms, is nowhere to be seen in moments of higher law making, according to proponents of ordinary politics.

The interpretation of Castoriadis provided in the last chapter was that – against his critics – the council system combines these two modes of politics. But in a way, the ambition of Castoriadis was one-sided, as it was primarily to imbue instituted politics with equal access to the instituting power, not to safeguard instituted reality from the possible dangers of the instituting power. This one-sidedness of Castoriadis's analysis is a product of his theory of the instituting society. Because something like a pure instituting power completely outside instituted politics is a logical absurdity, there is no reason to fear it. For Castoriadis, the enemy – so to speak – comes only from one side: from depoliticisation, bureaucracy, heteronomy. But for Arendt, both permanent revolution and depoliticisation are real dangers. In contrast to Castoriadis, Arendt argues that the employment of an absolute, constituent power in a state of nature has been the ambition of some revolutionary movements, as well as the theoretical consequence of the Hobbesian–Rousseauian–Sie-yèsian paradigm of sovereignty. As such, she is more attentive than Castoriadis to the dangers not just of apathy and elitism during normal politics, but also of the arbitrariness and groundlessness of a pure constituent power in a state of nature. While Castoriadis seeks to combine constituent and political form in this theory of council democracy, he clearly valorises the former over the latter, thereby coming close to the radical democratic conception of constituent power criticised in the Introduction. The interpretation of Arendt's council democracy provided below is instead focused on the relation between constituent power and constitutional form, and the potential dangers associated with both modalities of politics in their pure form. Although Arendt does not develop it systematically, throughout *On Revolution* she criticises two distinct modes of relating the constituent power to the constitutional form, namely what could be called *liberal constitutionalism* and *permanent revolution*, and provides her own alternative form of constitutionalism, in which the councils play a crucial role.

Liberal Constitutionalism: The Lethargy of the Public Realm

The first of these modalities of constitution-making can be termed liberal constitutionalism. According to this understanding, a constitution is a constraining device which is meant to set clear boundaries on political power. Liberal constitutionalists view political power as inherently vicious, and ever-expanding, hence a constitution needs to protect individual rights against organised state power. As Arendt argues, such a view of constitutionalism 'claims not a share in government but a safeguard against government' ([1963]

2006: 134). The defining mark of liberal constitutionalism is that the constituent power disappears in the newly established regime, and that the constitution can be revised by future generations only according to the constitutionally prescribed ways of amendment. The constituent power is conceptualised fully in legal terms. To step outside the constitutionally prescribed rules of amendment is to step directly into illegality. The moment of founding a new constitution is indeed a temporary moment; one that must be exhausted in ordinary politics due to the unpredictability of politics outside established legality.

It is possible to reconstruct Arendt's critique of liberal constitutionalism from her comments on the fate of the American Revolution. To do so, we must keep in mind that Arendt defines the object of constituent politics as the creation of a permanent regime which seeks not only to limit popular power and safeguard individual rights, but also to institutionalise power in such a manner that popular participation can become a reality in the everyday life of the republic. 'The notion of constitutional government', what I call liberal constitutionalism, Arendt reminds us, 'is nothing more or less than government limited by law, and the safeguard of civil liberties through constitutional guarantees' ([1963] 2006: 134). Such an exhaustion of constituent power in the established constitutional form is, according to Arendt, 'never intended to spell out the new revolutionary powers of the people, but on the contrary, was felt to be necessary in order to limit the power of government even in the newly founded body politic' ([1963] 2006: 134). But, Arendt continues, 'the main question' of politics is 'not how to limit power but how to establish it, not how to limit government but how to found a new one' ([1963] 2006: 139).

Arendt's famous statement that 'it was the Constitution itself, this greatest achievement of the American people, which eventually cheated them of their proudest possession' ([1963] 2006: 231), can unravel her critique of liberal constitutionalism. What is this proudest possession of the Americans, and how did the constitution rob them of it? 'The Constitution', Arendt contends,

> had given all power to the citizens, without giving them the opportunity of *being* republicans and of *acting* as citizens. In other words, the danger was that all power had been given to the people in their private capacity and that there was no space established for them in their capacity of being citizens. (Arendt [1963] 2006: 245; original emphasis)

Before the creation of the American constitution, town-hall meetings and self-ruling townships had governed the thirteen independent states. Also, the very process of constitution-making had involved the going back and forth between meetings in the confederated states and the Constitutional Convention. All this political activity was effectively put to an end with the ratification of the constitution. Now, according to Arendt, politics instead came to be the business of the members of Congress and the organs of the executive power. 'During the years of revolution', the citizens 'had been able to . . . act on their own and thus to participate in public business as it was being transacted from day to day', Arendt argued ([1963] 2006: 243). This changed, as 'by virtue of the Constitution, the public business of the nation as a whole had been transferred to Washington . . . it was the delegates of the people rather than the people themselves who constituted the public realm' ([1963] 2006: 243). The result, which is one of the primary vices in Arendt's political thinking in general, is the 'lethargy and inattention to public business, since the Constitution itself provided a public space *only* for the representatives of the people, and not for the people themselves' (Arendt [1963] 2006: 230; emphasis added). In conclusion, Arendt asserts that 'in this republic, as it presently turned out, there was no space reserved, no room left for the exercise of precisely those qualities, which had been instrumental in building it' ([1963] 2006: 224).

Arendt's critique of the American Constitution could be rephrased as a general critique of liberal constitutionalism: every genuine revolution is accompanied by widespread mass mobilisation and popular participation. The attention to public issues and the discussions of the pros and cons of the future regime which the revolutionary people are about to found are very much the order of the day. These moments of revolution and constitution-making are quintessentially characterised by what Arendt understands as political action: the co-creation of new constitutional beginnings, the bringing out of something politically new into the world. When the revolution ends with the ratification of a new constitution that inaugurates a constitutional regime with representative institutions and legally protected civil liberties, the intense business of acting together and caring for the public good is replaced by the professionalisation of politics and the withdrawal of ordinary people from the public realm. It might be government in the name *of* the people and *for* their private welfare, but it is not government *by* the people themselves. In this manner, the American Revolution, and the liberal constitutionalism of which it is an example, exhausts the constituent power in the constituted institutions and leaves the public sphere full of lethargic and privatised individual voters. This analysis could maybe suggest that Arendt was in favour of pure constituent politics in order for the genuine moments of political freedom to be extended as long as possible. But as I shall argue below, she is as critical of revolutions that do not come to an end, that is, permanent revolutions, as she is of revolutions that create only a limited, constitutional government.

Permanent Revolution: The Constituent Power in a State of Nature

Whereas Arendt's critique of liberal constitutionalism and the exhaustion of the constituent power can be excavated from her analysis of the American Revolution, her critique of a permanent revolution can be drawn from her analysis of the French one. At first sight it might be more difficult to understand why Arendt feared a permanent revolution as much as she feared a depoliticised regime. After all, Arendt can be deemed a pre-eminent theorist of new beginnings, celebrating the miraculous character of collective action that brings forth novel political forms. Some of her commentators have criticised her for being more attuned to extraordinary politics than to normal, constituted politics (Honig 1993: 93–4; Kateb 2000: 135). Canovan, for example, states that 'it is unfortunate that the same concern for rare events that gave her unparalleled insight into extraordinary politics should have led her to overlook normal politics altogether' (1978: 21). Although it is certainly true that Arendt has a keen eye for the generative character of political action, to deem her unashamedly critical of normal politics would be a mistake, as the object of revolution is precisely to create a stable, permanent regime for the exercise of freedom. Only by stabilising itself can the achievements of the constituent power be safeguarded. Arendt is highly critical of 'revolutions, which become permanent, which do not come to an end and do not produce their end, the foundation of freedom' ([1963] 2006: 135). The object of revolution is not to remain in a permanent movement without stabilisation, but 'to lay down the boundaries of the new political realm and to define the rules within it . . . to build a new political space within which the "passion for freedom" or the "pursuit of happiness" would receive the free play for generations to come' in order that the '"revolutionary" spirit could survive the actual end of the revolution' (Arendt [1963] 2006: 117).

By aspiring to make an *absolute* new beginning and rejecting all forms of constituted powers, the French revolutionaries had placed the constituent power in a state of nature. By following Sieyès and locating the constituent power in the unbound nation, the revolutionaries operated in a normative and legal vacuum in which the revolutionary terror could effectively follow. 'The experiences of the French Revolution with a people thrown into a "state of nature"', Arendt contends, opens the door for 'a violence which no institutionalized or controlled power could withstand' ([1963] 2006: 173). Because the French Revolution did not provide a lasting constitution, it kept instituting new 'revolutionary dictatorships, designed to drive on and intensify the revolutionary movement' (Arendt [1963] 2006: 150). A political system which seeks to found itself on such an ever-present, unbound constituent power 'is ever changing by definition' and 'its foundation is built on quicksand' (Arendt [1963] 2006: 154). This also became evident with the Russian Revolution, which in many respects mirrors central elements of the French experience. Where the revolutionaries do not produce a stable constitution but instead hold on to the constituent power, dictatorship, over-politicisation, violence and arbitrariness are possible outcomes. The Bolsheviks' termination of the Russian Constituent Assembly in early 1918 is a primary example of the 'permanentisation' of the revolution.

Hence, Arendt is faced with a dual problem: she wishes to avoid the exhaustion of the constituent power in normal politics, in order for the experience of freedom to live on in constituted politics. She also wishes to avoid the permanence of the constituent power, as the popular sovereign needs to give itself stable institutions for exercising freedom. In other words, the constituent power needs to be institutionalised in such a way that its excesses, arbitrariness and possibly violent nature are avoided, but which keeps its relation to freedom and the experience of new beginnings open. For this tough job, Arendt looked to none other institution than the council system.

By setting up the discussion in this way, certain similarities and differences with Castoriadis can be observed. Castoriadis positioned the council system between the instituting power and instituted society, but whereas something like a pure instituting power is nonsense according to Castoriadis, because the instituting dimension of society always emerges from within society as already instituted, Arendt locates in the French as well as in the Russian Revolution the ambition of the revolutionary founders to begin completely *ab novo* and hence employ the constituent power in a legal void. She also recognises that important figures in the tradition of sovereignty, such as Hobbes, Rousseau and Sieyès, had formulated such a conception in theoretical terms. Because she realises the possibility of such a groundless political project, her conceptualisation of the council system as a combination of constituent power and constituted form does indeed try to steer clear of the twin dangers of modern politics: depoliticisation and total politicisation.

Keeping the Constituent Power Alive: Beyond Liberal Constitutionalism and Permanent Revolution

In a crucial paragraph in *The Human Condition*, Arendt describes the fundamental frailty of human action, which is the precondition for political community. Human action is an experience that appears the moment people speak and act together; the moment collective speech and deed disappear, the political community is in principal dissolved again. Hence, the political community exists in actualisation, as 'power cannot be stored up and kept in reserve for emergencies, like the instruments of violence, but exists only in its actualization' (Arendt [1958] 1998: 200). Such a conceptualisation of politics does sound like the momentary, fleeting and episodic practice which Arendt has been criticised for. But after Arendt has discussed 'The Frailty of Human Affairs', as section 26 of *The Human Condition* is called, she discusses in section 27 the so-called 'Greek Solution' to the problem of the frailty of action. This solution is the establishment of the *polis*. According to Arendt, the 'function' of the *polis* was 'to enable men to do *permanently*, albeit under certain restrictions, what otherwise had been possible only as an *extraordinary* and *infrequent* enterprise' ([1958] 1998: 197; emphasis added). Moreover, 'the *polis* was supposed to *multiply* the occasions' for collective speech and deed, 'to *multiply* the chances for everybody to distinguish himself'; in short, and crucially for my argument, 'to make the *extraordinary* an *ordinary* occurrence of everyday life' (Arendt [1958] 1998: 197; emphasis added). This discussion elucidates how Arendt is not only concerned with the moment of constituting or with freedom as complete unboundedness. 'It is as though', she further argues, 'the wall of the *polis* and boundaries of law were drawn around an already existing public sphere, which however, without such stabilizing protection could not endure, could not survive the moment of action and speech'

(Arendt [1958] 1998: 198). Hence, Arendt could be taken to argue, the constituent dimension of politics, if it is to be sustained for longer periods of time, 'albeit under certain restrictions', is in need of ordinary politics, of institutionalisation and formalisation. As such, in the words of Hannah Pitkin (1998: 114), Arendt seeks 'a vision of "normal", ongoing ordinary politics that was not really normal or ordinary: not in accord with the now conventional understanding of politics, nor like the now ordinary practice of politics – petty, banal, and quotidian'. What is the relevance of this discussion to the interpretation of Arendt's council democracy? Andreas Kalyvas has aptly phrased her ambition – what he calls Arendt's substantial renewal of the socialist, council discourse – as the 'normalization of the extraordinary' (2008: 276). It is because of the novel combination of the extraordinary and the ordinary that Arendt is attracted to the council system.

Arendt opens the last chapter of *On Revolution* with a reflection on the fate of revolutionary thinking and the split between what I have called models of liberal constitutionalism and permanent revolution. According to Arendt, the outcome of historical experiences and theoretical models that valorise *either* constituent (permanent revolution) *or* constituted politics (liberal constitutionalism) signifies that an essential meaning of revolution and politics has been lost. As she asserts, 'the effort to recapture the lost spirit of revolution must, to a certain extent, consist in the attempt at *thinking together and combining meaningfully* what our present vocabulary presents to us in terms of opposition and contradiction' ([1963] 2006: 215–16; emphasis added). Participating in the act of founding involves paying *dual attention* to stability and novelty, to radical change and legal continuity, not just to one or the other, as the constitutional models that Arendt criticises assert. To elaborate on this, I quote Arendt in a rather lengthy passage:

> To the extent that the greatest event in every revolution is the act of foundation, the spirit of revolution contains two elements which to us seem irreconcilable and even contradictory. The act of founding the new body politic, of devising the new form of government involves the grave concern with the stability and durability of the new structure; the experience, on the other hand, which those who are engaged in this grave business are bound to have is the exhilarating awareness of the human capacity of beginning, the high spirits which have always attended the birth of something new on earth. Perhaps the very fact that

these two elements, the concern with stability and the spirit of the new, have become opposites in political thought and terminology . . . must be recognized to be among the symptoms of our loss. (Arendt [1963] 2006: 213–14)

In what way can the council system in Arendt's interpretation bring together these elements of revolution and constitution-making which have otherwise been divided from each other? In Chapter 2, I provided two different views on the councils. The *first* view is to regard the councils as temporary instruments of insurrection, what I call the Leninist position. After the successful overthrow of power, a process in which the councils had been absolutely instrumental, the councils must relinquish their power to the professional revolutionaries. The councils, in other words, cannot govern, but only destroy. The *second* view provided in some form by most council thinkers is that they also *in nucleus* preconfigure a new form of society. This obviously means that the councils are not only temporary organs, but also permanent organs – they are the institutional foundation of a future society. '[T]he councils, moreover, were always organs of *order* as much as organs of *action*', Arendt revealingly argues ([1963] 2006: 255; emphasis added). Such a combination of order and action, the fact that the councils 'invariably refused to regard themselves as temporary organs of revolution and, on the contrary, made all attempts at establishing themselves as permanent organs of government' (Arendt [1963] 2006: 256), shows that for Arendt the councils incarnate the dual character of the spirit of revolution, as involving both a care for the stability and durability of the republic and the exhilarating experience of novelty.

But how does Arendt imagine that the councils incorporate both of these elements of the revolutionary spirit? Must we not admit that constituent and constituted politics are ultimately incompatible? According to Arendt, as stressed before, the councils sprang spontaneously from the actions of the many. But although action in the Arendtian vocabulary is an experience, meaning that it disappears the moment the actors shy away from one another, the 'members of the councils were not content to discuss and "enlighten themselves" about measures taken by parties and assemblies'; instead, 'they consciously and explicitly desired the direct participation of every citizen in the public affairs of the country' (Arendt [1963] 2006: 255). The key to not abandoning the constituent power after the moment of foundation was quite simply to let the constituent power survive after the revolution, but in an institutionalised, de-revolutionised form. This could be achieved, in Arendt's mind, through a specific relation between local, regional and central councils, where the local councils would not be fully domesticated by the central council. As Arendt puts it,

> the common object was the foundation of a new body politic, a new type of republican government which would rest on 'elementary republics' in such a way that its own central power *did not deprive the constituent bodies of their original power to constitute.* (Arendt [1963] 2006: 259; emphasis added)

Such a 'new type of republican government', in which the power to constitute is retained, can be captured by what Arendt calls 'the federal principle', that is, 'the principle of league and association among separate units', which 'arises out of the elementary conditions of action itself' ([1963] 2006: 259). Arendt argues that historically, every time councils have appeared, some process of federalisation and integration has emerged, where local councils have delegated members to regional and national councils, but without relinquishing their power to constitute to these higher councils. Hence, this is Arendt's solution to the problem of the stark difference between constituent power and constitutional form that liberal constitutionalism and the permanent revolution thematise in different ways. A republic of councils would uphold the local councils' 'power to constitute' under normal politics, meaning that any number of citizens can constitute themselves in councils and require participation in regional and central councils. As Kalyvas has rightly phrased it, 'normal political action becomes a *constituted constitutional action*' (2008: 277; original emphasis). Thus, a republic of councils 'combined legal stability with constitutional change and institutional novelty' so that 'ordinary politics could still retain its dignity, even its extraordinary character, by turning the constitution into an unfinished project, open to further interventions, modifications, and amendments by an active *demos*' (Kalyvas 2008: 278). This unfinished character of the constitution through the ongoing participation in the councils amounts to what Woodrow Wilson called 'a kind of Constitutional Assembly in continuous session' (qtd in Arendt [1963] 2006: 192).

It is by imbuing normal politics in the councils with the qualities of the constituent power that we find Arendt's *republican* interpretation of the council system. Why is it republican? As discussed earlier, a republic in Arendt's understanding is not a fixed, final form in which conflict and effects of history have been eradicated. Instead, it is a political form where the act of foundation itself remains alive, and hence where a degree of constituent power remains active. Arendt sometimes thematises her council republic through the Roman concept of *augmentation*. According to Arendt, the strength of Roman republicanism was to understand normal politics as a continual amendment, or augmentation, of the foundations of the republic. The founding moment was in a way ever present, because the constitution was open to reinterpretation, enlargement and amendment:

> The very Roman concept of authority suggests that the act of foundation inevitably develops its own stability and permanence . . . 'augmentation' by virtue of which all innovations and changes remain tied back to the foundation which, at the same time, they augment and increase. (Arendt [1963] 2006: 194)

Hence, 'the very authority of the (American) Constitution resides in its capacity to be amended and augmented' (Arendt [1963] 2006: 194). Another way to say this is that a unique feature of council democracy is that it can be understood as a political form which welcomes self-transformation and augmentation, because it acknowledges the recurrent possibility of decay and corruption. It is striking that Arendt mentions Machiavelli as a thinker of augmentation early in *On Revolution* ([1963] 2006: 27), insofar as she argues that Machiavelli did not think of changes in the Roman political system as revolutions but as *rinovazione*, renovations. In *The Discourses*, Machiavelli comes close to the understanding of augmentation that Arendt ascribes to the council system's combination of constituent power and constituted form. Machiavelli states that 'the life of all mundane things is of finite duration' and they will eventually disintegrate if they are not taken 'back to their origins' ([1517] 2003: 385). According to Machiavelli, therefore, the primary way for political bodies to safeguard themselves is to ensure that it is possible to take them back to their origins, that is, to the moment when the constituent power was active: 'Hence those are better constituted and have a longer life whose institutions make frequent renovations possible' (Machiavelli [1517] 2003: 385).

Like Castoriadis's understanding of autonomy, the council republic is not a fixed, problem-free state of being. Neither does it imply a relation towards the world captured by absolute control as in the tradition of sovereignty. Rather, Arendt's vocabulary of augmentation, renewal, relative beginnings and 'constituted constituent power' testifies, firstly, to the dual preoccupation with both stability and novelty, and secondly, to the fact that absolute control in political affairs cannot be obtained. Instead, the consequence of this republican augmentation of the foundations in the councils is a device through which the almost inevitable process of decay (or depoliticisation, in Arendt's terminology) can be countered and momentarily stopped. Because the constituent moment is never truly over, and because the councils retain their original power to constitute, the constituted institutions will not confront the people as an alien force. Or, maybe more modestly, when institutions *do* begin to alienate themselves, and the relationship between masters and servants starts to reverse, the organised people in the councils have the possibility to reconstitute the polity and reassert the hierarchical relationship between the people and their institutions. As Bonnie Honig has also argued, by understanding the constitution as an unfinished project, the people is 'committing itself institutionally to continual world-building', such that 'this commitment to augmentation maintains a republic and its revolutionary spirit, by, in a curious sense, keeping its beginning always present' (1993: 112, 113).

In conclusion, by having constituted institutions of genuine political participation and self-government, which still have the power to constitute new organs and institutions, normal politics is infused with the creativity and freedom which are otherwise restricted to constitutional politics. As the republican concept of augmenting the foundation implies, normal politics, when conducted in institutions of self-government such as the councils, becomes a version of constitutional politics, because it is carried out in a manner similar to and with the spirit of the very foundation itself. It is thus possible, Arendt argues, that the revolutionary spirit can survive the revolutionary moment in a de-revolutionised form, if it is institutionalised in a way which mimics the revolution itself – meaning permanent institutions of self-government, deliberation and decision-making.

Conclusion

Arendt believed that the council system was an institutional expression of her political ideals of plurality (the council system's federalism), action (the council system's participatory character) and new beginnings (the council system's relation to the constituent power).

When discussing the Hungarian councils, I quoted the following evaluation by Arendt: 'The point is that the councils have always been undoubtedly democratic, but in a sense never seen before and never thought about', and as such, 'under modern conditions, the councils are the only democratic alternative we know' (1958a: 30). Now we can explicate this unseen democratic quality of the councils. The crucial significance of the council system is that it combines modes of politics which in their unmodified form are equally dangerous, namely total politicisation through a fully mobilised, homogenous people outside institutional and legal forms on the one hand, and, on the other hand, total depoliticisation with a lethargic population unable to participate in politics other than through periodic elections. Council democracy, Arendt speculated, could be conceptualised as a republican remedy to the depoliticising tendencies of liberal, normal politics, as well as to over-politicisation and the arbitrary elements of permanent revolution. The question of democratic politics, as seen through Arendt's council system, is not a politics without institutions or a politics that aims at finding fixed political forms with no need of augmentation, but instead a politics where the people are in control of their institutions; where they have the mechanisms to roll back institutions and to reconstitute them, when they begin to dominate and oppress. The council system, according to Arendt, is an example of such an institution because of its openness to participation and decision-making and because of the councils' retained power to constitute. Because the councils are both 'organs of order' and 'organs of action', they are able to keep the constituent moment alive. In short, the councils are 'spaces of de-alienation', because they provide the institutional means of combatting the becoming-independent of human creations.

Before turning to the book's last chapter, let us summarise the interpretive direction that council democracy has taken throughout the writings of Castoriadis, Lefort and Arendt. In their writings, the councils lose their status as predominantly belonging to the Marxist tradition, and instead of being primarily relevant for questions of capitalism, the emancipation of labour and organisation of the proletariat, the councils' primary importance for Castoriadis, Lefort and Arendt is related to the experiences with totalitarianism and to democracy as its counter-regime. By way of example: the political subject of 'the proletariat' is substituted by that of 'the people'; capitalism, parliamentarianism and the state, which were the key counter-concepts in early twentieth-century council theory, are mostly understood as examples of a larger process of separation between 'the people' and their creations – that is, the loss of constituent power. Revolution is understood not only as the break between specific modes of economic production, but also as the exercise of the human power to constitute. The discussions on the appropriate relations between the councils and the communist party become expressions of the conflict between disincarnated and incarnated models of power, between action and representation, and between autonomy and heteronomy. The relevance, hence, of the council system is transposed from the discourse of Marxism to the discourse of democracy.

As shown throughout the last three chapters, Castoriadis's, Lefort's and Arendt's interpretations of the councils engage directly with central questions of democratic theory, such as how 'the people' can govern, how the experience of freedom can be institutionalised, and how the excesses of popular self-rule can be countered. It is not so much that the language of Marxism becomes redundant, but instead that Castoriadis, Lefort and Arendt expand the questions that the councils can pose and the possible answers they can provide. The shift from Marxism to democracy can be formulated even more forcefully by accentuating another similarity between Castoriadis, Lefort and Arendt. They are all post-foundational thinkers, meaning that they understand politics to be a distinctively worldly practice whose principles ought not to be found in nature, religion or science. Although Castoriadis is the one who emphasises this aspect the most, they all agree that human beings themselves create their political institutions, hierarchies and principles. The evaluation of this self-creation of society or the people's constituent power obviously differs, but all three thinkers understand politics as a practice that cannot be domesticated by transcendental and extra-human figures of thought. Moreover, Castoriadis, Lefort and Arendt agree that a fundamental distinction can be drawn between forms of governments that recognise this fact of politics as post-foundational and forms of governments that do not. Consequently, for these thinkers, the advent of totalitarianism is a reaction to the lack of foundations in modern, democratic politics. Hence, totalitarianism seeks to institute heteronomy by concealing society's self-institution (Castoriadis); it establishes a non-debatable, absolute law (Arendt), and resurrects a figure which fully incarnates the place of power (Lefort). The reason for stressing this shared post-foundationalism is that as the relevance of the councils shifts from the Marxist discourse to the discourse of totalitarianism and democracy, the councils also become relevant for the question of the institution of society as such. This is because Castoriadis, Lefort and Arendt understand the relation between totalitarianism and democracy as hinging on the recognition of politics as an endeavour without absolutes. As the councils are born in revolution, and as revolution testifies to the human creation of new political forms, the councils are related to this fundamental activity of politics. In other words, they relate to the constituent power.

It is in the context of this relation between council democracy and constituent power that the three thinkers take markedly different routes. The chief difference between Castoriadis and Lefort, both in terms of their vision of council democracy, but also in their political theory writ large, could be designated as a distinction between a *strategy of reconstitution* and a *strategy of pluralisation*. In Castoriadis's strategy of reconstitution, the chief political danger stems from heteronomy; from the 'becoming-independent' of institutions in particular and human creations in general. The mode of countering this alienation is through the reconstitution of institutions, which in turn involves a re-experience of agency and freedom. Hence, the danger to politics stems from *forms* and *formalisation*, and the remedy available comes from the constituent power. In Lefort's strategy of pluralisation, in contrast, the chief political danger stems from the lack of division of power and from 'the people' as an undifferentiated and formless mass. The remedy is to pluralise the number of political claims within the polity, that is, within constituted politics.

The chief difference between these two different strategies is the role which the constituent power – the exceptional, the extraordinary, the emergency – plays. For Castoriadis, the constituent power is the source of renewal; for Lefort, the constituent power is a source of homogenous and incarnated forms of power. For Lefort, an allusion to the *extraordinary* refers to a revolutionary mode of politics whose excesses cannot be controlled, and which seeks to fully occupy the place of power. Although Lefort's strategy of pluralisation is viable to a certain extent, I contend that it has its limits. At a certain point, pluralisation must be replaced by partisanship and action; at a certain point, democratic politics must risk the inherent tragedy of acting and putting forward a positively formulated political project. At a certain point, the council system loses its politico-historical specificity if it is pluralised into too many opposing logics. Ultimately, the problem, in my reading of Lefort, is that his theory of democracy becomes too paralysing, moderate and defensive, as

the trace of totalitarianism disrupts the possibilities of transformatory political projects altogether.

As a way to break this impasse, I have reconstructed Arendt's
vision of council democracy as one which is equally critical of pure
constituent power and pure constituted power. As the formlessness
and arbitrariness often associated with constituent power has its
own dangers, the council system in Arendt's analysis is a way to
balance these features. On the one hand, in the face of inevitable
decay, alienation and ossification, Arendt imagined the council system as an institutional mechanism for continually re-countering
alienation and re-experiencing freedom. Council democracy, as
reconstructed in the political thought of Arendt, is a political form
which is able to reintroduce an element of constituent power into
itself by revitalising its own political structures. On the other hand,
in the face of permanent revolution, absolute beginnings and a constituent power in a state of nature, Arendt imagined the council
system as a stabilising mechanism, a housing structure, which could
check the fundamental arbitrariness of constituent power without
exhausting it. Arendt could thus be taken to provide the following,
meta-historical argument: in theocratic, authoritarian, monarchical
and totalitarian forms of government, the people in no way control the institutions that govern society. These institutions are truly
alien to them, separate from them and hence a dominating force.
With secularisation and the modern revolutions, the extra-human
absolutes which legitimate non-democratic forms of government
have, at least theoretically, vanished, and a new legitimating subject
has entered the scene: the people.

With her novel interpretation of council democracy, Arendt can
be understood as providing an answer to the question of how democratic forms of government can avoid the same fate as all forms of
governments before them, namely political alienation and domination. The answer is that such challenges cannot be eradicated fully,
but that the continual augmentation of the foundation – that is, the
combination of constituent power and political form – is needed in
order to continually reclaim control over the institutions brought
into the world by the constituent power of 'the many'.

Chapter 6
The Politics of Form
Council Democracy between Transformatory Politics and Political Form

Popular politics outside institutions, through spontaneous actions, occupations of public spaces and the creation of new, nascent institutions, often face the critique that it is too unruly, too uncontrollable, illegal, and even violent. Historically, this critique has been levelled time and time again against democracy.[1] To such critics, no laws or norms guide democratic action, and hence, it is an often-rehearsed move to associate democracy with anarchy, thus giving popular action the traits of a lawless state of exception. The same is true for many commentators on constituent power. By referring predominantly to the Sieyèsian–Schmittian version, constituent power is often criticised because of its affinities with the worst elements of sovereignty, namely its normative arbitrariness, its political subjectivity of homogeneity, its discretionary violence and its lawless groundlessness. In evaluations of council democracy in contemporary political theory, the Sieyèsian–Schmittian conception of constituent power is frequently mapped onto the council system by sympathetic and critical commentators alike. According to two of the former, Massimiliano Tomba and Artemy Magun, the councils are associated with a constituent power in complete contradiction to constituted politics. Hence, Magun argues, 'councils are an analogue to what Sieyès called "constituent power" – the *formless, pre-legal* sovereign democratic authority that precedes the constitution and the government and operates to create them' (2007: 69; emphasis added). According to Tomba, the soviet form 'expresses a kind of democratic *excess*, which democratic constitutionalism seeks to tame and put to sleep within the political *form*' (2017: 504; emphasis added). In short, they regard the councils as a formless, constituent power antithetical to political form – as a type of political action that is inherently unable to formalise and institutionalise itself.

Moreover, they position this power in opposition to constitutional-ism, thus reproducing the liberal understanding of a constitution as merely a constraining device. In short, they equate council democracy with Sieyèsian–Schmittian constituent power.

Critics of council democracy often proceed along similar lines. Habermas argues that 'the idea of council democracy . . . displayed only a minimal degree of institutionalisation', which means that council democracy 'was always utopian; today it is still less workable, given the regulatory and organizational needs of modern societies' (1996: 480–1). A form of council politics, Habermas contends, which is solely founded upon 'voluntary associations', is bound to never leave the state of nature and will be caught in 'the fluid condition of foundation' and is hence ultimately 'anarchistic' (1996: 480). Habermas thus argues that council democracy is trapped in a constituent moment, and that the idea that society can govern itself directly through processes of face-to-face deliberation is untenable for modern society.[2]

Martin Jay makes a similar evaluation of the councils in his article 'No Power to the Soviets' written in the aftermath of the 1989–90 revolutions, as he argues 'that the old reliance on workers' councils as the placeholder of redemption will no longer suffice . . . the soviets died in practice a long time ago; now they are likely to die in theory as well' (1990: 69). Jay's argument is that 'although the ideal of maximizing participatory involvement has by no means been abandoned, the necessity of some institutional framework mediating between rulers and the ruled is now widely accepted', and 'democratic theory' has 'moved beyond the sterile dichotomy of direct versus representative' democracy (1990: 67). The councils, it seems from the evaluations of both supporters and critics, are caught in the dynamics of constituent/constituted power, formlessness/political form and anarchy/sovereignty.

At the most fundamental level, these evaluations of council democracy take as their starting point a presumably clear-cut division between constituent power and political form. While I have argued in previous chapters that this is neither an accurate interpretation of the political thinking of Arendt and Castoriadis, for example,[3] nor of the historical councils or of most theories of council democracy developed in the interwar period, I want to formulate the argument differently in this chapter. It is one thing to 'rescue' council democracy from the category of the extraordinary, the exceptional and (Schmittian) constituting power by also highlighting its stabilising, formal and institutional features; it is a different, more productively formulated task to argue that from the council system itself an *alternative* understanding of constituent power can be developed, where constituting and institutionalisation, power and form, spontaneity and organisation, are not 'binary oppositions, non-negotiable and without overlap', as Bonnie Honig argues (1995: 144) in relation to Arendt's political thinking, but intertwined and combined in what I call a *council democratic constituent power*. It is hence not my ambition to argue that council democracy is not really associated with constituent power and revolutionary politics after all – that it is solely 'the form at last discovered' – but to argue that an *alternative* understanding of constituent power, where constituent politics and political form are combined instead of kept apart, can be developed through the historical experiences with council democracy and their theoretical interpretations.

As demonstrated throughout the book, the evaluation of the Russian soviets in the aftermath of the Russian Revolution often involved regarding them as *either* too formless to govern *or* as too formalised to express a genuine revolutionary will. Instead of trying to conclude this debate by associating the councils with *either* form *or* formlessness, interwar council communists such as Korsch and Pannekoek sought to think the councils from the intersection between political form and constituent power. Moreover, a similar argument is provided in Marcuse's evaluation of the councils as 'organized spontaneity', Castoriadis's interpretation of the councils as institutionalised spaces for society's self-institution, and Arendt's proclamation of the councils as 'organs of order as much as organs of action'. Therefore, the historical experiences with the councils, as well as their theoretical interpretations, often express the dual nature of council democracy: democracy as insurrection and as self-government.

This dual nature is the fundamental principle of council democracy, insofar as it bridges the clear-cut distinction between constituent and constituted politics which is the precondition for the survival of the constituent power after the moment of revolution. Council democracy hence provides an alternative understanding of the exception, extraordinary politics and constituent power compared with the dominant Sieyèsian–Schmittian conception of constituent power. In contrast to this conception, the experiences with council democracy disclose a notion of constituent power that involves *immanent principles*, a *plural constituting subject*, an *active conception of citizenship* and a *politicised public sphere*.

Such conceptualisation of the constituent power is important, because it reassesses our evaluation of popular politics outside, below and against established political structures. Moreover, council democratic constituent power, as I shall discuss in this chapter, also provides an important institutional corrective to much radical democratic theory. While radical democratic theories of constituent power do not fall into the Sieyèsian–Schmittian camp, as they are often developed as alternatives to its unitary and decisionistic notion of the people and its power, thinkers like Negri, Wolin and Rancière reproduce one of the central tenets of Sieyèsian–Schmittian constituent power, namely the antagonistic relation between constituent power and political form. By advancing a concept of democracy in contrast to any institutionalisable ideal, radical democrats stress the inevitably inegalitarian form of social organisation that institutions seem to require. For radical democrats, it is not only the question of exchanging an inegalitarian, oppressive form of government or constituted order for another, more egalitarian and free form of government. Instead, by pointing to the intimate relation between constituent power and democracy, radical democrats are able to differentiate between *any* institutionalised version of democracy and the democratic ideal of popular self-government itself. The problematic consequence of associating (radical) democracy with this specific understanding of constituent power, that is, the antagonistic relation between constituent power and political form, is that democracy itself becomes momentary, unable to ever institutionalise itself.

While council democracy shares with radical democracy the critique of the impoverished understanding of democracy within liberalism, as well as the critique of the decisionistic, unitary subject in Sieyèsian–Schmittian constituent power, council democracy proposes a historically grounded way to bridge the antagonistic gap between constituent power and political form entailed in many theories of radical democracy. The aim, hence, is to contribute to radical democratic theory by providing a way to understand political institutions apart from domination, representation, discipline and elitism. In short, what does it mean for institutions to be radically democratic? Council democratic constituent power, I argue, expresses how contestation and struggle against established institutions can carry within itself immanent principles of legitimacy and nascent forms of legality.

'A nation never leaves the state of nature': The Sieyèsian–Schmittian Concept of Constituent Power

As the concept of council democratic constituent power is developed in opposition to the Sieyèsian–Schmittian concept of constituent power, this section briefly introduces the latter conceptualisation. With their theories of constituent power, Sieyès and Schmitt seek to theorise the relation between the people and its constitution. Sieyès's original formulation of constituent power is meant to discredit monarchical power in the initial phase of the French Revolution by arguing that the Crown is merely a *constituted* office subject to will of the *constituent* power of the nation. Schmitt's ambition, by contrast, was to show that liberal constitutionalism in general, and the German Weimar Constitution in particular, is unable to understand the political nature of the decision on the constitutional form, which leads to continuing crisis and instability. Despite the 150 years between the two interpreters of constituent power, their theories are remarkably similar.

As argued by Loughlin, 'Sieyès clearly explains the logic of the concept of constituent power as it has been received by the modern discourse' (2010: 225). In the famous pamphlet 'What is the Third Estate?', which was one of the many singular sparks that torched the revolutionary flame in Paris in 1789, Sieyès describes the constituent power of the people as above constituted politics, as 'the nation exists prior to everything; it is the origin of everything. Its will is always legal. It is law itself' (2003: 136). Sieyès uses a famous metaphor of political thought to describe the formlessness of the constituent power, as it 'never leaves the state of nature', because it 'is independent of all forms . . . it is the source and supreme master of all positive laws' (2003: 138). The act of constituting is both temporally prior to and politically superior to all constituted political forms. 'It would be ridiculous', Sieyès argues, 'to suppose that the nation itself was bound by the formalities or the constitution to which it had subjected those it mandated' (2003: 136). Therefore, the constituent power cannot alienate its power to constituted authorities, 'but even if it could', Sieyès contends, 'a nation *should* not subject itself to the restrictions of positive form. To do so would expose it to the irretrievable loss of its liberty' (2003: 137; original emphasis). Constituent power as ultimate liberty, hence, is completely unbound by laws, norms and political forms. Although it is hugely influential, commentators on Sieyèsian constituent power regularly point to its paradoxical nature. While constituent power is the highest power of the polity and designates the people's power to freely create their own constitutional forms, constituent power exists only outside the polity in which it cannot appear. Although constituent power is the foundation of legality, it cannot coexist with law (Loughlin 2003: 100; Del Lucchese 2016: 182). Moreover, constituent power is enacted in the name of the people, although the legitimate subject of this power comes only after the very act of constituting (Derrida 1986). Constituent power, then, while it is the source of constitutional forms, procedural norms and positive law, is itself formless, normless and lawless. Despite constituent power being the ultimate foundation for ordinary, normal politics, it is itself an exceptional, extraordinary power.

By building on Sieyès's original theory, Schmitt was able to tie constituent power together with discussions on decisionism, the state of exception and dictatorship in a way that radicalised the Sieyèsian formulation. Schmitt is an exponent of legal decisionism, suggesting that the legitimacy of the constitution does not originate in formal processes, rational deliberation or from legal substance, but originates from the concrete decision taken by the sovereign. The legal order does not guide the decision; the decision, on the contrary, institutes the legal order. 'There exists no norm that is applicable to chaos', Schmitt argues; 'for a legal order to make sense, a normal situation must exist, and he is sovereign who definitively decides whether this normal situation actually exists' (1985: 13). Schmitt's understanding of sovereignty relates to his concept of constituent power via the two different notions of dictatorship that he developed in *Dictatorship*: commissarial dictatorship and sovereign dictatorship ([1921] 2014: 1–13, 111–31).

Commissarial dictatorship, theorised firstly by the Romans, has the limited task of restoring order to the polity in times of crisis. It is a constituted power established by a higher authority with a definite aim. In situations of emergency, the commissarial dictator operates outside the laws of the polity and cannot be held accountable for his actions, as long as he does not violate the mandate he has been given. The commissarial dictator, hence, suspends the constitution in order to defend it. But he cannot change or abolish the constitution; this is only the right of the true sovereign. The sovereign dictator, instead, has the object not of restoring the established order, but of creating a novel political order by drafting a new constitution (Schmitt [1921]

2014: 119). The sovereign dictator is hence a *constituent* power and is as such not limited by any laws, has no mandate and no time frame.

The purpose of the sovereign dictator is to make a concrete decision on the political form of the polity. As a constituent power, 'the sovereign decision is an absolute beginning, and the beginning is nothing else than a sovereign decision. It springs out of a normative nothingness and from a concrete disorder' (Schmitt qtd in Kalyvas 2004: 323). As such, 'while the commissarial dictatorship is authorized by a constituted organ and has an identity in the existing constitution, sovereign dictatorship exists only *quoad exercitium* [in relation to what it does], and it derives directly from the amorphous *pouvoir constituant*' (Schmitt [1921] 2014: 127). This suggests that Schmitt's constituent power, like the Sieyèsian version, ought to be understood from the position of exceptionality. In *Constitutional Theory*, Schmitt defines constituent power as 'the political will, whose power or authority is capable of making the concrete, comprehensive decision over the type and form of its own political existence' ([1928] 2008: 125). The sovereign dictator as a constituent power is thus visible only in moments of revolution, crisis and founding. Consequently, the subject that emerges in such exceptional times *must be* a sovereign dictator regardless of whether this constituent subject is a monarch, an aristocratic body or the people. 'In a very general sense, any exception from a condition conceived of as normal can be called a dictatorship', Schmitt revealingly argues ([1921] 2014: 128). From the French Revolution onwards, the constituent power has been in the hands of the people, according to Schmitt ([1928] 2008: 126–30), meaning that every new constitution is implicitly the will of the people – at least through their tacit consent or lack of revolt.

Schematically, we can identify the traits of Schmitt's constituent power as the following: firstly, the constituent power is prior to legality, and as such it is the normless and extra-legal source of all norms and legality. Secondly, and consequently, the constituent power 'cannot be a regulated procedure, through which the activity of the constitution-making power would be bound' (Schmitt [1928] 2008: 130). No rules assist the people as a constituting subject because if it were assisted by rules, the people would merely be a constituted entity. In the language developed throughout the book, Schmitt's constituent power is antithetical to form, as the constituting subject 'can change its forms and give itself continually new forms of political existence. It has the complete freedom of political self-determination. It can be the *"formless formative capacity"'* (Schmitt [1928] 2008: 129; emphasis added). Thirdly, it is necessary to stress the fundamental abyssal character of Schmitt's constituent power and hence the complete lawlessness of this type of politics. This is expressed in a powerful paragraph from *Dictatorship*:

> The theory of the *pouvoir constituant* is incomprehensible simply as a form of mechanistic rationalism. The people, the nation, the primordial force of any state – these always constitute new organs. From the infinite, incomprehensible abyss of the force [*Macht*] of the *pouvoir constituant*, new forms emerge incessantly, which it can destroy at any time and in which its power is never limited for good. It can will arbitrarily. The content of its willing has always the same legal value like the content of a constitutional definition. Therefore it can intervene arbitrarily. (Schmitt [1921] 2014: 123)

By combining elements of Rousseau and Sieyès, Schmitt gives the constituent power three classical traits of sovereignty: it is indivisible, unrepresentable and non-transferable. The subject of Schmittian constituent power, 'the People', is hence a homogenous subject without internal differences. Moreover, it is a subject that cannot deliberate, but only will. Hence, Schmitt argues, 'the natural form of the direct expression of a people's will is the assembled multitude's declaration of their consent or their disapproval, the *acclamation*' ([1928] 2008: 131; original emphasis). Although the people is the origin of all constituted organs, it can never act itself, but is reduced by Schmitt to a brute force only capable of expressing itself through acclamation. This means that the constituting people can act and speak only through personalistic representation by a leader, a president, a *Führer* – a sovereign dictator, in short (Raimondi 2016). To be a citizen of Schmitt's constituent politics is hence to be a part of a mass subject, a shouting mob, an unlimited force that can express itself only in an oversimplified affirmation or rejection, pleasure or pain. The public sphere of Schmittian constituent power is one of public visibility, in which the people are gathered together without any other means of articulation than acclamation in the plebiscite (Körösenyi 2005).

Hence, Schmitt operates with a clear-cut distinction between exceptional and normal politics, constituent power and political form. Furthermore, normal politics is always subordinated to constituent politics, as the constituting people 'expresses itself in continually new forms, producing from itself these ever renewing forms and organizations. It does so, however, without ever subordinating itself, its political existence, to a conclusive formation' (Schmitt [1928] 2008: 128). It is *this specific* conceptualisation of constituent power which I argue council democracy takes issue with and transcends. If this were indeed the only way to understand constituent power, the critics would be right to point out the dangers inherent in the concept. Moreover, these traits of lawlessness, anti-institutionalism and normlessness are levelled not only against constituent power, but often against democracy itself. Therefore, the ambition of developing an alternative conception of constituent power through the historical experiences with council democracy and its theoretical interpretations is thus also an attempt to address the claim that democratic politics is deprived of norms, legality and political forms. To stipulate the stakes involved in such a task, it can be argued that equating democracy with lawlessness is foundational for Western political thinking, as this critique originally emerged with the ancient critics of Athenian democracy, Plato and Aristotle. I revisit their critique of democracy from the perspective of constituent power in the following section.

Is Democracy a Constitutional Form?

The fact that the council system both historically and theoretically can be interpreted through notions of form and formlessness, constituent power and constitutional order, relates it to one of the oldest questions of the Western political tradition, namely the question of political forms and democracy. The theory of political forms originates in classical times, where, most famously, Plato and Aristotle developed a classification of constitutions depending on their mode of ruling and the subject of ruling. These classifications gave rise to three good forms of government – monarchy, aristocracy and *politeia* – and three vicious forms – tyranny, oligarchy and democracy. Such typologies express the conviction that politics naturally falls into pre-established forms which seek to realise certain values. There is no politics excessive to these forms, according to such thinking, as all modes of political existence must be classified according to these forms. Formlessness, in short, is not a feature of political life.

Confusion surrounds the constitutional form of democracy, however. According to Aristotle, the concrete expression of democracy's principles of liberty and equality is to rule and be ruled in turn – that is, rotation and lottery. For such a system to function, it requires institutionalisation (Aristotle 1958: 1317b1–5, 258). Plato also counts liberty and equality as the primary principles of democracy and mentions how this form of government rests on 'equal rights and opportunities of office' and 'appointment to office being as a rule by lot' (Plato 1955: 557a–b, 292). Again, such equal rights to office require formal procedures to be established. Hence, the democratic constitution has, just like any other constitution, a set of institutions and procedures which secure the realisation of its principles. This is, however, where the confusion begins. When Aristotle (1958: 1292a24, 168) discusses the existing democracies in the ancient world, he differentiates between five forms of democracy, gradually more inclusive and to a lesser extent governed by law. While the first four forms are governed by law, in the fifth form, 'the people, not the law, is the final sovereign' (Aristotle 1958: 1292a24, 168). When the people are sovereign, according to Aristotle, the authority of the magistrates is destabilised, demagogues have free play, and the polis is governed by decrees. We have, in other words, encountered a conceptual slippage from democracy as a constitutional form to democracy as beyond constitutional form. Aristotle concludes

> that a democracy of this type is not a true constitution. Laws should be sovereign on every issue, and the magistrates and the citizen body should only decide about detail. The conclusion, which emerges, is clear. Democracy *may* be a form of constitution; but this particular system, under which everything is managed merely by decrees, is not even a democracy, in any real sense of the word. (Aristotle 1958: 1292a30–1, 169; emphasis added)

Democracy *may* be a form of constitution, and it *may* not. It depends on whether it is governed by positive law. In the classical typology, though, the vicious political constitutions – tyranny, oligarchy and democracy – are precisely characterised by the fact that they are *not* governed by law. But now Aristotle argues that if democracy is not governed by law, and the people is sovereign, democracy ceases to be a political form at all and so forfeits its very status as a constitution. Consequently, there is something qualitatively different with the lawless rule of the many (democracy), which does not characterise the lawless rule of the few or the one (oligarchy and tyranny). Oligarchy and tyranny, although not governed by law, still operate with a structure of rule, insofar as the few or the one rules the many.

But in a democracy, Aristotle suggests, if there is no law, neither is there a structure of rule, as everyone does as he pleases. Hence, democracy becomes intrinsically related to anarchy. This suggests that the sovereignty of the people needs to be domesticated by law in order to become a constitutional form at all. Popular power needs to be tamed by form, otherwise 'it grows despotic; flatterers come to be held in honour; it becomes analogous to the tyrannical form of single-person government' (Aristotle 1958: 1292a27, 168). Put crudely, democracy as a constitutional form *does not exist*: either the rule of the many is constitutionalised in a *politeia* – government of the many by law – or it is pure anarchy.

Plato also vividly describes democracy as the complete ignorance of form. In a democracy, 'everything is full of the spirit of liberty' (1955: 563d, 300), as 'the teacher fears and panders to his pupils . . . the young as a whole imitate the elders, argue with them and set themselves up against them' (1955: 563a, 300); the 'father and son change places, the father standing in awe of his son, and the son neither respecting nor fearing his parents, in order to assert what he calls his independence' (Plato 1955: 562e, 299–300). In addition, there is 'no distinction between citizen, alien and foreigner' (Plato 1955: 563a, 300). The hierarchies that make society governable are absent in a democracy. Because of its 'excessive desire for liberty', democracy is an *'anarchic* form of society, with plenty of variety, which treats men as equal, whether they are equal or not' (Plato 1955: 562c, 299; 558c, 294; emphasis added). 'In a democracy', Plato argues in conclusion,

> there's no compulsion either to exercise authority if you are capable, or to submit to authority if you don't want to; you needn't fight if there's a war, or you can wage a private war in peacetime if you don't like peace; and if there's any law that debars you from political or judicial office, you will none the less take either if they come your way. (Plato 1955: 558a, 293)

Democracy, it would seem, respects no authority; it is volatile and unstable and cannot be embodied in a form, as it exceeds formalisation due to its 'excessive desire for freedom'. Despite the ambition of classifying all political regimes through the six-fold classification, democracy is not a constitutional form after all, according to Plato and Aristotle, because democratic life itself is antithetical to form. This might be why we seldom speak of democracy as such, but instead of *representative* democracy, *liberal* democracy, *constitutional* democracy, *elite* democracy or *minimalist* democracy, as if democracy can exist only if another force domesticates its formlessness into a stable form and dominates its excessive desire for freedom with the rigidity of a constitution. In other words, critics of popular action regard the formalisation of democracy as necessary in order for anarchy not to emerge, and they equate democracy exclusively with *constituted* politics – that is, politics *in* already established institutions.

Radical Democracy: Upholding the Antagonism between Constituent Power and Political Form

Many radical democrats accept the critique of democracy as anarchical, turn the argument on its head, and make the constituent power pivotal for their theories of democracy. Distinctions like those between constituent and constituted power, democratic constitutionalism and constitutional democracy, and politics and police (Negri 1999: 1–35; Wolin 1994: 39; Rancière 2010: 36–7) aim in different ways to wrest free the democratic ideal from its present liberal institutionalisation. By pointing to the intimate relation between constituent power and democracy, radical democrats are able to differentiate between the institutional set-up of contemporary representative democracy and the democratic ideal of popular self-government itself. To be involved in self-government, these thinkers argue, much like Castoriadis and Arendt, is to participate in *constituting* the forms of political life, not only participating in them as already *constituted*. Representative democracy and postwar liberal constitutionalism have effectively sealed off the possibility of popular constitutional reformulation, which creates the need, radical democrats argue, for a new understanding of democracy modelled on the constituent power and its extralegal legitimacy and extraconstitutional freedom. For radical democrats, it is a question not only of exchanging one constituted order for another, more democratic one, but also of realising that every institutionalised form of politics inevitably requires a division between governors and governed, thereby accepting the so-called 'iron law of oligarchy'. It is for this reason that democracy appears to be 'fugitive' to Wolin or 'an-archic' in Rancière's view. Moreover, although radical democrats make constituent power central to their political interventions, they do not simply replicate the Sieyèsian–Schmittian conception. In fact, these thinkers at times come close to conceptualising constituent power in a way that is compatible with the council democratic constituent power I develop below, and hence in conflict with the Sieyèsian–Schmittian conception. Negri, for example, does not understand constituent power in terms of a homogenous subject, pre-political citizenship and a depoliticised, non-dialogic public sphere like the Schmittian version, but as the creation of plural forms of subjectivity (the multitude), participatory practices (action) and politicised public spaces (the commons).

But some radical democrats do agree with the Sieyèsian–Schmittian understanding of constituent power in one key aspect, namely on the antagonistic distinction between constituent power and constituted power. Negri, for example, conceptualises the relation between constituent and constituted power as parasitic (1999: 229). Rancière understands 'the part that has no part' as the genuine subject of democratic agency; that is, democratic agency can only be practised in relation to the transformation of an already established (police) order (2010: 33). Wolin, as I shall discuss below, posits an absolute gap between democracy and political form and subscribes to an understanding of institutional politics as apathetic, limited and elitist.

With this in mind, the aim of the remainder of the chapter is to develop a concept of *council democratic constituent power*, which is not to be understood as a sweeping critique of radical democrats and their understanding of constituent power, because council democracy shares many normative convictions with radical democracy. Instead, my ambition is to develop an institutional approximation of the principles of radical democracy, namely to provide a historically grounded way to bridge the gap between theories of radical democracy and institutional politics. In short, the aim is to answer the question: what does it mean for institutions to be radically democratic? The very possibility of asking this question is precluded when radical democrats advance their theories of democracy through the clear-cut distinction between constituent power and political form, as democracy and institutionalisation invariably fall on either side of the distinction.

Whereas critics of democracy – ancient and modern – have stressed the excessive nature of popular rule, radical democrats shift the evaluation of democratic power as formless, that is, as constituent power, from a negative to a positive register. Whereas liberals regard the formalisation of democracy as necessary for avoiding anarchy, radical democrats regard institutionalisation as the death of the constituent capabilities of the *demos*. Whereas thinkers of political forms make democracy exclusively equal to *constituted* politics, radical democrats equate democracy purely with *constituent* politics. The very distinction between constituent power and political form breaks down in council democracy, as the councils in the twentieth century disclose a mode of politics with equal attention to the freedom to act anew (constituent power) and the care for stability (political form), thereby aiming to preserve the democratic order through its continual self-transformation.[4] In order to explicate the need to go beyond the distinction between constituent and constituted power, and the consequent disregard for institutions inherent in many theories of radical democracy, I discuss below one influential exponent of the radical democratic disregard for institutional politics and the understanding of democracy solely through the constituent power. Sheldon Wolin's formulations provide an illustrative vantage point for my argument that council democracy can productively be interpreted as a way to combine constituent power and political form instead of keeping them conceptually and politically apart.

At the end of *Politics and Vision*, Wolin states that 'as a starting-point it is necessary to reject the classical and modern conception that ascribes to democracy "a" proper or settled form' (2004: 601). To Wolin, 'the democracy we are familiar with is a constitutionalized democracy, democracy indistinguishable from its constitutional form', and such political *form*alism 'seeks to repress democracy' (1996: 36). This conception of the relation between democracy and form has characterised 'virtually all canonical political theorists from Plato to Jean Bodin', and 'the impression left by these accounts was of a natural incompatibility, lack of proper fit between democracy and the sort of law-defined, institutionally constrained political structure represented by a constitution' (Wolin 1994: 31). Therefore, Wolin accepts the critique that democracy is formless, but instead of lamenting the transgressive nature of popular power, Wolin makes it the *sine qua non* of democracy. This redefinition provides Wolin with a programmatic characterisation of democracy:

> Democracy is not primarily a set of institutions . . . Democracy permits all manner of dress, behavior, and belief: it is in*formal*, indifferent to *form*alities . . . Thus democracy is wayward, inchoate, unable to rule. It does not naturally con*form*. It is inherently formless. (Wolin 1994: 50; original emphasis)

This formulation does have affinities with Schmitt's notion of constituent power as a 'formless formative capacity', which in turn has several conceptual consequences. Firstly, for Wolin and other radical democrats, the institutionalisation of democracy equals bureaucratisation and domestication. Democracy cannot be equated with any kind of normal politics, hence becoming an exceptional experience – 'revolutionary and excessive, irregular and spasmodic' (Wolin 1994: 48). The momentary character of democratic politics, essentially, makes it a 'bitter experience, doomed to succeed only temporarily' (Wolin 1996: 43). Secondly, 'democracy needs to be reconceived as something other than a form of government'; it instead becomes 'a political moment, perhaps *the* political moment . . . democracy is a rebellious moment' (Wolin 1996: 43; original emphasis). As such, democracy is in sharp opposition to any kind of normal politics.

Although I will not go into detail with Negri and Rancière, both uphold the distinction between constituent power and political form and the consequent disregard for institutional politics. Rancière, much like Wolin, interprets democracy as a form of constituent politics insofar as 'democracy is not a political regime in the sense that it forms one of possible constitutions which define the ways in which people assemble under a common authority. Democracy is the very institution of politics itself' (2010: 32). For Negri, 'constituent power resists being constitutionalized', because 'the paradigm of constituent power is that of a force that bursts apart, breaks, interrupts, unhinges any preexisting equilibrium and any possible continuity' (1999: 1, 11). Ultimately, by associating democracy solely with constituent power, Wolin and other radical democrats reproduce something akin to the Hobbesian conception of political life that envisions politics as occurring *only* in two distinct modes: either absolute sovereignty or absolute anarchy. In the former conception, politics is inextricably linked to regularity, obedience and alienation; in the latter conception, politics is indistinguishable from anarchy, creation and excess. There is 'no continuity', as expressed by Negri. Consequently, radical democrats like Wolin, Negri and Rancière reproduce a central tenet of Schmitt's constituent power, namely the unbridgeable gap between constituent power and political form. The argument I will pursue below is that the historical practices of workers' councils, instead, can be interpreted as a combining constituent power and political form with the aim of preserving the constituent power of the revolutionary moment in ordinary politics. I do not regard council democracy as a fundamental critique of radical democracy, therefore, but as strengthening one of its main weaknesses by going beyond the terms of its own discourse – namely by developing a notion of constituent power that does not rest on a fundamental antagonism to institutionalisation.

Council Democratic Constituent Power

'The way the beginner starts whatever he intends to do', Arendt proclaims, 'lays down the law of action for those who have joined him in order to partake in the enterprise and bring about its accomplishment' ([1963] 2006: 205). This book has analysed the 'new beginnings' of workers' councils in the twentieth century and the emerging political form of council democracy. The basic feature of these experiences and interpretations of the councils is, I have argued, the conviction that the councils were both *organs of insurrection* and *organs of self-government*. This is absolutely central. This duality is apparent in Anweiler's (1974: 4) basic characteristics of the councils, as organs with a revolutionary origin, but also as organs of self-government. It is captured by Pannekoek's statement that 'the workers' councils growing up as organs of fight will at the same time be organs of reconstruction' (2003: 51), by Korsch's (1929) interpretation of Marx's Commune as oscillating between form and formlessness, by Marcuse's idea of the councils as 'organized spontaneity' (2005: 126) and by Arendt's proclamation of the councils as 'organs of order as much as organs of action' ([1963] 2006: 255). Every time a historical actor or a political thinker has articulated the councils as *embryos*, *germs*, *nucleuses* or *harbingers* prefiguring a future society, they have implicitly alluded to this dual character of council democracy as a practice of insurrection and as a form of self-government. It is from this dual character that a distinct council democratic conceptualisation of constituent power, in contrast to the Sieyèsian–Schmittian and the radical democratic versions, can be theorised.

As argued, a crucial feature of Sieyèsian–Schmittian constituent power is its normative groundlessness. Consequently, when democracy becomes associated with this version of constituent power, which is the case for both Schmitt and some contemporary radical democrats, democracy itself becomes a formless, normless and lawless regime – or simply no regime at all, as Plato and Aristotle argued. In contrast, council democratic constituent power is also beyond law, as it is the origin of a new regime, but it is not deprived of norms,

forms or institutions. There are, instead, *immanent* principles in council democratic constituent power, as there already in the moment of
foundation are forms and principles that guide action. What are these
immanent principles that save the act of founding council democracy
from its own arbitrariness? When discussing Athenian democracy,
Wolin notes how 'rotation and lot both function to limit effects of
institutionalization: they are, paradoxically, *institutions that subvert institutionalization*' (1994: 43; emphasis added). Democracy, in
this formulation, incorporates institutions – namely institutions that
subvert formalisation, ossification and alienation. Or reformulated:
democracy has its own political forms, which undermine formalisation; democratic forms institutionalise constituent power without
exhausting it. The fundamental principle I detect from the duality of
the councils as organs of insurrection and organs of self-government
is the mutual intertwinement of constituent power and constituted
form; the continuation of extraordinary politics in a de-revolutionised form during ordinary times. Consequently, the councils continually had the ambition of establishing themselves as self-ruling organs
without a bureaucratic stratum in times of crisis; they continually
developed institutional mechanisms for combatting alienation and
hierarchy such as imperative mandate and instant recall during normal politics; and they sought to expand the council movement by
multiplying the formation of councils in all spheres of society. Moreover, the councils continually sought to differentiate themselves from
hierarchical institutions such as liberal parliamentarianism and party
communism. In order to actualise this principle of stabilising the constituent after the revolution without repressing it, I argue that council
democracy expresses a distinct understanding of *political subjectivity*, *citizenship* and *the public sphere*, which clearly differentiates it
from Schmittian constituent power.

The Political Subjectivity of Council Democracy

The experiences with council democracy disclose a new kind of
political subjectivity, which is both plural and concrete instead of
homogenous and essentialist. In Schmitt's constituent power, the
people is unitary, homogenous and abstract, hence it can be represented by the One: the dictator, the leader, the president. In the
case of Schmitt's commissarial exception, internal conflict cannot
be allowed, and order must be restored at all costs because of the
fundamental unity of the people. The subject – or *subjects*, to be

precise – of council democracy is instead plural and concrete. The Russian soviets were stratified into workers', peasants' and soldiers' councils, and hence did not operate through the fictional membership of 'the people', but through the concrete functions of society. In the first article of the Soviet Constitution of 1918,[5] these plural and concrete bodies are made the foundation of the Russian Soviet Federated Socialist Republic insofar as 'Russia is declared to be a republic of the Soviets of Workers', Soldiers', and Peasants' Deputies' (Constitution of the Russian Soviet Federated Socialist Republic 1918: Article 1).

Arendt also notes the plural and concrete character of the subjects of council democracy, as the first observation she makes, after she concludes that the experiences in Russia 1917 and in Hungary 1956 'show in bare outlines what a government would look like and how a republic was likely to function if they were founded upon the principles of the councils' ([1963] 2006: 258), is that the revolutions were made up of 'the most disparate kinds of councils', of 'disparate groups' of 'neighbourhood councils . . . in all residential districts', 'revolutionary councils that grew out of fighting in the streets', 'councils of writers and artists, born in the coffee houses', 'students and youths' councils at the universities', 'workers' councils in the factories, councils in the army, among civil servants, and so on' ([1963] 2006: 258–9). In all cases Arendt describes the specificity of 'the disparate' milieu of the various councils – living side by side in the same residential districts, fighting together in the streets, born in discussions at the coffee houses, at the universities, in the army and so on. As these concrete sites of struggle produce different experiences, Arendt overcomes the temptation of speaking about 'the people' as the driving force of the councils, but instead she continually emphasises the concrete and plural character of their political subjectivity. This is another way to elucidate how council democratic constituent power does not revert to a state of nature like the Sieyèsian–Schmittian version. It is simply not the case that there exist no institutions in the revolutions initiated by the councils. By integrating the concrete and plural groups of the revolution into the constitution as the foundation of public authority, as done in the Soviet Constitution of 1918, council democracy does not function via dichotomies of individual/sovereign, lawlessness/sovereignty and formlessness/form.

Moreover, it is through this understanding of political subjectivity that imperative mandate and instant recall, and their differences to parliamentarianism, can be reassessed. If the political subject is one and indivisible, it can only will one thing, hence a single assembly can represent the interests of the people (Hobbes 1994: 146; Schmitt [1928] 2008: 242–7). If the political subject is indivisible, it can shout in singular voice through acclamation in the plebiscite. By contrast, if the political subject is plural and concrete, institutional forms are needed to maintain this plurality and concreteness. Such a subject needs multiple arenas for deliberation and decision-making because it is itself multifarious. Through mandate and recall, the 'disparate' groups that comprise the plural subject stay in existence 'as disparate'. Mandate and recall are hence institutional mechanisms applied to avoid unification by insisting that the concrete and different milieus that constituted the different councils stay concrete and different. Imperative mandate is a way to ensure that the spontaneous organs of the revolution live on in ordinary politics because they retain the power to call back and reinstruct their delegates. It is, as Wolin aptly phrased it, an institution that subverts institutionalisation. The mechanisms of mandate and recall consequently disclose a continuity between insurgent practices and constituted politics – that is, continuity between constituent power and political form, which I have argued is the basic principle of council democracy. It is thus the ambition of the councils to uphold their concrete and plural character beyond the moment of foundation and make this political subjectivity the foundation of constituted public authority.

Council Democratic Citizenship

Council democratic citizenship is entirely different from being a citizen in Schmitt's commissarial or sovereign exception. Whereas the citizen of the Schmittian exceptions is a pre-political entity of national or ethnic standing or an abstract, juridical subject, council democratic citizenship is performatively created through action. To be a citizen, in short, is to participate in a council; hence, the dynamic of inclusion/exclusion is defined in terms of action, not in terms of birth or ethnicity. Therefore, a citizen in council democracy is not defined in terms of being – what the citizen 'is' – but in terms of action – what the citizen 'does'. As a form of action, citizenship is understood as a form of participation that contests the established order, while simultaneously attempting to constitute new political forms. In the words of Castoriadis, in council democracy 'all sections of the nation abandon their passivity and conformity to the old order, all strive to take an active part in its destruction and in the shaping of the new order' (1993a: 254). Council democratic citizenship is hence not a juridical category granted from above by the state or achieved through a primordial contract before politics, but a political category enacted from below through the council system. Consequently, citizenship is not formulated in the modality of *ruling* like the Aristotelian conception – a citizen is one who rules and is ruled in turn – or the modality of *electing* as in parliamentary democracy. Neither is it formulated in the modality of *passivity* as in the commissarial exception, nor in the modality of *acclamation* as in plebiscitary democracy. Instead, citizenship is defined in the modality of *acting* and *constituting*. Consequently, the councils retrieve the original meaning of citizenship as taking active part in the political life of the city, as in council democracy 'individuals become actively interested in public affairs as if these were their own personal affairs – and *this is indeed what they actually are*' (Castoriadis 1993a: 261; original emphasis).

Active citizenship is manifested in times of extraordinary politics, as political differences and existing norms become the object of conflict. But it is not equal to pure transgression. Entailed in active citizenship is a way of caring for the continuation of this mode of action and the necessary institutional means for such continuation. Council democracy thus runs counter to the two images of 'the people' in Schmittian constituent power. Here, 'the people' is either passive and obedient, as the temporary state of emergency requires a tranquil public so as to restore order (commissarial exception), or it acts arbitrarily as a founding, homogenous entity (sovereign exception). The active citizenship of the councils proposes an active performance, but not a mob-like transgression. It is instead a practice of 'organized spontaneity', as Marcuse called it. Just as the conception of political subjectivity discloses a continuity between constituent power and political form, so does council democratic citizenship. Citizenship as performative action emerges in moments of rebellion, but as the Soviet Constitution of 1918, for example, suggests, participation in the councils is also the precondition for citizenship during normal politics. The citizen comes into being not by being born into a homogenous subject or through a hypothetical contract in a fictitious state of nature, but through concrete action in the public space.

The Public Sphere of Council Democracy

The varying conceptions of the public sphere are another parameter of difference between Schmittian constituent power and council democratic constituent power. In his discussion of the Hungarian councils, Castoriadis provides the following description of the revolutionary situation in Russia in 1917 and in Hungary in 1956:

> The revolution is the state of overheating and fusion of society, accompanied by the general mobilization of all categories and strata and the breaking up of all established barriers. It is this character that makes understandable the extraordinary liberation and multiplication of the creative potential of society during revolutionary periods, the breaking up of the repetitious cycles of social life, the sudden *opening* of history. (Castoriadis 1993a: 254; original emphasis)

Whereas the public sphere of Schmitt's commissarial exception is characterised by depoliticisation, the public sphere of council democracy amounts to a politicisation of society and its *opening* up to self-transformation and conflict. In the Roman Republic, where the concept of commissarial dictatorship originates, it was forbidden to assemble in the squares once a dictator was appointed (Tuori 2016). In the states of emergency of modern constitutional regimes, political rights are limited as long as a threat is challenging the polity. Hence, the public sphere is nullified and a personalistic form of power with royal prerogatives is revived. By contrast, the politicisation of the public sphere is intensified in council democracy, which amounts to the principle that in moments of crisis, it is the citizens themselves who solve the problems of society – not an appointed, constituted officer like the commissarial dictator. Consequently, the public sphere of council democracy is truly public, insofar as it becomes open for the citizenry as a space of contestation and deliberation of issues of shared interest and common concern.

In relation to the public sphere, it can again be argued that a continuity between constituent power and political form exists in council democracy. In modern liberal-constitutional regimes, the bill of rights is formulated as individual rights and without describing the further material conditions for exercising such rights. As Tomba aptly suggests, a council democratic public sphere is formulated in 'the grammar of freedom' and not in the grammar of rights (2017: 506). Articles 13–17 of the 1918 Soviet Constitution list the freedom of conscience, expression, assembly, association and access to knowledge, and each article specifies the material conditions for exercising these freedoms. Hence, the local soviet is constitutionally responsible for offering to 'the working class and to the poorest peasantry furnished halls, and takes care of their heating and lighting appliances' (Constitution of the Russian Soviet Federated Socialist Republic 1918: Article 15), that is, freedom of assembly; the soviets hand 'over to the working people and the poorest peasantry all technical and material means for the publication of newspapers, pamphlets, books, etc., and guarantees their free circulation throughout the country' (Article 14), that is, freedom of expression; and the soviets 'abolished all obstacles which interfered with the freedom of organization and action of the workers and peasants, offers assistance, material and other, to the workers and the poorest peasantry in their effort to unite and organize' (Article 16), that is, freedom of association. This 'grammar of freedom' enables a deliberate recreation of a public sphere during *ordinary* politics that resembles the public sphere of *extraordinary* politics to a considerable degree. By constitutionally providing the material and concrete means for participation in public life, the councils themselves seek to preserve the constituent power in constituted form.

Conclusion

Together these council democratic conceptualisations of political subjectivity, citizenship and the public sphere amount to a relation of continuity between constituent power and political form, which discloses the ambition of institutionalising the constituent power in ordinary politics after the moment of foundation. Hence, the constituent power exercised in the council system is not formless but entails the creation of institutions that seek to subvert bureaucratisation and to uphold the plurality and concreteness of the constituting subjects, an active conception of citizenship and a politicisation of the public sphere. They are 'institutions that subvert institutionalization', as Wolin (1994: 43) argued was the case of specifically *democratic* political forms.

As a result, council democracy seeks to steer clear of two dangers often associated with constituent politics: on the one hand, it seeks to go beyond the fetishism of *form*, as no form can guarantee the practices of self-government in perpetuity. Council democracy is not an attempt to find a political form which is not in need of active participation and continual, deliberate reconstitution. Hence, council democracy does not seek to exhaust the constituent power in ordinary politics, only to stabilise it. On the other hand, council democracy avoids the fetishism of *formlessness* central to Sieyèsian–Schmittian understandings of constituent power.

Moreover, council democratic constituent power provides an important institutional approximation of the principles inherent in many theories of radical democracy. Whereas radical democrats like Negri, Wolin and Rancière distance themselves from Schmitt's unitary, constituting subject, the depoliticised, non-deliberative and acclamatory public sphere and the pre-political, ethnic-national understanding of citizenship, they reproduce the clear-cut, antagonistic relation between constituent power and political form. For many radical democrats, genuine democratic politics cannot take institutional form, as institutions limit and domesticate the constituent power. While this argument establishes a productive incongruence between the democratic ideal of popular self-government and every concrete institutionalisation of this ideal, it also makes democracy an episodic experience, which cannot be sustained for longer periods of time. What council democracy offers radical democratic politics is a way of understanding institutions beyond the language of domination, bureaucracy and elitism – beyond what Marx called 'repressive' institutions and towards a more 'expansive' understanding of institutional politics. The councils disclose a conception of constituent power that is not 'some kind of paroxysm', but which instead functions as 'the prefiguration' of ordinary, participatory politics (Castoriadis 1988b: 96). Castoriadis puts it brilliantly:

> It is therefore essential that revolutionary society, from its very beginning, furnish itself with a network of institutions and modes of operation . . . It is essential too that revolutionary society should create for itself, at each step, those *stable forms* of organization that can most readily become effective *normal mechanisms* for the expressions of popular will, both in 'important matters' and in everyday life (which is, in truth, the first and foremost of all 'important matters'). (Castoriadis 1988b: 96; emphasis added)

Integral to council democratic constituent power is thus the creation of 'stable forms' and 'normal mechanisms' for expressing popular power. The stability of these forms and the normalcy of these mechanisms is what bridges 'important matters' and 'everyday life', because such a distinction is obsolete, as it is grounded upon a clear-cut division between constituent power and constituted politics. 'In this sense', Castoriadis argues – and this is the ambition of council democracy, I would add – 'the main problem of post-revolutionary society is the creation of institutions that allow for the continuation and the development of this autonomous activity, without requiring heroic feats twenty-four hours a day' (1993a: 262).

Council democratic constituent power is thus not devoid of forms but involves the creation of forms of insurrection, which are *at the same time* forms of self-government. The immanent principle of council democracy is that its insurrectionary forms ought also to be able to function as ordinary forms of self-government. In contrast to Lenin, who argued that the soviets could function only as organs of insurrection, the practices of the historical councils as well as the interpretative direction I have followed suggest that the genuine aim of the councils was to survive the revolution as organs in which society could be reconstituted without resorting to a conception of constituent politics as a lawless state of nature, and without resurrecting the homogenous, unified people as the origin of all law.

Conclusion
Council Democracy and Contemporary
Movements of Occupation

This book has been about different *visions* of council democracy, developed by various political thinkers of the last 150 years. The visions are united in the ambition of transcending the distinctions between politics and economics, state and society, public and private, legislation and execution, rulers and ruled, which liberal democracy and modern capitalism have sought to naturalise and exploit. Instead of natural law, communicative reason, divine right or dynastic privilege, thinkers of council democracy have legitimised the political order with reference to the constituent power of the people, thereby accepting that modern politics is devoid of natural foundations and pre-given principles. No finality or conclusiveness can be experienced in the realm of politics, interpreters of council democracy suggest, which is why a free, autonomous and democratic polity must have continual access to its constituent, transformative powers. This vision of council democracy, powerfully thematised in different ways by Castoriadis, Lefort and Arendt in the post-war era and as a *visionary* (in the Wolinian sense) attempt to rethink politics after the tragedies of totalitarianism, is no less relevant today.

Twentieth-century politics has mainly been characterised by hierarchical forms of political organisation, such as parliaments, parties and unions, fundamentally centred around the principle of representation. The present crisis of democracy, and the flagrant mismatch between globalised capitalism and democratic decision-making nested in the nation-state, is a testimony to the fact that the principle of representation itself is in crisis. While technocratic, undemocratic liberalism abandons the very idea of a political relation between rulers and ruled, populists develop an illiberal, anti-representative idea of democracy based on logics of popular homogeneity and incarnation. While the citizenry of contemporary Western democracies does not feel represented by the present political elites, none of these major alternatives to contemporary representative democracy has experimented with novel forms of political participation, popular mobilisation or organisational structure.

The clearest, most genuinely *popular* response to the crisis of representative democracy and the uncontrollable nature of twenty-first-century global capitalism has been anti-austerity Square movements like *Occupy* in America, *Indignados* in Spain and *Aganaktismenoi* in Greece, which emerged after the global financial crisis of 2007–8. In a broader political, cultural and geographical context, the *commune* or the *council* has been reinvented by the Zapatistas in Mexico, the Global Justice movement, in the struggle against neo-liberalisation in Bolivia, in the communal councils in Venezuela, in the Kurds' struggle against ISIS in Rojava and in the opposition to dictatorship during the Arab Spring. Central tactics employed by twentieth-century workers' councils such as worker recuperation of factories and occupations of public spaces have been pivotal for contemporary anti-capitalist, radical democratic struggle and experimentation.

These various political movements might not have been directly inspired by the twentieth-century council movements, but in their horizontality, their lack of leaders and their experimentation with new forms of solidarity, mobilisation and organisation, they share with the twentieth-century council movement at least three principles.[1] The *first* principle is that of *self-management* or what Castoriadis would call *autonomy*, which considers representation a distortion of democracy. Contemporary Square and council movements have in common a distinct way of engaging people in politics: councils, communes, occupations and encampments encourage citizens to act and organise themselves. Even though there can still be a delegatory function in the council system as well as in the Squares of Zuccotti Park, Syntagma, Puerta del Sol, Tahrir and Gezi Park – like the councils' imperative mandate or the spokespersons or sub-committees of the occupied Squares – their primary aim is to make people *organise their own life*, whether this be in the workplace, in the neighbourhood or somewhere else.

The *second* principle shared by contemporary movements of occupation and the council movement is the idea that politics should not be limited to what has become the dominant arena for politics. From Marx's communal analysis through the interwar council communists to Castoriadis, Lefort and Arendt, all agreed that council democracy is a political form that can transfer politics from parliaments and the apparatuses of the state to other spheres of society that need to be democratised. The Square movements can be seen as reactivating the ambition of transferring politics to places, which due to the hegemony of global capitalism and liberal democracy have effectually become non-political or anti-political places. The occupation of public squares, like the councils' occupation of the workplace, barracks and neighbourhoods, ceases to limit politics to already confined spaces as well as the activity of political decision-making to already privileged elites. In the words of Castoriadis, which the Occupy movements succinctly rephrased in the simple slogan 'We are the 99%':

> what is at stake here is the 'deprofessionalization' of politics, the abolition of politics as a special and separate sphere of activity and skill, and, conversely, the universal *politicization* of society, which means just this: the business of society is, in act and not in words, everybody's business. (Castoriadis 1993a: 261; original emphasis)

The *third*, and most important principle shared by council democracy and the contemporary Square movements is the dynamic between constituent power and political form, which stands at the centre of this book. Although critics of the Square movements have deemed them anarchical, disorganised, enraged and without realistic political goals, in this way advancing the same critique levelled against democracy since Plato and Aristotle and repeated by opponents of democracy such as Thomas Hobbes, Edmund Burke and James Madison, such critics have generally overlooked how what could be called the constituent power of the Square movements – the initial spontaneous occupation of public spaces and creation of short-lived, self-governing 'Square republics' – did not operate in any anarchical fashion, nor did their constituent power disappear after the occupation of the highly symbolic squares. The encampments themselves, much like John Reed's depiction of the storming of the Winter Palace, were in no way devoid of procedures, germinal institutions or nascent, shared understandings of legitimacy, as critics of democracy have always argued. The plurality of sub-committees, the federated working groups, the daily general assemblies and the procedural mechanism of hand waving, clapping and the human microphone are examples from the Occupy movements of what Wolin called *institutions that subvert institutionalisation*; institutions and procedures aimed at upholding the plurality, equality, autonomy and freedom of Squares' initial constituent power. Moreover, just

as the ambition of the council movements was never only to overthrow the monarchical regimes in which they appeared or merely to
occupy the symbolic Winter Palaces throughout Europe, the aim of
the Square movements was never only to set up encampments in the
centres of capitalist metropolises. Instead, they aimed to create 'a
general assembly in every backyard' and 'on every street corner', in
every workplace and neighbourhood, thereby aspiring 'to make the
extraordinary an *ordinary* occurrence of everyday life', as I have let
Arendt argue numerous times ([1958] 1998: 197; emphasis added).

As recently claimed by Judith Butler (2015: 154–92), freedom of
assembly is at once the precondition for popular sovereignty, for the
very utterance of 'we, the people', and at the same time a constant
threat to every statist, parliamentary institutionalisation of popular
sovereignty. Freedom of assembly, consequently, much like council
democracy, entails a combination of constituent power and political
form. In the closing pages of Michael Hardt and Antonio Negri's
Assembly (2017), they write that

> The general assemblies instituted by social movements in every
> encampment and occupation of recent years, with their efforts to open
> participation to all and their rules to encourage those traditionally dis-
> advantaged to speak first . . . should be understood as symptoms of
> a growing political desire for new democratic modes of participation
> and decision-making. But the demands and practices of these social
> movements continually overflow the traditional framework of political
> rights. Their actions certainly do declare their right to assemble – their
> right to the streets, the squares, and the city as a whole – but they fill
> these rights with new social content. The significance of these move-
> ments may best be understood, in fact, as an enrichment of the freedom
> of association central to modern labour movements. From the tradition
> of strikes at the workplace are emerging forms of social strike. (Hardt
> and Negri 2017: 293–4)

The assemblies in Zuccotti Park, Syntagma Square, Puerta del Sol,
Tahrir Square and Gezi Park hoped for a continuation of their
constituent power, as the enormous civil society initiatives, social
cooperation and immense creation of new organisations after the
occupations came to an end testify (Wiltshire 2013; Newman 2016).
Hence, reminiscent of the idea of a *council democracy constituent power* developed in the last chapter, contemporary occupiers
realised the important task of translating the initial burst of constituent power into social, cooperative initiatives around new practices

of 'the commons'. Only in this way can the constituent power of the many steer between the Scylla of pure constituted politics and the exhaustion of constituent power (note, for example, how similar movements in Spain and Greece were replaced by political parties such as Podemos and Syriza,[2] just like the Russian soviets were replaced by the Bolshevik party) and the Charybdis of disorganised insurrection and revolutionary violence. By stressing the combination of constituent power and political form, contemporary Square movements – like the vision of council democracy developed in this book – aspired to perform practices of continual political self-alteration, but without the normlessness of revolutionary politics and without the hierarchy and elitism of normal parliamentary politics. The legacies of council democracy, deliberately or not, could come to shape the future of democracy, which in its present crisis might survive only by being radicalised.

Notes

Introduction

1. For a short version of this argument, see Popp-Madsen (2020a).
2. Two of the most influential contemporary interpreters of constituent power, Antonio Negri and Andreas Kalyvas, have both argued this point. According to Negri, 'to speak of constituent power is to speak of democracy' (1999: 1). In the phrasing of Kalyvas, 'constituent power is the truth of modern democracy' (2013).
3. For a critique of Rancière and Wolin along these lines, see Myers (2016); Kateb (2001).
4. The Tsar and his family were not killed during the Russian Revolutions, but in July 1918 by the Ural Regional Soviet and with instructions from Vladimir Lenin.

Chapter 1

1. In Berlin, during the German Revolution of 1918–19, the councils were only in power from November to December 1918 (Hoffrogge 2011); in Hungary, the councils only exercised power from March to August 1919 (Carsten 1972: 50–9); and in countries such as Austria, Italy and Britain, the various council formations never reached considerable power in national politics (Haumer 2015; Di Paola 2011; Gluckstein 1995). The Hungarian councils of 1956, on which Castoriadis, Lefort and Arendt extensively draw, only existed for about two weeks.
2. The first article of the first *de facto* constitution of post-1917 Russia reads: 'Russia is hereby proclaimed a Republic of Soviets of Workers', Soldiers' and Peasants' Deputies. All power, centrally and locally, is vested in these Soviets' (Lenin 1918).
3. For one discussion of relations between class interest and representative institutions, see McCormick (2011).
4. Friedrich Ebert was the first President of Germany from 1919 to 1925 and a leading member of the SPD.

Chapter 2

1. Originally entitled *The Task of the Proletariat in the Present Revolution*, but generally known as the *April Theses*.

Chapter 3

1. For two recent exceptions, see Holman (2018) and Popp-Madsen (2020b).
2. Examples of recent analyses of Castoriadis and democratic theory that omit the council tradition are Breckman (2013), Klooger (2009) and Adams (2011). Brian Singer (1979, 1980, 2015) provides a rarely detailed analysis of Castoriadis's entire project but does not mention a single word about the council system. By contrast, Christos Memos (2014) has analysed Castoriadis's writings on the council system, but does not connect them to his later writings on autonomy.
3. Institutions in Castoriadis's vocabulary mean both concrete institutional complexes, and also laws, norms, traditions and so on. 'Institution' of society is thus its 'world' of significations, its imaginary, its hierarchies and structures (Castoriadis 2007a: 95).
4. For the relation between Castoriadis's instituting power and the concept of the constituent power, see Kalyvas (1998, 2013).
5. 'Those who believe that I am inspired exclusively by ancient history simply have not read me completely. My reflection began not with Athenian democracy (only in 1978 did I truly start working on it) but with the contemporary workers' movement' (Castoriadis 1997b: 414).

Chapter 4

1. Libertarianism in this context has nothing to do with the ultra-liberalism of the anglophone tradition. Libertarianism in this context signifies *left-wing* anti-authoritarianism.
2. For such an understanding of radical democracy, see for example Wolin (1996) and Rancière (2010) as well as my discussion of radical democracy in Chapter 6.
3. The only monograph on Lefort's thought, Bernard Flynn's (2005) otherwise excellent introduction to Lefort, has nothing to say on the issue of the councils or socialist democracy. The only collective volume featuring analyses of a range of different aspects of Lefort's thinking by leading Lefort scholars, *Claude Lefort: Thinker of the Political* (edited by Martín Plot, 2013), also neglects Lefort's interpretations of the council system (Arato's brief remarks in chapter 8 of the volume are an exception). Analyses of Lefort by political theorists and intellectual historians such as Warren Breckman (2013), Samuel Moyn (2009), Oliver Marchart (2007), Raf Geenens (2007) and Carlo Accetti (2015)

all discuss Lefort's theory of democracy, but none reflects on Lefort's notion of socialist democracy or the self-limiting democracy of the councils.

4. The traditional cry, when a monarch dies, 'The King is dead, long live the King', testifies to the dual – finite and infinite – body of the monarch.

5. The most thorough discussion of savage democracy is by Miguel Abensour (2011b); see also Nelson (2019).

6. In Aristotle's edition of the classic typology, democracy is the perverted form of the government of the many, whereas the good form is called *politeia*. In later Roman editions, such as in Polybius and Cicero, democracy is the good form of rule of the many, whereas the perverted is labelled 'mob-rule', see Hansen (2010: 517–21).

Chapter 5

1. Exceptions are Muldoon (2016: 596–607), Totschnig (2014) and Kalyvas (2008: 254–91).

2. Along the same lines, James Miller has called Arendt's analysis of the council system a 'distorting lens' almost 'comical to anyone versed in history', as 'her gloss on revolutionary history begins to sound like so much wishful thinking' (1979: 182, 181). According to Seyla Benhabib, Arendt's council 'model is flawed, because more often than not, it seems to fly in the face of realities' (2000: 165). Even John F. Sitton, who is generally sympathetic to Arendt's vision of council democracy, finds that 'Arendt fundamentally misinterprets the council tradition', as she does not 'appreciate exactly what is at stake' (1987: 94). Arendt's alleged lack of exact historical understanding has also been criticised by McConkey (1991) and Medearis (2004).

3. Although, she then added directly afterwards: 'And yet perhaps, after all – in the wake of the next revolution' (Arendt 1969: 233).

4. In her analysis of the Israeli *kibbutzim*, her proposal for collaborative Jewish–Arab council communities, and her plans for World War II federal restoration, one could argue that Arendt starts conceptualising council-like structures, but although she discusses local organs of political participation, they have so little in common with the historical councils that I will not include them in Arendt's council discussions.

5. Arendt would agree with Castoriadis that regime forms relying on extra-human absolutes are essentially authoritarian: 'The source of authority in authoritarian government is always a force external and superior to its own power; it is always this source, this external force which transcends the political realm' (Arendt 1961d: 97).

6. See also Kalyvas (2008: 200–10) for this argument.

7. As Arendt observes, 'the liberal thinker is apt to pay little attention to this because of his conviction that all power corrupts and that the constancy of progress requires constant loss of power, no matter what its origin might be' (1961d: 97).

8. In Arendt's only reference to Schmitt in her published work, in a footnote to 'What is Freedom?', Arendt argues that 'among the modern political theorists, Carl Schmitt is the most able defender of the notion of sovereignty. He recognizes clearly that the root of sovereignty is the will: Sovereign is he who wills and commands' (1961e: 296).

9. This is obviously wrong, as the history of the political theory of council democracy provided in Chapter 2 testifies.

Chapter 6

1. According to Hobbes, democracy 'undoes today all that was concluded yesterday' because outside established institutions the people exists only in 'the confusion of a disunited multitude' (1994: 120–1, 111). According to Madison, 'democracies have been spectacles of turbulence and contention; have been found incompatible with personal security or the rights of property; and have in general been as short in life as they have been violent in their deaths' (1961: 76). In the evaluation of Ellen Meiksins Wood, 'the main issue dividing democrats from anti-democrats . . . was whether the labouring multitude, the *banausic* or menial classes, should have political rights, whether such people are able to make political judgements. This is a recurring theme not only in ancient Greece, where it emerges very clearly in Plato's philosophy, but in debates about democracy throughout most of Western history' (2011: 39).

2. I agree with the latter part of Habermas's argument, but contend that it is a caricature understanding of the councils, which ultimately reproduces Lenin's final understanding of the soviets as organs exclusively useful for insurrection.

3. Because of Castoriadis's dichotomy between society as instituting and as instituted, some critics argue that he envisions an irreducible gap between politics as instituting and politics as instituted, between constituent power and political form (Zerilli 2002: 544; Habermas 1987a; Cohen 2005: 16–17; Honneth 1984). They argue that Castoriadis only locates moments of freedom, autonomy and genuine politics in the process of instituting society; that is, that Castoriadis advances a vision of politics as *solely* extraordinary, revolutionary, formless and constituent. In this way, Castoriadis has been accused of advancing a Schmittian theory of decisionism and exceptional politics (Breckman 1998: 40; Howard 1977: 286–7). When interpreting Castoriadis through his writings on the council system, such a reading, which solely privileges society as instituting, as well as maintaining an irreducible gap between instituting and instituted society, cannot be sustained. In a similar manner, Arendt has been criticised for only having an eye for the extraordinary moments of politics in such a way that she has only disdain for ordinary politics (Canovan 1978; Honig 1993; Kateb 1987, 2000). This accusation centres on Arendt's conceptualisation of political action as miraculous, constituting and world-building. Again, similarly to Castoriadis, the drawback of privileging

202 Visions of Council Democracy

the extraordinary dimension of politics – according to Arendt's critics on this matter – is that Arendt is unintentionally proposing what Kalyvas (2004: 321) has called 'a veiled theory of decisionism'. Jean Cohen and Andrew Arato have voiced a similar critique, as in their reading of Arendt they argue that although she 'renounces the politics of any kind of permanent revolution based on the continuous functioning of a *pouvoir constituant*', her conceptualisation of action as an 'unlimited power, inevitably returning us to a model of permanent revolution, could not yield any institutionalization of stable political foundations'. Consequently, 'the difficulty or even self-contradiction inherent in a project aiming at the embodiment of the revolutionary spirit in enduring institutions' must be realised (Cohen and Arato 1992: 193). Hence, critics of Arendt's allegedly exclusive focus on extraordinary politics argue that by proposing a theory of decisionism, she is not capable of superseding the concept of sovereignty which she so desperately seeks to overcome with her concepts of plurality, natality and federalism. With her writings on the council system, a reading of Arendt that stresses her exclusive privileging of the extraordinary dimension of politics becomes increasingly difficult, as she deliberately seeks to combine novelty and stability in a council republic established 'in such a way that its own central power *did not deprive the constituent bodies of their original power to constitute*' (Arendt [1963] 2006: 259; emphasis added).
4. One interpreter of constituent power, Andreas Kalyvas, comes very close to this interpretation of the council tradition (2008: 254–91).
5. Throughout the following sections I refer to the Soviet Constitution of July 1918. It might be perplexing that this document can tell anything about the council system. As the Bolsheviks controlled the soviets after the October Revolution, the argument could be made that the 1918 Soviet Constitution is merely an expression of Bolshevik power. But according to Anweiler, who is indeed very sceptical of the Bolsheviks' usurpation of soviet power, the 1918 Soviet Constitution can reasonably be understood as a codification of how the soviets functioned from February to October 1917. See Anweiler (1974: 224–5); Tomba (2017: 503–4).

Conclusion

1. For a further elaboration on these three principles, see Popp-Madsen and Kets (2020).
2. For a discussion of the relation between horizontality and leadership as well as direct democracy and representation in the Square movements, see Prentoulis and Thomassen (2013).

Bibliography

Abensour, Miguel (2011a) *Democracy against the State: Marx and the Machiavellian Moment*. Cambridge: Polity Press.

Abensour, Miguel (2011b) '"Savage Democracy" and the "Principle of Anarchy"', in *Democracy against the State: Marx and the Machiavellian Moment*. Cambridge: Polity Press, pp. 102–24.

Accetti, Carlo (2015) 'Claude Lefort: Democracy as the Empty Place of Power', in Breaugh, M., Holman, C., Magnusson, R., Mazzocchi, P. and Penner, D. (eds) *Thinking Radical Democracy: The Return to Politics in Post-War France*. Toronto: University of Toronto Press, pp. 121–40.

Ackerman, Bruce (1988) 'Neo-Federalism?', in Elster, J. (ed.) *Constitutionalism and Democracy*. Cambridge: Cambridge University Press, pp. 153–94.

Adams, Suzi (2011) *Castoriadis's Ontology: Being and Creation*. New York: Fordham University Press.

Anweiler, Oskar (1974) *The Soviets: The Russian Workers, Peasants, and Soldiers Councils, 1905–1921*. New York: Pantheon Books.

Arato, Andrew (1984) 'The Democratic Theory of the Polish Opposition: Normative Intentions and Strategic Ambiguities'. Working Paper no. 15. Notre Dame, IN: Helen Kellogg Institute for International Studies.

Arato, Andrew (1990) 'Thinking the Present: Revolution in Eastern Europe. Revolution, Civil Society and Democracy', *PRAXIS International*, 10 (1+2), pp. 25–38.

Arato, Andrew (2013) 'Lefort, the Philosopher of 1989', in Plot, M. (ed.) *Claude Lefort: Thinker of the Political*. Basingstoke: Palgrave Macmillan, pp. 114–23.

Arendt, Hannah (1958a) 'Totalitarian Imperialism: Reflections on the Hungarian Revolution', *The Journal of Politics*, 20 (1), pp. 5–43.

Arendt, Hannah (1958b) 'Totalitarianism', *Meridian*, 2 (2), 1.

Arendt, Hannah (1961a) 'The Concept of History: Ancient and Modern', in *Between Past and Future: Six Exercises in Political Thought*. New York: Penguin Books, pp. 41–90.

Arendt, Hannah (1961b) 'Preface: The Gap between Past and Future', in *Between Past and Future: Six Exercises in Political Thought*. New York: Penguin Books, pp. 3–16.

Arendt, Hannah (1961c) 'Truth and Politics', in *Between Past and Future: Eight Exercises in Political Thought*. New York: Penguin Books, pp. 227–64.

Arendt, Hannah (1961d) 'What is Authority?', in *Between Past and Future: Six Exercises in Political Thought*. New York: Penguin Books, pp. 91–142.

Arendt, Hannah (1961e) 'What is Freedom?', in *Between Past and Future: Six Exercises in Political Thought*. New York: Penguin Books, pp. 143–72.

Arendt, Hannah (1968) *The Origins of Totalitarianism*. New York: Harcourt Brace.

Arendt, Hannah (1969) 'Thoughts on Politics and Revolution', in *Crises of the Republic*. New York: Harcourt Brace, pp. 199–233.

Arendt, Hannah (1970) *On Violence*. New York: Harcourt Brace.

Arendt, Hannah (1979) 'On Hannah Arendt', in Hill, M. (ed.) *Hannah Arendt: The Recovery of the Public World*. New York: St. Martin's Press, pp. 341–54 .

Arendt, Hannah [1958] (1998) *The Human Condition*. Chicago: University of Chicago Press.

Arendt, Hannah (2005) 'Montesquieu's Revision of the Tradition', in *The Promise of Politics*. New York: Schocken Books, pp. 63–9.

Arendt, Hannah [1963] (2006) *On Revolution*. New York: Penguin Books.

Aristotle (1958) *Politics*. Oxford: Oxford University Press.

Avrich, Paul (1991) *Kronstadt, 1921*. Princeton, NJ: Princeton University Press.

Azzellini, Dario (ed.) (2015) *An Alternative Labour History: Worker Control and Workplace Democracy*. London: Zed Books.

Bakunin, Mikhail (1870) *Letter to Albert Richard*. Marxists Internet Archive, <https://www.marxists.org/reference/archive/bakunin/works/1870/albert-richard.htm> (last accessed 3 September 2020).

Bakunin, Mikhail (1871) 'The Paris Commune and the Idea of the State', in *Writings on the Paris Commune*. St Petersburg: Red and Black Publishers, pp. 75–87.

Bakunin, Mikhail (1970) *God and the State*. New York: Dover.

Benhabib, Seyla (2000) 'The Embattled Public Sphere: Hannah Arendt, Jürgen Habermas, and Beyond', in Ullmann-Margalit, E. (ed.) *Reasoning Practically*. Oxford: Oxford University Press, pp. 164–81.

Bernstein, Jay (1989) 'Praxis and Aporia in Habermas' Critique of Castoriadis', *Revue européenne des sciences sociales*, 23 (86), pp. 111–23.

Bernstein, Richard (1996) *Arendt and the Jewish Question*. Cambridge: Polity Press.

Blokker, Paul (2009) 'Democracy Through the Lens of 1989: Liberal Triumph or Radical Turn?', *International Journal of Politics, Culture and Society*, 22 (3), pp. 273–90.

Bodin, Jean (1992) *On Sovereignty: Four Chapters From the Six Books of the Commonwealth*. Cambridge: Cambridge University Press.

Bonnet, Alberto (2014) 'The Idea of Councils Runs Through Latin America', *South Atlantic Quarterly*, 113 (2), pp. 271–83.

Bosteels, Bruno (2017) 'State or Commune: Viewing the October Revolution from the Land of Zapata', *Constellations*, 24 (4), pp. 570–9.

Bourinet, Phillippe (2016) *The Dutch and German Communist Left*. Leiden: Brill.

Breckman, Warren (1998) 'Cornelius Castoriadis contra Postmodernism: Beyond the "French Ideology"', *French Politics and Society*, 16 (2), pp. 30–42.

Breckman, Warren (2013) *Adventures of the Symbolic: Post-Marxism and Radical Democracy*. New York: Columbia University Press.

Brennan, Jason (2016) *Against Democracy*. Princeton, NJ: Princeton University Press.

Bricianer, Serge (1978) *Pannekoek and the Workers Councils*, St Louis: Telos Press.

Butler, Judith (2012) *Parting Ways: Jewishness and the Critique of Zionism*. New York: Columbia University Press.

Butler, Judith (2015) *Notes Towards a Performative Theory of Assembly*. Cambridge, MA: Harvard University Press.

Canovan, Margaret (1978) 'The Contradictions of Hannah Arendt's Political Thought', *Political Theory*, 6 (1), pp. 5–26.

Canovan, Margaret (1992) *Hannah Arendt: A Reinterpretation of Her Political Thought*. Cambridge: Cambridge University Press.

Carr, Edward (1952) *A History of Soviet Russia*. London: Macmillan Press.

Carsten, Flemming (1972) *Revolution in Central Europe, 1918–1919*. London: Maurice Temple Smith.

Castoriadis, Cornelius (1987) *The Imaginary Institution of Society*. Cambridge, MA: The MIT Press.

Castoriadis, Cornelius (1988a) 'General Introduction', in *Political and Social Writings, vol. 1*. Minneapolis: University of Minnesota Press, pp. 3–36.

Castoriadis, Cornelius (1988b) 'On the Content of Socialism, II', in *Political and Social Writings, vol. 2*. Minneapolis: University of Minnesota Press, pp. 90–154.

Castoriadis, Cornelius (1988c) 'On the Regime and against the Defense of the USSR', in *Political and Social Writings, vol. 1*. Minneapolis: University of Minnesota Press, pp. 44–55.

Castoriadis, Cornelius (1988d) 'The Proletarian Revolution against Bureaucracy', in *Political and Social Writings, vol. 2*. Minneapolis: University of Minnesota Press, pp. 57–89.

Castoriadis, Cornelius (1988e) 'Proletariat and Organization, I', in *Political and Social Writings, vol. 2*. Minneapolis: University of Minnesota Press, pp. 193–222.

Castoriadis, Cornelius (1988f) 'Socialism or Barbarism', in *Political and Social Writings, vol. 1*. Minneapolis: University of Minnesota Press, pp. 76–106.

Castoriadis, Cornelius (1991a) 'The Greek Polis and the Creation of Democracy', in *Philosophy, Politics, Autonomy: Essays in Political Philosophy*. Oxford: Oxford University Press, pp. 81–123

Castoriadis, Cornelius (1991b) 'Power, Politics, Autonomy', in *Philosophy, Politics, Autonomy. Essays in Political Philosophy*. Oxford: Oxford University Press, pp. 143–74.

Castoriadis, Cornelius (1991c) 'The Social-Historical: Mode of Being, Problems of Knowledge', in *Philosophy, Politics, Autonomy: Essays in Political Philosophy*. Oxford: Oxford University Press, pp. 33–46.

Castoriadis, Cornelius (1993a) 'The Hungarian Source', in *Political and Social Writings, vol. 3*. Minneapolis: University of Minnesota Press, pp. 250–71.

Castoriadis, Cornelius (1993b) 'Socialism and Autonomous Society', in *Political and Social Writings, vol. 3*. Minneapolis: University of Minnesota Press, pp. 314–31.

Castoriadis, Cornelius (1997a) 'Democracy as Procedure and Democracy as Regime', *Constellations*, 4 (1), pp. 1–18.

Castoriadis, Cornelius (1997b) 'Done and To Be Done', in *The Castoriadis Reader*. Oxford: Blackwell Publishing, pp. 361–417.

Castoriadis, Cornelius (2007a) 'Primal Institution of Society and Second-Order Institutions', in *Figures of the Thinkable*. Stanford, CA: Stanford University Press, pp. 91–101.

Castoriadis, Cornelius (2007b) 'What Democracy?', in *Figures of the Thinkable*. Stanford, CA: Stanford University Press, pp. 118–50.

Christofferson, Michael (2004) *French Intellectuals against the Left: The Antitotalitarian Moment of the 1970s*. Oxford: Berghahn Books.

Cohen, Jean (2005) 'The Self-Institution of Society and Representative Government: Can the Circle be Squared?', *Thesis Eleven*, 80 (1), pp. 9–37.

Cohen, Jean and Arato, Andrew (1992) *Civil Society and Political Theory*. Cambridge, MA: The MIT Press.

Connolly, William (2017) *Aspirational Fascism: The Struggle for Multifaceted Democracy under Trumpism*. Minneapolis: University of Minnesota Press.

Constitution of the Russian Soviet Federated Socialist Republic (1918) Marxists Internet Archive, <https://www.marxists.org/history/ussr/government/constitution/1918/index.htm> (last accessed 3 September 2020).

Daniels, Robert (1953) 'The State and Revolution: A Case Study in the Genesis and Transformation of Communist Ideology', *American Slavic and East European Review*, 12 (1), pp. 22–43.

Daniels, Robert (1965) *The Conscience of Revolution: Communist Opposition in Soviet Russia*. Cambridge, MA: Harvard University Press.

Declaration of the Lyon Commune (1870) <https://www.libertarian-labyrinth.org/bakunin-library/a-poster-from-the-lyon-commune-1870/> (last accessed 15 October 2020).

Del Lucchese, Filippo (2016) 'Spinoza and Constituent Power', *Contemporary Political Theory*, 15 (2), pp. 182–204.

d'Entrèves, Maurizio Passerin (1994) *The Political Philosophy of Hannah Arendt*. London: Routledge.

Derrida, Jacques (1986) 'Declarations of Independence', *New Political Science*, 7 (1), pp. 7–15.

Di Paola, Pietro (2011) 'Factory Councils in Turin, 1919–1920: "The Sole and Authentic Social Representatives of the Proletarian Class"', in Ness, I. and Azzellini, D. (eds) *Ours to Master and to Own: Workers' Control from the Commune to the Present*. Chicago: Haymarket Books, pp. 130–47.

Dirik, Dilar (2016) 'Building Democracy without the State', *Roar Magazine*, 1, pp. 32–41.

Dubigeon, Yohan (2017) *La democratie de conseils*. Paris: Klincksieck.

Eley, Geoff (2002) *Forging Democracy: The History of the Left in Europe, 1850–2000*. Oxford: Oxford University Press.

Fehér, Ferenc and Heller, Ágnes (1983) *Hungary 1956 Revisited: The Message of a Revolution a Quarter of a Century Later*. Winchester, MA: Allen & Unwin.

Figes, Orlando (1998) *A People's Tragedy. The Russian Revolution: 1891–1924*. New York: Penguin Books.

Finchelstein, Federico (2017) *From Fascism to Populism in History*. Oakland, CA: University of California Press.

Flynn, Bernard (2005) *The Philosophy of Claude Lefort: Interpreting the Political*. Evanston, IL: Northwestern University Press.

Geenens, Raf (2007) 'Contingency and Universality? Lefort's Ambiguous Justification of Democracy', *Research in Phenomenology*, 37 (3), pp. 443–55.

Gerber, John (1989) *Anton Pannekoek and the Socialism of Workers' Self-Emancipation 1873–1960*. Dordrecht: Kluwer Academic Publishers.

Gluckstein, Donny (1983) 'The Workers' Council Movement in Western Europe', *International Socialism Journal*, 18 (2), pp. 1–29.

Gluckstein, Donny (1995) *The Western Soviets: Workers' Councils Versus Parliament, 1915–1920*. London: Bookmarks.

Gluckstein, Donny (2011) 'Workers' Councils in Europe: A Century of Experience', in Ness, E. and Azzellini, D. (eds) *Ours to Master and to Own: Workers' Control from the Commune to the Present*. Chicago: Haymarket Books, pp. 32–47.

Gombin, Richard (1975) *The Origins of Modern Leftism*. Harmondsworth: Penguin Books.

Gombin, Richard (1978) *The Radical Tradition: A Study in Modern Revolutionary Thought*. London: Methuen.

Gorter, Herman (1920) *Open Letter to Comrade Lenin*. Marxists Internet Archive, <https://www.marxists.org/archive/gorter/1920/open-letter/> (last accessed 3 September 2020).

Gramsci, Antonio (1994a) 'The Conquest of the State', in *Pre-Prison Writings*. Cambridge: Cambridge University Press, pp. 108–14.

Gramsci, Antonio (1994b) 'Unions and Councils', in *Pre-Prison Writings*. Cambridge: Cambridge University Press, pp. 115–20.

Gramsci, Antonio (1994c) 'Workers' Democracy', in *Pre-Prison Writings*. Cambridge: Cambridge University Press, pp. 96–100.

Grunberger, Richard (1973) *Red Rising in Bavaria*. London: Arthur Barker.

Habermas, Jürgen (1977) 'Hannah Arendt's Communications Concept of Power', *Social Research*, 44 (1), pp. 3–24.

Habermas, Jürgen (1987a) 'Excursus on Cornelius Castoriadis', in *The Philosophical Discourse of Modernity: Twelve Lectures*. Cambridge: Polity Press, pp. 327–35.

Habermas, Jürgen (1987b) *The Theory of Communicative Action, vol. 2: Life-World and System: A Critique of Functionalist Reason*. Boston: Beacon Press.

Habermas, Jürgen (1996) 'Popular Sovereignty as Procedure', in *Between Facts and Norms*. Cambridge: Polity Press, pp. 463–90.

Hansen, Mogens Herman (2010) 'The Mixed Constitution Versus the Separation of Powers: Monarchical and Aristocratic Aspects of Modern Democracy', *History of Political Thought*, 31 (3), pp. 509–31.

Hardt, Michael and Negri, Antonio (2017) *Assembly*. Oxford: Oxford University Press.

Haumer, Peter (2015) 'The Austrian Revolution of 1918–1919 and Working Class Autonomy', in Azzellini, D. (ed.) *An Alternative Labour History: Worker Control and Workplace Democracy*. London: Zed Books, pp. 120–56.

Haynes, Mike (2006) 'Hungary: Workers' Councils against Russian Tanks', *International Socialism*, 112 (2), pp. 81–106.

Hobbes, Thomas (1994) *Leviathan*. Indianapolis: Hackett Publishing.

Hobsbawm, Eric (1973) 'Hannah Arendt on Revolution', in *Revolutionaries*. New York: Meridian Books, pp. 201–8.

Hobsbawm, Eric (1994) *The Age of Extremes, 1914–1991*. New York: Vintage Books.

Hoffrogge, Ralf (2011) 'From Unionism to Workers' Control: The Revolutionary Shop Stewards in Germany, 1914–1918', in Ness, E. and Azzellini, D. (eds) *Ours to Master and to Own: Workers' Control from Commune to the Present*. Chicago: Haymarket Books, pp. 84–103.

Holman, Christopher (2018) 'The Councils as Ontological Form: Cornelius Castoriadis and the Autonomous Potential of Council Democracy', in Muldoon, J. (ed.) *Council Democracy: Towards a Democratic Socialist Politics*. London: Routledge, pp. 131–49.

Honig, Bonnie (1993) *Political Theory and the Politics of Displacement*. Ithaca, NY: Cornell University Press.

Honig, Bonnie (1995) 'Towards an Agonistic Feminism: Hannah Arendt and the Politics of Identity', in Honig, B. (ed.) *Feminist Interpretations of Hannah Arendt*. University Park, PA: Pennsylvania State University Press, pp. 135–66.

Honneth, Axel (1984) 'Rescuing the Revolution with an Ontology: On Cornelius Castoriadis' Theory of Society', *Thesis Eleven*, 14 (1), pp. 62–78.

Howard, Dick (1977) *The Marxian Legacy*. Basingstoke: Macmillan Press.

Ingram, James (2006) 'The Politics of Claude Lefort's Political: Between Liberalism and Radical Democracy', *Thesis Eleven*, 87 (1), pp. 33–50.

Jacobetti, Suzanne (1988) 'Hannah Arendt and the Will', *Political Theory*, 16 (1), pp. 53–76.

Jay, Martin (1990) 'No Power to the Soviets', *Salmagundi*, 88/89, pp. 64–71.

Jefferson, Thomas (1999) *Political Writings*. Cambridge: Cambridge University Press.

Johnson, Martin (1996) *The Paradise of Association: Political Culture and Popular Organizations in the Paris Commune of 1871*. Ann Arbor: The University of Michigan Press.

Jonsson, Stefan (2013) *Crowds and Democracy: The Idea and Image of the Masses from Revolution to Fascism*. New York: Columbia University Press.

Kalyvas, Andreas (1998) 'The Radical Instituting Power and Democratic Theory', *Journal of the Hellenic Diaspora*, 24 (1), pp. 9–28.

Kalyvas, Andreas (2001) 'The Politics of Autonomy and the Challenge of Deliberation: Castoriadis Contra Habermas', *Thesis Eleven*, 64 (1), pp. 1–19.

Kalyvas, Andreas (2004) 'From the Act to the Decision: Hannah Arendt and the Question of Decisionism', *Political Theory*, 32 (3), pp. 320–46.

Kalyvas, Andreas (2005) 'Popular Sovereignty, Democracy, and the Constituent Power', *Constellations*, 12 (2), pp. 223–44.

Kalyvas, Andreas (2008) *Democracy and the Politics of the Extraordinary: Max Weber, Carl Schmitt, and Hannah Arendt*. Cambridge: Cambridge University Press.

Kalyvas, Andreas (2013) 'Constituent Power', *Political Concepts: A Critical Lexicon*, 3 (1), <http://www.politicalconcepts.org/constituent-power/> (last accessed 3 September 2020).

Kalyvas, Andreas (2014) 'Solonian Citizenship: Democracy, Conflict, Participation', *Il Pensiero Politico. Rivista di Storia Delle Idee Politiche e Sociali*, 34, pp. 19–36.

Kantorowicz, Ernst (1957) *The King's Two Bodies: A Study in Medieval Political Thought*. Princeton, NJ: Princeton University Press.

Karalis, Vrasidas (ed.) (2014) *Cornelius Castoriadis and Radical Democracy*. Leiden: Brill.

Kateb, George (1983) 'Arendt and Representative Democracy', *Salmagundi*, 60, pp. 20–59.

Kateb, George (1987) 'Death and Politics: Hannah Arendt's Reflections on the American Constitution', *Social Research*, 54 (3), pp. 605–16.

Kateb, George (2000) 'Political Action: Its Nature and Advantages', in Villa, D. (ed.) *The Cambridge Companion to Hannah Arendt*. Cambridge: Cambridge University Press, pp. 130–48.

Kateb, George (2001) 'Wolin as a Critique of Democracy', in Botwinik, A. and Connolly, W. E. (eds) *Democracy and Vision: Sheldon Wolin and the Vicissitudes of the Political*. Princeton, NJ: Princeton University Press, pp. 39–57.

Kets, Gaard and Muldoon, James (2019) *The German Revolution and Political Theory*. Cham: Palgrave Macmillan.

Kioupkiolis, Alexandros and Katsambekis, Giorgos (eds) (2016) *Radical Democracy and Collective Movements Today: The Biopolitics of the Multitude versus the Hegemony of the People*. London: Routledge.

Klooger, Jeff (2009) *Castoriadis: Psyche, Society, Autonomy*. Leiden: Brill.

Klooger, Jeff (2012) 'The Meaning of Autonomy: Project, Self-Limitation, Democracy and Socialism', *Thesis Eleven*, 108 (1), pp. 84–98.

Körösenyi, András (2005) 'Political Representation in Leader Democracy', *Government and Opposition*, 40 (3), pp. 358–87.

Korsch, Karl (1929) *Revolutionary Commune*. Marxists Internet Archive, <https://www.marxists.org/archive/korsch/1929/commune.htm> (last accessed 3 September 2020).

Kropotkin, Peter (1880) 'The Paris Commune', in *Writings on the Paris Commune*. St Petersburg: Red and Black Publishers, pp. 89–101.

Kuhn, Gabriel (ed.) (2012) *All Power to the Councils!: A Documentary History of the German Revolution of 1918–1919*. Oakland, CA: PM Press.

Laclau, Ernesto and Mouffe, Chantal (1985) *Hegemony and Socialist Strategy: Towards a Radical Democratic Politics*. London: Verso.

Lefort, Claude (1956) 'The Hungarian Insurrection', in Anon. (trans. and ed.) *A Socialisme ou Barbarie Anthology: Autonomy, Critique, and Revolution in the Age of Bureaucratic Capitalism*. [Online] <http://notbored.org/SouBA.pdf> (last accessed 3 September 2020), pp. 201–23.

Lefort, Claude (1958) 'Organization and Party', in Anon. (trans. and ed.) *A Socialisme ou Barbarie Anthology: Autonomy, Critique, and Revolution in the Age of Bureaucratic Capitalism*. [Online] <http://notbored.org/SouBA.pdf> (last accessed 3 September 2020), pp. 309–18.

Lefort, Claude (1975) 'Interview with Lefort', *Anti-Mythes*, 14, pp. 173–92.

Lefort, Claude (1976a) 'The Age of Novelty', *Telos*, 29, pp. 23–38.

Lefort, Claude (1976b) 'La question de la revolution', *Esprit*, 460 (9), pp. 206–12.

Lefort, Claude (1986a) 'The Image of the Body in Totalitarianism', in *The Political Forms of Modern Society: Bureaucracy, Democracy, Totalitarianism*. Cambridge, MA: The MIT Press, pp. 292–306.

Lefort, Claude (1986b) 'Novelty and the Appeal of Repetition', in *The Political Forms of Modern Society: Bureaucracy, Democracy and Totalitarianism*. Cambridge, MA: The MIT Press, pp. 122–36.

Lefort, Claude (1986c) 'Totalitarianism without Stalin', in *The Political Forms of Modern Society: Bureaucracy, Democracy and Totalitarianism*. Cambridge, MA: The MIT Press, pp. 52–88.

Lefort, Claude (1988a) 'The Permanence of the Theologico-Political?', in *Democracy and Political Theory*. Cambridge: Polity Press, pp. 213–55.

Lefort, Claude (1988b) 'The Question of Democracy', in *Democracy and Political Theory*. Cambridge: Polity Press, pp. 9–21.

Lefort, Claude (2012) *Machiavelli in the Making*. Evanston, IL: Northwestern University Press.

Lenin, Vladimir (1905a) *The Dissolution of the Duma and the Tasks of the Proletariat*. <https://www.marxists.org/archive/lenin/works/1906/dissolut/index.htm> (last accessed 16 October 2020).

Lenin, Vladimir (1905b) *Socialism and Anarchism*. Marxists Internet Archive, <https://www.marxists.org/archive/lenin/works/1905/nov/24.htm> (last accessed 3 September 2020).

Lenin, Vladimir (1917a) *Letter to the Central Committee Members*. Marxists Internet Archive, <https://www.marxists.org/archive/lenin/works/1917/oct/24.htm> (last accessed 3 September 2020).

Lenin, Vladimir (1917b) *Letters From Afar*. Marxists Internet Archive, <https://www.marxists.org/archive/lenin/works/1917/lfafar/third.htm#v23pp64h-320> (last accessed 3 September 2020).

Lenin, Vladimir (1917c) *On Dual Power*. Marxists Internet Archive, <https://www.marxists.org/archive/lenin/works/1917/apr/09.htm> (last accessed 3 September 2020).

Lenin, Vladimir (1917d) *Speech on the Attitude Towards the Provisional Government*. Marxists Internet Archive, <https://www.marxists.org/archive/lenin/works/1917/jul/07.htm> (last accessed 3 September 2020).

Lenin, Vladimir (1917e) *The State and Revolution*. Moscow: Foreign Languages Publishing House.

Lenin, Vladimir (1917f) *The Tasks of the Proletariat in the Present Revolution*. Marxists Internet Archive, <https://www.marxists.org/archive/lenin/works/1917/apr/04.htm> (last accessed 3 September 2020).

Lenin, Vladimir (1917g) *To Workers, Soldiers and Peasants!* Marxists Internet Archive, <https://www.marxists.org/archive/lenin/works/1917/oct/25-26/25b.htm> (last accessed 3 September 2020).

Lenin, Vladimir (1918) *Declaration of Rights of the Working and Exploited People*. Marxists Internet Archive, <https://www.marxists.org/archive/lenin/works/1918/jan/03.htm> (last accessed 3 September 2020).

Lenin, Vladimir [1920] (1940) *'Left-Wing' Communism: An Infantile Disorder*. New York: International Publishers.

Levitsky, Steven and Ziblatt, Daniel (2018) *How Democracies Die*. London: Penguin.

Lindemann, Albert (1974) *The Red Years: European Socialism Versus Bolshevism, 1919–1921*. Berkeley: University of California Press.

Loughlin, Martin (2003) *The Idea of Public Law*. Oxford: Oxford University Press.

Loughlin, Martin (2010) *Foundations of Public Law*. Oxford: Oxford University Press.

Loughlin, Martin and Walker, Neil (2007) 'Introduction', in Loughlin, M. and Walker, N. (eds) *The Paradox of Constitutionalism: Constituent Power and Constitutional Form*. Oxford: Oxford University Press, pp. 1–8.

Lucardie, Paul (2014) *Democratic Extremism in Theory and Practice: All Power to the People*. New York: Routledge.

Luxemburg, Rosa (1906) *The Mass Strike, the Political Party and the Trade Unions*. Marxists Internet Archive, <https://www.marxists.org/archive/luxemburg/1906/mass-strike/> (last accessed 3 September 2020).

Luxemburg, Rosa (2012a) 'National Assembly or Council Government?', in Kuhn, G. (ed.) *All Power to the Councils!: A Documentary History of the German Revolution of 1918–1919*. Oakland, CA: PM Press, pp. 113–15.

Luxemburg, Rosa (2012b) 'A Pyrrhic Victory', in Kuhn, G. (ed.) *All Power to the Councils!: A Documentary History of the German Revolution of 1918–1919*. Oakland, CA: PM Press, pp.116–18.

McConkey, Mike (1991) 'On Arendt's Vision of the European Council Phenomenon: Critique from a Historical Perspective', *Dialectical Anthropology*, 16 (1), pp. 15–31.

McCormick, John (2007) 'People and Elites in Republican Constitutions, Traditional and Modern', in Loughlin, M. and Walker, N. (eds) *The Paradox of Constitutionalism: Constituent Power and Constitutional Form*. Oxford: Oxford University Press, pp. 107–25.

McCormick, John (2011) *Machiavellian Democracy*. Cambridge: Cambridge University Press.

Machiavelli, Niccolò [1517] (2003) *The Discourses*. London: Penguin Classics.

Machiavelli, Niccolò (2005) *The Prince*. Oxford: Oxford University Press.

Madison, James (1961) 'Federalist No. 10', in Kesler, C. (ed.) *The Federalist Papers*. New York: Signet Classics.

Magun, Artemy (2007) 'The Post-Communist Revolution in Russia and the Genesis of the Representative Democracy', *Redescriptions: Yearbook of Political Thought and Conceptual History*, 11, pp. 61–78.

Mandel, David (2011) 'The Factory Committee Movement in the Russian Revolution', in Ness, E. and Azzellini, D. (eds) *Ours to Master and to Own: Workers' Control from the Commune to the Present*. Chicago: Haymarket Books, pp. 104–29.

Marchart, Oliver (2007) *Post-Foundational Political Thought: Political Difference in Nancy, Lefort, Badiou and Laclau*. Edinburgh: Edinburgh University Press.

Marcuse, Herbert (2005) 'On the New Left', in *The New Left and the 1960s: Collected Papers of Herbert Marcuse, vol. 3*. New York: Routledge, pp. 122–7

Marx, Karl (1992a) 'A Contribution to the Critique of Hegel's Philosophy of Right', in *Early Writings*. London: Penguin Classics, pp. 243–58.

Marx, Karl (1992b) 'Critique of Hegel's Doctrine of the State', in *Early Writings*. London: Penguin Classics, pp. 57–198.

Marx, Karl (1992c) 'On the Jewish Question', in *Early Writings*. London: Penguin Classics, pp. 211–42.

Marx, Karl (1996a) 'The Civil War in France', in *Later Political Writings*. Cambridge: Cambridge University Press, pp. 163–207.

Marx, Karl (1996b) '"Preface" to A Contribution to the Critique of Political Economy', in *Later Political Writings*. Cambridge: Cambridge University Press, pp. 158–62.

May, Todd (1994) *The Political Philosophy of Poststructuralist Anarchism*. University Park, PA: Pennsylvania State University Press.

Medearis, John (2004) 'Lost or Obscured? How V. I. Lenin, Joseph Schumpeter and Hannah Arendt Misunderstood the Council Movement', *Polity*, 36 (3), pp. 447–76.

Memos, Christos (2014) *Castoriadis and Critical Theory: Crisis, Critique and Radical Alternatives*. Basingstoke: Palgrave Macmillan.

Michell, Allen (1965) *Revolution in Bavaria 1918–1919: The Eisner Regime and the Soviet Republic*. Princeton, NJ: Princeton University Press.

Miller, James (1979) 'The Pathos of Novelty: Hannah Arendt's Image of Freedom in the Modern World', in Hill, M. A. (ed.) *Hannah Arendt: The Recovery of the Public World*. New York: St. Martin's Press, pp. 177–208.

Molnár, Miklós (1971) *Budapest 1956: A History of the Hungarian Revolution*. Winchester, MA: Allen & Unwin.

Mounk, Yascha (2018) *The People vs. Democracy: Why Our Freedom is in Danger and How to Save It*. Cambridge, MA: Harvard University Press.

Moyn, Samuel (2009) 'Marxism and Alterity: Claude Lefort and the Critique of Totality', in Breckman, W., Gordon, P. E., Moses, A. D., Moyn, S. and Neaman, E. (eds) *The Modernist Imagination: Intellectual History and Critical Theory*. Oxford: Berghahn Books, pp. 99–116.

Muldoon, James (2015) 'Arendt's Revolutionary Constitutionalism: Between Constituent Power and Constitutional Form', *Constellations*, 22 (4), pp. 596–607.

Muldoon, James (2016) 'The Origins of Hannah Arendt's Council System', *History of Political Thought*, 37 (4), pp. 761–89.

Muldoon, James (ed.) (2018) *Council Democracy: Towards a Democratic Socialist Politics*. London: Routledge.

Müller, Jan-Werner (2011) *Contesting Democracy: Political Thought in Twentieth-Century Europe*. New Haven, CT: Yale University Press.

Müller, Jan-Werner (2014) '"The People Must Be Extracted from within the People": Reflections on Populism', *Constellations*, 21 (4), pp. 483–93.

Müller, Jan-Werner (2016) *What is Populism?* University Park, PA: Pennsylvania State University Press.

Nancy, Jean-Luc and Lacoue-Labarthe, Philippe (1997) *Retreating the Political*. London: Routledge.

Myers, Ella (2016) 'Presupposing Equality: The Trouble with Rancière's Axiomatic Approach', *Philosophy & Social Criticism*, 42, pp. 45–69.

Negri, Antonio (1999) *Insurgencies: Constituent Power and the Modern State*. Minneapolis: University of Minnesota Press.

Negri, Antonio (2004) *Factory of Strategy: 33 Lessons on Lenin*. New York: Columbia University Press.

Negri, Antonio (2017) 'Soviet: Within and Beyond the "Short Century"', *South Atlantic Quarterly*, 116 (October), pp. 835–49.

Nelson, Bryan (2019) 'Lefort, Abensour and the Question: What is "Savage" Democracy?', *Philosophy & Social Criticism*, 45 (7), pp. 844–61.

Ness, Immanuel and Azzellini, Dario (eds) (2012) *Ours to Master and to Own: Workers' Control from the Commune to the Present*. Chicago: Haymarket Books.

Newman, Saul (2016) 'Occupy and Autonomous Political Life', in Kioupkiolis, A. and Katsambekis, G. (eds) *Radical Democracy and Collective Movements Today: The Biopolitics of the Multitude versus the Hegemony of the People*. London: Routledge, pp. 93–110.

Pannekoek, Anton (1920) *World Revolution and Communist Tactics*. Marxists Internet Archive, <https://www.marxists.org/archive/pannekoe/tactics/ch04.htm> (last accessed 3 September 2020).

Pannekoek, Anton (2003) *Workers Councils*. Edinburgh: AK Press.

Pelz, William A. (2018) *A People's History of the German Revolution 1918–1919*. London: Pluto Press.

Pettit, Philip (2012) *On the People's Terms: A Republican Theory and Model of Democracy*. Cambridge: Cambridge University Press.

Pitkin, Hannah (1998) *The Attack of the Blob: Hannah Arendt's Concept of the Social*. Chicago: University of Chicago Press.

Plato (1955) *The Republic*. London: Penguin Books.

Plot, Martín (ed.) (2013) *Claude Lefort: Thinker of the Political*. Basingstoke: Palgrave Macmillan.

Popp-Madsen, Benjamin Ask (2018) 'The Self-Limiting Revolution and the Mixed Constitution of Socialist Democracy: Claude Lefort's Vision of Council Democracy', in Muldoon, J. (ed.) *Council Democracy: Towards a Democratic Socialist Politics*. London: Routledge, pp. 168–88.

Popp-Madsen, Benjamin Ask (2020a) 'Between Constituent Power and Political Form: Toward a Theory of Council Democracy', *Political Theory* [online first], <https://doi.org/10.1177/0090591720925435> (last accessed 3 September 2020).

Popp-Madsen, Benjamin Ask (2020b) 'From Workers' Councils to Democratic Autonomy: Rediscovering Cornelius Castoriadis' Theory of Council Democracy', *Critical Horizons: A Journal of Philosophy and Social Theory*, 21 (4), pp. 318–44.

Popp-Madsen, Benjamin Ask and Kets, Gaard (2020) 'Workers' Councils and Radical Democracy: Towards a Conceptual History of Council Democracy from Marx to Arendt', *Polity*.

Poulantzas, Nikos (1978) *State, Power, Socialism*. London: Verso.

Prentoulis, Marina and Thomassen, Lasse (2013) 'Political Theory in the Square: Protest, Representation, Subjectification', *Contemporary Political Theory*, 12, pp. 166–84.

Priban, Jiri (2002) *Dissidents of Law: On the 1989 Velvet Revolutions, Legitimations, Fictions of Legality and Contemporary Version of the Social Contract*. Farnham: Ashgate Publishing.

Pribicevic, Branko (1959) *The Shop Stewards' Movement and Workers' Control, 1910–1922*. Oxford: Blackwell Publishing.

Rabinowitch, Alexander (1997) 'The October Revolution', in Acton, E., Cherniaev, V. and Rosenberg, W. G. (eds) *Critical Companion to the Russian Revolution 1914–1921*. London: Arnold, pp. 81–92.

Rachleff, Peter (1976) *Marxism and Council Communism: The Foundation for a Revolutionary Theory for Modern Society*. New York: Revisionist Press.

Raimondi, Sara (2016) 'From Schmitt to Foucault: Inquiring the Relationship between Exception and Democracy', *Democratic Theory*, 3 (1), pp. 52–70.

Rancière, Jacques (1999) *Disagreement: Politics and Philosophy*. Minneapolis: University of Minnesota Press.

Rancière, Jacques (2010) 'Ten Theses on Politics', in *Dissensus: On Politics and Aesthetics*. New York: Bloomsbury, pp. 27–44.

Reed, John (1966) *Ten Days That Shook the World*. New York: Penguin Books.

Ross, Kristin (2015) *Communal Luxury: The Political Imagination of the Paris Commune*. London: Verso.

Rousseau, Jean-Jacques (2002) *The Social Contract and the First and Second Discourses*. New Haven, CT: Yale University Press.

Rühle, Otto (1920a) *Moscow and Ourselves*. Marxists Internet Archive, <https://www.marxists.org/archive/ruhle/1920/moscow-and-ourselves.htm> (last accessed 3 September 2020).

Rühle, Otto (1920b) *The Revolution is Not a Party Affair*. Marxists Internet Archive, <https://www.marxists.org/archive/ruhle/1920/ruhle02.htm> (last accessed 3 September 2020).

Rühle, Otto (1924) *From the Bourgeois to the Proletarian Revolution*. Marxists Internet Archive, <https://www.marxists.org/archive/ruhle/1924/revolution.htm> (last accessed 3 September 2020).

Runciman, David (2018) *How Democracy Ends*. London: Profile Books.

Schecter, Darrow (1994) *Radical Theories: Paths beyond Marxism and Social Democracy*. Manchester: Manchester University Press.

Scheuerman, William (1998) 'Revolutions and Constitutions: Hannah Arendt's Challenge to Carl Schmitt', in Dyzenhaus, D. (ed.) *Law as Politics: Carl Schmitt's Critique of Liberalism*. Durham, NC: Duke University Press, pp. 252–80.

Schmitt, Carl (1985) *Political Theology: Four Chapters on the Concept of Sovereignty*. Chicago: University of Chicago Press.

Schmitt, Carl [1928] (2008) *Constitutional Theory*. Durham, NC: Duke University Press.

Schmitt, Carl [1921] (2014) *Dictatorship: From the Origin of the Modern Concept of Sovereignty to the Proletarian Class Struggle*. Cambridge: Polity Press.

Shipway, Mark (1987) 'Council Communism', in Rubel, M. and Crump, J. (eds) *Non-Market Socialism in the Nineteenth and Twentieth Centuries*. Basingstoke: Palgrave Macmillan, pp. 104–26.

Sieyès, Emmanuel (2003) 'What is the Third Estate?', in *Political Writings: Including the Debate between Sieyès and Tom Paine in 1791*. Indianapolis: Hackett Publishing, pp. 92–162.

Singer, Brian (1979) 'The Early Castoriadis: Socialism, Barbarism and the Bureaucratic Thread', *Canadian Journal of Political and Social Theory*, 3 (3), pp. 35–56.

Singer, Brian (1980) 'The Later Castoriadis: Institution under Interrogation', *Canadian Journal of Political and Social Theory*, 4 (1), pp. 75–101.

Singer, Brian (2015) 'Cornelius Castoriadis: Auto-Institution and Radical Democracy', in Breaugh, M., Holman, C., Magnusson, R., Mazzocchi, P. and Penner, D. (eds) *Thinking Radical Democracy: The Return to Politics in Post-War France*. Toronto: University of Toronto Press, pp. 141–64.

Sirianni, Carmen (1980) 'Workers' Control in the Era of World War I: A Comparative Analysis of the European Experience', *Theory and Society*, 9 (1), pp. 29–88.

Sirianni, Carmen (1982) *Workers Control and Socialist Democracy: The Soviet Experience*. London: Verso.

Sitrin, Marina and Dario Azzellini (2014) *They Can't Represent Us! Reinventing Democracy from Greece to Occupy*. London: Verso Books.

Sitton, John (1987) 'Hannah Arendt's Argument for Council Democracy', *Polity*, 20 (1), pp. 80–100.

Skinner, Quentin (1981) *Machiavelli: A Very Short Introduction*. Oxford: Oxford University Press.

Smirnov, Nikolai (1997) 'The Soviets', in Acton, E., Cherniaev, V. and Rosenberg, W. G. (eds) *Critical Companion to the Russian Revolution 1914–1921*. London: Arnold, pp. 429–37.

Smith, Steve (1983) *Red Petrograd: Revolution in the Factories*. Cambridge: Cambridge University Press.

Smith, Steve (1997) 'Factory Committees', in Acton, E., Cherniaev, V. and Rosenberg, W. G. (eds) *Critical Companion to the Russian Revolution 1914–1921*. London: Arnold, pp. 346–58.

Sturmthal, Adolf (1964) *Workers Councils: A Study of Workplace Organization on Both Sides of the Iron Curtain*. Cambridge, MA: Harvard University Press.

Tampio, Nicholas (2016) 'Political Theory and the Untimely', *Political Theory*, Guides Through the Archives, 2 (1), pp. 1–7.

Tomba, Massimiliano (2017) 'Politics Beyond the State: The 1918 Soviet Constitution', *Constellations*, 24 (4), pp. 503–15.

Tomba, Massimiliano (2018) 'Who's Afraid of the Imperative Mandate?', *Critical Times*, 1 (1), pp. 108–99.

Totschnig, Wolfhart (2014) 'Arendt's Argument for the Council System: A Defense', *European Journal of Cultural and Political Sociology*, 1 (3), pp. 266–82.

Trotsky, Leon (1907) *1905*. Marxists Internet Archive, <https://www.marxists.org/archive/trotsky/1907/1905/ch08.htm> (last accessed 3 September 2020).

Trotsky, Leon (1932) *The History of the Russian Revolution, Vol. 1*. London: Victor Gollancz.

Tuori, Karius (2016) 'Schmitt and the Sovereignty of Roman Dictators: From the Actualization of the Past to the Recycling of Symbols', *History of European Ideas*, 41 (1), pp. 98–102.

United Nations (1957) *Report of the Special Committee on the Problem of Hungary*, General Assembly Official Records: Eleventh Session, Supplement No. 18 (A/3592). New York: United Nations.

van der Linden, Marcel (1997) 'Socialisme or Barbarie: A French Revolutionary Group', *Left History*, 5 (1), pp. 7–37.

van der Linden, Marcel (2004) 'On Council Communism', *Historical Materialism*, 12 (4), pp. 27–50.

Wallis, Victor (2011) 'Workers' Control and Revolution', in Ness, I. and Azzellini, D. (eds) *Ours to Master and to Own: Workers' Control from the Commune to the Present*. Chicago: Haymarket Books, pp. 10–31.

Weymans, Wim (2005) 'Freedom through Political Representation: Lefort, Gauchet and Rosanvallon on the Relationship between State and Society', *European Journal of Political Theory*, 4 (3), pp. 263–82.

Williams, Gwyn (1975) *Proletarian Order: Antonio Gramsci, Factory Councils and the Origins of Italian Communism, 1911–1921*. London: Pluto Press.

Wiltshire, Jon (2013) 'After Syntagma: Where are the Occupiers Now?', *Open Democracy*, <https://www.opendemocracy.net/en/opensecurity/after-syntagma-where-are-occupiers-now/> (last accessed 3 September 2020).

Wolin, Richard (2001) *Heidegger's Children: Hannah Arendt, Karl Löwitz, Hans Jonas and Herbert Marcuse*. Princeton, NJ: Princeton University Press.

Wolin, Sheldon (1994) 'Norm and Form: The Constitutionalizing of Democracy', in Euben, J. P., Wallach, J. R. and Ober, J. (eds) *Athenian Political Thought and the Reconstruction of American Democracy*. Ithaca, NY: Cornell University Press, pp. 29–59.

Wolin, Sheldon (1996) 'Fugitive Democracy', in Benhabib, S. (ed.) *Democracy and Difference: Contesting the Boundaries of the Political*. Princeton, NJ: Princeton University Press, pp. 31–45.

Wolin, Sheldon (2004) *Politics and Vision*. Princeton, NJ: Princeton University Press.

Wood, Ellen Meiksins (2011) *Citizens to Lords: A Social History of Western Political Thought from Antiquity to the Late Middle Ages*. London: Verso.

Zerilli, Linda (2002) 'Castoriadis, Arendt and the Problem of the New', *Constellations*, 9 (4), pp. 540–53.

Index

EU representative:
Easy Access System Europe
Mustamäe tee 50, 10621 Tallinn, Estonia
Gpsr.requests@easproject.com

www.ingramcontent.com/pod-product-compliance
Lightning Source LLC
Chambersburg PA
CBHW070844300326
41935CB00039B/1417